THE REIGN OF ELIZABETH I

Covering the period from 1558 to 1603, *The Reign of Elizabeth I* looks at all the important aspects of the reign of the last of the Tudor monarchs. Using a range of sources and considering the ideas of different historians, Stephen J. Lee covers government and foreign policy, Elizabeth's relations with Parliament, the religious settlement, the reactions of Catholics and Puritans, aspects of the economy, society and culture, and connections between England and the Celtic regions of the British Isles. Each chapter combines a historiographical survey with historical analysis.

Stephen J. Lee was formerly head of history at Bromsgrove School. He has published over twenty books, including *European Dictatorships* (2nd edition, Routledge, 2000) and, in this series, *Gladstone and Disraeli* (Routledge, 2005).

QUESTIONS AND ANALYSIS IN HISTORY

Edited by Stephen J. Lee, Sean Lang and Jocelyn Hunt

Other titles in the series:

Modern History

Imperial Germany, 1871–1918
Stephen J. Lee

The Weimar Republic
Stephen J. Lee

Hitler and Nazi Germany
Stephen J. Lee

The Spanish Civil War
Andrew Forrest

The Cold War
Bradley Lightbody

Stalin and the Soviet Union
Stephen J. Lee

Parliamentary Reform, 1785–1928
Sean Lang

British Foreign and Imperial Policy, 1865–1919
Graham D. Goodlad

The French Revolution
Jocelyn Hunt

The First World War
Ian C. Cawood and David McKinnon-Bell

Anglo-Irish Relations, 1798–1922
Nick Pelling

Churchill
Samantha Heywood

Mussolini and Fascism
Patricia Knight

Lenin and Revolutionary Russia
Stephen J. Lee

Gladstone and Disraeli
Stephen J. Lee

Russia and the USSR, 1855–1991
Stephen J. Lee

Early Modern History

The English Wars and Republic, 1636–1660
Graham E. Seel

The Renaissance
Jocelyn Hunt

Tudor Government
T. A. Morris

Spain, 1474–1598
Jocelyn Hunt

The Early Stuart Kings, 1603–1642
Graham E. Seel and David L. Smith

The Mid Tudors: Edward VI and Mary, 1547–1558
Stephen J. Lee

THE REIGN OF ELIZABETH I

1558–1603

STEPHEN J. LEE

LONDON AND NEW YORK

First published 2007
by Routledge
2 Park Square, Milton Park, Abingdon, Oxon OX14 4RN

Simultaneously published in the USA and Canada
by Routledge
270 Madison Ave, New York, NY 10016

Routledge is an imprint of the Taylor & Francis Group, an informa business

© 2007 Stephen J. Lee

Typeset in Akzidenz Grotesk, Perpetua and Scala Sans by
RefineCatch Limited, Bungay, Suffolk
Printed and bound in Great Britain by
TJ International Ltd, Padstow, Cornwall

British Library Cataloguing in Publication Data
A catalogue record for this book is available from the British Library

Library of Congress Cataloging in Publication Data
Lee, Stephen J., 1945–
  Reign of Elizabeth I / Stephen J. Lee.
      p. cm. – (Questions and analysis in history)
  Includes bibliographical references.
1. Elizabeth I, Queen of England, 1533–1603.   2. Great Britain—History—
Elizabeth, 1558–1603.   3. Great Britain—Politics and government—1558–1603.
4. Great Britain—History—Elizabeth, 1558–1603—Historiography.   5. Great
Britain—History—Elizabeth, 1558–1603—Problems, exercises, etc.   I. Title.
  DA355.L36 2007
  942.05'5—dc22   2007007660

ISBN10: 0–415–30212–9 (hbk)
ISBN10: 0–415–30213–7 (pbk)
ISBN10: 0–203–08947–2 (ebk)

ISBN13: 978–0–415–30212–8 (hbk)
ISBN13: 978–0–415–30213–5 (pbk)
ISBN13: 978–0–203–08947–7 (ebk)

For Charlotte

CONTENTS

INTRODUCTION

The *Questions and Analysis* series is based on the belief that the student actively benefits from explicit interpretation of key issues and help with source-based technique. Each volume therefore separates narrative from analysis and sources; it follows an overall structure of Background, Analyses and Sources.

This volume, *The Reign of Elizabeth I*, adds a further dimension. Sixth-form and university courses have given more and more importance to historical debates, requiring proficiency in historiography as well as in history. The format takes this development into account. Some Analyses focus mainly on historical explanation, some on historiographical interpretation; many provide a combination of the two. The number of Analyses in each chapter depends on appropriate subdivisions of the topic covered. About half the Sources are 'primary', while the remainder are 'secondary', giving examples of differing lines of interpretation. Suggested approaches are provided to one source-based question in each of Chapters 1 to 8.

It is hoped that the student or general reader will want to contribute to the debate in these chapters. Having a wide range of ideas is bound to stimulate more. Provided that they can be substantiated, they are all valid – and they all count. This is what makes history so creative.

1

ELIZABETH AND HER GOVERNMENT

BACKGROUND

Elizabeth is generally seen as one of the most popular monarchs in the whole of English history. From the time that she ascended the throne she was always far more accessible to the people than were other rulers. She courted popularity more directly and assiduously than any of her predecessors or successors, partly through official propaganda, partly through her own actions and speeches (see Source 1.3 below).

Her attributes have been extensively documented in many biographies. Her key strength was a strong intellect. She was a classical scholar, adept in both Latin and Greek, and also acquired linguistic skills in French, Italian and Spanish. Such academic abilities and skills could be put to direct practical use. She was able to bring sharp powers of analysis to the political process and therefore saw through carelessly constructed arguments. Similarly she was able more than most other monarchs – and certainly more so than Mary or Henry VIII – to disconnect her own personal feelings from the political issues over which she presided. In this respect her intellect was very much in control of her emotions. She also displayed total self-confidence, although she was cautious and circumspect in her dealings with officials or with foreign ambassadors. She was able to castigate verbally anyone from ministers of state down to members of her household, and had a particular dislike of the obvious pursuit of self-interest. By and large, she recognised qualities in others and was a good judge of character when it came to making a choice of ministers. She was also inclined to pragmatic opportunism and was instinctively distrustful of positions based on ideology.

Elizabeth did, however, possess a number of serious defects which at times impeded the process of effective government. She frequently became involved in minor issues, finding it hard to delegate. It was also very difficult to obtain a decision from the Queen: she was notorious both for her procrastination and for her sudden changes of mind. This was partly because she was able to see so many different sides to an issue and wanted to explore the intricacies involved. There were also contradictions in her personality: she combined nervous energy and occasional lethargy; charm and irritability; resolution and indecision; self-control and temper. Although she has been praised for her religious moderation, she could as easily fall behind draconian measures: for example, her reign (1558–1603) produced 65 per cent of the documented cases of torture during the period 1540–1640. Examples of all these areas of her personality will be found throughout this book.

In the absence of the modern system of party politics and prime minister, government was in a very real sense conducted by the Queen herself. She was directly responsible for all the state departments, including the Privy Council, Exchequer and Chancery. Like all monarchs of the period, her right to this power was uncontested, as can be seen in an extract from *Mirror for Magistrates* (see Source 1.1 below). Whether or not she had a significant impact on the governing institutions of the time is the subject of Analysis 1. She was served by five prominent ministers. William Cecil (from 1571 Lord Burghley) was Principal Secretary (1558–72), then Lord Treasurer (1572–98). He also held the post of Master of the Court of Wards (1562–98). Robert Dudley (Earl of Leicester) was a prominent member of the Privy Council, with aspirations to Cecil's offices. Sir Christopher Hatton served as Lord Chancellor between 1587 and 1591. Sir Francis Walsingham was second Secretary of State from 1573 until his death in 1590; he had also been ambassador to France (1570–73) and was sent on a special embassy to Scotland in 1583. Robert Devereux, Earl of Essex, was not given any of the key offices of state, although he became a Privy Councillor in 1593 and, as Earl Marshal, was given command of the Queen's armies in 1597. Their roles and importance are compared in Analysis 2.

ANALYSIS 1: ASSESS THE CHANGES IN AND EFFECTIVENESS OF ELIZABETH'S GOVERNMENT.

The Queen's servants presided over and operated institutions which had existed for centuries. At the centre was the Privy Council, the history of which was one of continuity. As with her predecessors, Elizabeth maintained it as the single most important institution in decision-making and the formation of policy. Yet she did introduce one major change, which was really a reversion to the practices of Henry VIII: the Privy Council was returned to the smaller size of the days of Thomas Cromwell, after its expansion to forty members under Edward VI and fifty during the reign of Mary. How well did this work?

On the one hand, a more compact Council was more likely to produce an agreed and coherent policy. A small inner ring, usually of five, developed within the broader membership of between nine and thirteen. Elizabeth clearly thought this helped the formulation of coherent policy when she said that 'a multitude doth make rather discord and confusion than good counsel'.[1] The Privy Council was able to develop a convention whereby the Queen did not attend meetings but considered it her main function to receive its recommendations and, upon this basis, to make a decision. This enabled a small body of Councillors to go through the preliminary stages of open discussion without being either distracted by numbers or constrained by the royal presence. The smaller Council also had sufficient self-confidence to impose its control over the House of Commons. At times it could even pressurise the Queen, either by mobilising public opinion or by activating Parliament.

On the other hand, smaller numbers within the Council meant that there was likely to be more factional infighting. This was especially the case during the second period of Elizabeth's reign. In the immediate term this might be an attempt to discredit a specific minister, like Cecil, who was bringing stability. Over a longer period rivalry was lubricated by patronage. This meant that recommendations were made by some individuals within the Council for reasons of personal gain rather than in the national interest. For example, the differences over whether England should intervene in the Netherlands were due as much to the rivalry over personal patronage from the Queen as to genuine differences of foreign policy. At the same time, patronage did not act as a means of polarising positions into a more stable and predictable form of support and opposition; factions based on patronage were not, therefore, the early equivalent of party politics. Overall, the smaller Council tended to accentuate the advantages and disadvantages.

When it worked well it was quite exceptional and there is no real equivalent in the whole century to the work of the four great statesmen associated with it. Conversely, its size meant that any real factional conflict was likely to be particularly destabilising, which tended to exacerbate crises.

Local government also saw considerable continuity. It still depended largely on the co-operation of those members of the local aristocracy who served in the capacity of Justice of the Peace or Lord Lieutenant. JPs were responsible for enforcing statute law by deciding on disputes. Elizabeth also continued the use of special commissions. These were very much in line with the work of the commissioners of Henry VIII in the dissolution of the monasteries. Elizabeth used a similar process in enforcing the 1559 religious settlement. However, the reign also saw some changes, particularly the expanding role of existing officials. JPs were given extra duties such as the enforcement of the Poor Law, economic regulation and the maintenance of highways. Lords Lieutenant also assumed a larger role. Their initial responsibility during the reign of Henry VII had been for local militia. Under Elizabeth, they were appointed to every county and were given responsibility for supervising the work of JPs, raising loans and enforcing the orders of the Privy Council.

How effective was this pattern of local government? There were certainly advantages. It was, for example, administration on the cheap, which therefore fitted into the financial constraints of the Elizabethan system. At this stage there was no real alternative since that would have involved a professional and paid bureaucracy. In any case, this would have been inappropriate during the period since the social hierarchy was dominated by the magnates. The JP system by and large ensured their loyalty, whereas the insertion of an impersonal bureaucracy would have created considerable resentment. There was also a series of natural checks and balances. The local potential for rebellion was normally neutralised by two influences. One was the centrifugal force of nationalism, stronger during the Elizabethan period than before, partly because of the increased external threat and partly because of the propaganda from the court and the growth of the Elizabethan cult. The other was the centripetal force of conflicting local interests. Whenever there was the threat of a local uprising it was quite likely to collapse because of the intrusion of local rivalries. This was evident in the Northern Rising of 1569 and the Essex revolt of 1601.

But there were also deficiencies. One was the problem of implementing the decisions of central government. Many JPs were reluctant to become fully involved in their duties, seeing their position largely as a social adornment. The tendency of officials to misuse their position to accumulate personal profit was always likely in a period in which there was no official remuneration. And, despite the obstacles in the way, rebellion could never be discounted. There was always the problem of the questionable loyalty of some of the magnates: the Earl of Derby, who was sympathetic to the Catholics, was in charge of the militia in Lancashire – England's most consistently Catholic area. The 1590s saw a decline in the overall efficiency of local government as carrying out normal functions was complicated by a run of bad harvests, increased poverty and higher assessments for militia rates and ship money.

Elizabethan financial administration saw virtually no changes. Elizabeth's policy was the strictest possible budgeting rather than the extension of the range of financial administration or the scope of its institutions. Hence her reign was far from innovatory: indeed, it could be said that there were fewer alterations during the period covered by this book than at any other time – certainly by comparison with earlier monarchs. For example, the tendency of the Yorkist kings, together with Henry VII and Henry VIII, had been to divert financial management from the Exchequer to the household. The reigns of Edward VI and Mary saw the revival of the Exchequer, a development which continued during the reign of Elizabeth until the Exchequer had largely recovered its former influence.

The main strength in financial policy was the control over expenditure to produce an increase in ordinary revenue from £200,000 to £300,000 per annum; at certain stages there was even a moderate surplus on the annual account. Elizabeth managed to settle the debts left by Mary and to develop a substantial cash reserve. Tight budgeting was complemented by the increase in revenue through the sale of crown lands worth more than £600,000, more frequent parliamentary taxation, and forced loans. Elizabeth avoided the more drastic expedient, favoured by some of her predecessors, of debasing the coinage – even though she had to finance a war with Spain and the conquest of Ireland.

Any defence of the Elizabethan finances should not, however, conceal the defects. These related to a lack of any real vision in the overall supervision of the administration. Little attempt was made to gain a complete perspective of the relationship between revenues and inflation: it has been estimated that, while inflation increased by 75 per cent during the reign, the revenues were increased by only 25 per cent. Hence Elizabeth was forced to resort especially to parliamentary taxation. This, of course, might have become an alternative source of regular supply. But no steps were taken to convert the extraordinary into the ordinary. Historians have also criticised the roles of the Privy Council and the Exchequer. The Council had the ultimate responsibility for the economy. It did receive information and statistics from the Exchequer, but generally speaking it was unable to handle the details of financial business. This was strange, since it was quite capable of handling the minutiae, even trivia, of individual judicial cases. According to J.D. Alsop, the Council remained 'relatively unused to its role as the principal superintendent of state finance'.[2] In addition, 'The Exchequer was adrift, moving where the currents of economic change, vested interests, the blossoming patronage system, and so on, would take it'.[3] Here, as elsewhere, Elizabethan administration might well have benefited from a greater degree of innovation.

Even so, we should not be too ready to blame the problems of Elizabeth's reign, even of its last decade, for the eventual collapse of the Stuart regime. The crises confronting James I and Charles I were usually more immediate, and recent historiography has rightly moved towards a shorter-term view of the origins of the Civil War and away from connecting it up with the Elizabethan period.

Questions

1. 'Little innovation and not much consolidation.' Is this a fair comment on the development of administration under Elizabeth?
2. How much did Elizabethan administration depend on Elizabeth?

ANALYSIS 2: COMPARE THE ROLES AND IMPORTANCE OF ELIZABETH'S MAIN POLITICAL SERVANTS.

Elizabeth's officials make for interesting comparison in terms of how they conceived their respective roles; the strength and consistency of their views; their political and administrative effectiveness; the extent to which they were able to work with others; and their relationship with the Queen.

The one minister who was quite clear as to his role was Cecil, who pursued a line of moderation in all things. His family had its origins in the gentry and had established its reputation as servants of the crown. This was a tradition which Cecil himself was determined to continue. 'Serve God', he said, 'by serving the queen, for all other service is indeed bondage to the devil.'[4] This meant a low-key approach to the pursuit of personal interests and a patient harmony with others. Although he did occasionally risk alienating his colleagues by battling for his own views, as for example in the 1590s over Essex, he usually settled for a line of less resistance. This was in contrast to the Earl of Leicester. Of less humble origins, he had risen through the court. His family had been more prominent than the Cecil's in royal service, Sir Edmund Dudley under Henry VII and the Earl of Northumberland as Lord President of the Council under Edward VI. As a result, Leicester was far more conscious of his personal position and was prepared to resort to devious means to undermine that of Cecil. Even further along the spectrum than Leicester was the Earl of Essex, who inherited his title at the age of nine. He has been seen as the incarnation of aristocratic chivalry and culture. He was, however, highly volatile, spent extravagantly and was always in debt. Walsingham was the reverse – closer to Cecil. He was private, withdrawn, and highly organised and methodical in his work. At the same time, he was more interested than Cecil in the arts and was a patron of Spenser and others.

There were also significant contrasts in attitudes and ideas. Cecil was inclined towards pragmatism and moderation in religious matters, although he instinctively favoured the Edwardian variant of Protestantism. Walsingham preferred the aims of the Puritans. It is arguable that he was more genuine in his views than Cecil, but the latter was more in tune with the views of the Queen, who therefore found his support indispensable. Leicester was also more inclined towards the radical Protestant position, although he was equally prepared to play the conservative card if it suited him to do so. Hatton was the most public in his views, but usually for reasons of policy. In 1587, for example, he spoke to Parliament of the dangers posed by Catholics abroad and at home, of the oppression of the Inquisition in the Netherlands. His personal views were less important. He was unsympathetic to the Puritan cause and certainly lacked the strong Protestant beliefs of Walsingham. As for Essex, he was the most pragmatic of all, having no apparent ideological orientation at all.

The Tudor period required two major skills of the top royal servants. One was practical administration, the other policy-making. Cecil combined the two most effectively. He brought to administration an attention to detail and accuracy. He was also adept at solving problems, the legacy of his education at Cambridge and the Inns of Court in London. At the same time, he was extensively involved in the essential policy formation, whether the Elizabethan religious settlement, or negotiations in foreign policy with France, Spain and Scotland, or relations with Parliament, or domestic crises such as the Northern Rebellion of 1569.

Leicester had very different political skills. These were used less in the interests of administration than in securing his own advancement and were therefore directed at destabilising Cecil's position. There is, however, increasing evidence to show that Leicester gradually moved away from his acrimonious dislike of Cecil and was more prepared to co-operate with him during the more stable period of the 1570s and 1580s. Walsingham was somewhat more remote as an administrative figure. But he did have a good eye for detail and an excellent style for written correspondence and memoranda. He was also above reproach as far as his honesty and loyalty were concerned. Perhaps his greatest strength, however, was his versatility as a diplomat, which meant that Elizabeth was able to use his services in France, before he became Secretary, and again in 1583 in Scotland. Hatton, as Lord Chancellor, had particularly strong contacts with Parliament. It was he who acted as the main channel between the legislature and the executive. Hatton also provided strong links outside the court, which he used to bring stability to his additional role as Lord Lieutenant of Northamptonshire – where he worked especially well with his two deputies, Knightley and Montagu. Essex, by contrast, played little direct part in the administrative process, except as demanded by his position as Privy Councillor from 1593. His interests were more in terms of military expeditions, whether to France or Ireland. Here, however, he proved generally ineffectual. He failed to achieve anything lasting in the expeditions he led against Spain between 1595 and 1597, while his attempt to put down the Earl of Tyrone's rebellion in Ireland in 1599 was a disaster – largely because he disobeyed instructions.

An essential political skill was being able to work with others and to avoid conflicts. In an era which lacked even rudimentary party politics, it was usual for interest groups or factions to develop around specific individuals, lubricated by patronage. The least prone to the inevitable abuses of this system was Cecil, whose background induced him to avoid making himself a target for resentment. By contrast, Leicester was the core of faction, based on his own interests. Far from controlling faction, he sometimes became dangerously caught up within it – as, for example, in his abortive attempt to secure Norfolk's marriage with Mary Queen of Scots in 1569. He also targeted Cecil directly, aiming to secure his dismissal. Essex too was directly involved in factional feuds. For example, after his appointment to the Privy Council, it was expected that he would work in tandem with Cecil. In practice, he did what he could to undermine Cecil's position, taking over where Leicester had left off. Essex went well beyond even the accepted conventions of the day by supplementing patronage with intimidation. He took the ultimate step by trying to force the Queen to grant him ascendancy over all other ministers. He was therefore the only one who ended up on the scaffold for converting faction into rebellion. There is no evidence that Walsingham entered into the factional conflicts of the court. Generally speaking, he worked well with Cecil and there were occasions when the two collaborated closely to secure the Queen's agreement to a line of policy. If this failed they were even prepared to act secretly, as they did in securing the execution of Mary Queen of Scots in 1587.

The relationship between the leading ministers and the Queen varied widely. Cecil was probably closest to her viewpoint. He shared her instinctive moderation in ideology and caution in policy. He backed her parsimonious attitude to financial dealings and shared her prefer-ence for avoiding financial reform or change. He also tended towards her caution in foreign policy. Leicester had a much closer personal relationship with the Queen, whom he came close to marrying in 1559–60. Essex also had dealings with Elizabeth not normally associated with a political servant. But she was less prepared to tolerate his excesses than Leicester's. Walsingham probably had the least direct influence on the Queen, who did not have quite the same personal dependence on him as on Cecil, or personal feelings as for Leicester and Essex. Yet she respected his professionalism, even though he appeared remote and aloof. The one servant who seemed to combine the Queen's affec-tion (rumour occasionally implied more) with her respect for his judge-ment was Hatton. Certainly he made a change from the unpredictability of Leicester and the tantrums of Essex.

To what extent did these servants actually influence the Queen? Recent historical interpretation has shown occasional attempts by Cecil to pressurise the Queen indirectly through instructions to English ambassadors abroad as to what to report. He also implemented certain key policies without consultation, such as the execution of Mary Queen of Scots in 1587, or the use of Parliament to generate opposition to the Queen's marriage policy. On the other hand, it is possible to overdo this revision. Such action was the exception rather than the rule, and Cecil's preferred approach was one of patient persuasion and the search for a common ground. Leicester sought to enhance his position by exploiting the Queen's good opinion of him. He flattered and cajoled, where Cecil persuaded; he dressed extravagantly, where Cecil was sober, even sombre. He also attempted, although unsuccessfully, to pressurise the Queen into dismissing Cecil by stating that the latter's unpopularity threatened civil war. By and large, the Queen retained overall control, deciding on the stages of his promotion. Essex, like Leicester, com-bined exploiting the Queen's good will and periodically flouting her instructions. For example, he left the court in 1589 to take part in the Portugal Expedition, against the Queen's instructions. The reverse applied in 1599 when he returned from Ireland before he had carried out her orders there. He was convinced that he could put pressure on the Queen where others had failed. This explains his attempt in 1601 to apply force to make her increase his political power. Elizabeth, however, showed decisive action, occasioned no doubt by loss of patience.

Of the other two ministers, Walsingham tended to speak his mind and apply pressure more directly than Cecil. This was especially the case over the situation in the Netherlands and France. He urged the Queen to intervene on behalf of Anjou and the Huguenots in 1573 and again to become involved against Spain in the Netherlands. On both occasions she resisted his forceful arguments, preferring to take lesser measures such as a subsidy to the Elector of the Palatinate to provide mercenary support for Anjou. Nevertheless, Walsingham did provide the sort of perspective which the Queen needed to consider and, even if she did not take his advice, this must have helped shape her eventual decision. At least she knew she could receive from him a view which was neither loaded with considerations of personal advancement nor coloured by personal affection. Hatton, too, was prepared to argue his view strongly, and took a leading part against Mary Queen of Scots, denouncing her in Parliament in October 1585 by referring to the 'horrible and wicked practices and attempts caused and procured by the Queen of Scots so called'.[5] Hatton was therefore a key factor in persuading Parliament to put pressure on the Queen when he saw the necessity. He also articulated his views about the main dangers confronting England in that same forum.

Of all the ministers who served Elizabeth – and there are many more than have been covered here – Cecil was probably the most important. He dominated the age, in terms of his length of service and his overall influence. He has been variously dealt with by historians. The traditional view is that he played very much a secondary role to the Queen; more recent evidence has shown that he took the initiative more frequently and that he had a strong capacity for duplicity. Overall, he is still seen as the statesman who combined most harmoniously the political and administrative skills, and who provided the most effective overall support for the Queen. Leicester's overall reputation has been somewhat less favourable. He is generally seen as able and charismatic but, above all, as a destabilising influence – to whom the Queen was strongly attracted but had the common sense to cut down to size. On the other hand, it is possible to go too far in stereotyping Leicester.

During the 1570s there was growing evidence of co-operation with Cecil. It is difficult to say anything positive about Essex unless one focuses on his flamboyance and intellectual interests. In many ways his was a wasted career. He had all the attributes of a Renaissance man; but he was impatient, petulant and ruthless without having the political instinct to know when to stop. He therefore lacked the sort of safeguards which prevented Leicester from pursing the same path to self-destruction. Walsingham was the type of minister needed in every government – one who spoke his mind, usually on the basis of strong beliefs. Yet, at the same time, his personality enabled him to co-operate with Cecil. It is small wonder that the partnership between these two and Hatton has been seen politically as the key stabilising factor of the reign.

Questions

1. Place the five men covered in this Analysis in order of the value of their contributions to the Queen's government. Justify your choice.
2. 'Elizabeth seemed to be drawn personally more to those ministers who gave her problems than to those who did not.' Do you agree?

ANALYSIS 3: CONSIDER THE OVERALL ASSESSMENTS MADE OF THE QUEEN AND HER REIGN.

During her reign Elizabeth was given a variety of roles. The perception of these has been influenced by the age in which works on her were produced.

She was projected at the time as England's saviour from the threats of papism and Spanish domination, as the architect of a moderate religious settlement, as the focus of effective government and as the inspiration behind a cultural resurgence. Other positive assessments were made after her death. William Camden, who lived through Elizabeth's reign, had been particularly influenced by Lord Burghley, although he wrote his *Annales: The True and Royall History of the famous Empresse Elizabeth* between 1608 and 1617. Sir Robert Naunton was also fulsome in his praises, partly a reflection of disillusionment with the growing problems of the reign of Charles I and a yearning for a past 'golden age'.

Historians of the nineteenth century were more divided. T. Macaulay, J. Lingard (1855)[6] and J.A. Froude (1904)[7] were generally critical of Elizabeth's rule, while J.R. Green (1874)[8] and M. Creighton (1896) were laudatory; Creighton, for example, believed that 'She represented England as no other ruler ever did.'[9] These two approaches reflected the priorities of individual writers. For Macaulay the evolution of parliamentary history was particularly important (considered in Chapter 2). Froude considered that the main achievement of the Tudor period was the Reformation, which Elizabeth merely completed (considered in Chapter 3), in the process leaving significant problems for the future. Lingard, a Catholic priest as well as a historian, was more inclined to consider the negative features of the reign, especially the persecution of recusant and seminary priests (chapter 4). More positive perceptions were influenced by the imperial expansion of Britain in the late nineteenth century, in the name of another great Queen: Victorians frequently equated their achievements with those of the Elizabethans. The positive outlook continued well into the twentieth century in the work of A.F. Pollard (1910)[10] and in what was for many years considered the greatest of all biographies of Elizabeth: written in 1934 by J.E. Neale,[11] this projected her as a Queen of the Renaissance, fully in control of the political situation.

Neale provided a direct link with the post-war period and the revival of the interest in Elizabeth I during the 1950s, when praise for the Queen and her achievements reached a new peak. In 1950 S.T. Bindoff wrote of 'that line of statesmen-monarchs than whom, indeed, no wiser or mightier ever adorned the English throne, and of whom she herself . . . was in the fullness of her genius the superb and matchless flower'.[12] According to A.L. Rowse,[13] 'All historians now know that it was Elizabeth who ruled in England' and that 'when she was gone, her work stood clear and unmistakable'.[14] Such views were influenced partly by the times in which these historians wrote: Britain had just experienced a major war under the leadership of Churchill, and was, of course, entering a new Elizabethan era. It was also experiencing the ideological rivalry of the Cold War, which Neale compared with the religious antipathies of the sixteenth century. 'Had it not been for her, the broad way of English life would have been narrowed and an experiment made with what we today term the ideological state.'[15] (See Chapters 5 and 6.) The Elizabethan cult was therefore renewed within the context of some of the most renowned and reputable historical writing of the day. The reign had produced moderation as an alternative to extremism and balance as an alternative to chaos.

Since then there has been a considerable amount of reconsideration, influenced, among others, by C. Haigh[16] and A.G.R. Smith.[17] Some historians have been much more openly critical of Elizabeth's government. G. Donaldson argued that she 'allowed problems to build up in her later years' and that her reign 'ended in anti-climax, in decline and almost in failure'.[18] Such criticisms have been made of Elizabeth's religious policies and achievements (considered in Chapters 3, 4 and 5), her relations with Parliament (Chapter 2) and her foreign policy (Chapter 6). Within the context of the present chapter, revisionism has affected the assessment of Elizabeth's role as monarch and the functioning of her ministers and institutions. There is, however, no cut-and-dried transformation – rather a shifting of emphasis and balance, with periodic revivals of the emphasis on positive achievement.

The context of the reign in the sixteenth and seventeenth centuries

Placing the reign within the context of 'early modern' English history has produced four distinctive sets of arguments, two 'looking back' and two 'looking forward'.

The traditional retrospective view is that the Elizabethan period saw internal recovery and the achievement of new heights after a period of 'mid-Tudor crisis' under Edward VI (1547–53) and Mary (1553–58).[19] The obvious supporters of this thesis were those who attached most importance to the influence of Elizabeth – for example, Green, Creighton and, more recently, Neale and Rowse. An alternative twist has been to point to a bridge between Henry VIII's innovatory achievements and Elizabeth's fulfilment of them – a bridge across the chasm of the reigns of Edward VI and (especially) Mary. G.R. Elton, for example, argued that Henry VIII provided a Tudor 'revolution in govern-ment',[20] which was subsequently endangered by his two successors. Fortunately, the premature deaths of Edward VI and Mary meant that 'Good government came back in the nick of time.'[21] Bindoff similarly called Mary's reign 'a dangerous corner',[22] while W.R.D. Jones referred in 1973 to the Tudor 'high noons' of Henry VIII and Elizabeth, in con-trast to the 'trouble-shadowed reigns of Edward VI and Mary'.[23] Some of this has now been substantially revised. D. Loades,[24] A.G.R. Smith,[25] P. Williams[26] and many others have shown that the mid-Tudor period was one of achievement in two senses – consolidation of Henry VIII's changes and further innovation in its own right. These approaches affect the overall interpretation of Elizabeth's reign: if it followed a period of positive development, was its achievement any less than if it had followed a political vacuum?

This is a recurring theme in the chapters which follow – as is the 'look forward' into the seventeenth century. On the one hand, Elizabeth's reign has been seen as a respite, after which England experienced deepening crisis on the 'high road to civil war'. Both Camden and

Naunton, for example, contrasted the positive statecraft of Elizabeth with the failings of James I and Charles I. More recently, both Rowse and Neale have emphasised the resilient balance of radical and conservative forces under Elizabeth. According to Rowse, England was a 'small society – tough, vigorous and pulsating with energy', which 'accomplished those extraordinary achievements and made the age the most remarkable in our history'.[27] The collapse of this balance and energy projected England into crisis, rebellion and civil war. There is also a mirror-image of this version – that Elizabeth's reign actually stored up dangers for the future: Donaldson, for example, argued that many of the problems of the next reign 'were not of James's making'; rather, they were the 'damnosa hereditas of Elizabeth, a sovereign utterly careless of the well-being of her kingdom after her own demise'.[28] In complete contrast to this approach is one of the major revisionist interpretations concerning the seventeenth century, which is reflected in Chapters 2 and 5. C. Russell and others have argued that the Civil War was not the end of a 'high road' but, to vary the metaphor, had shallower roots in the crisis of Charles I: 'Both the religious and the financial problem had been plainly visible by the 1550s, and they had not created civil war in ninety years since then'.[29] Similarly, both Haigh[30] and Guy[31] have loosened the connection (whether positive or negative) between Elizabeth and the Civil War by questioning the 'balance' attributed by Neale.

The phases of the reign

The reign of Elizabeth has traditionally been seen as one of high achievement, ending in uncertainty and crisis. There was, in other words, a basic contrast between two phases divided at about 1590. This is based on the premise that the Queen herself, through her considerable political skills and her extensive popularity, was directly responsible for the stability from 1558 through to the 1580s. She it was who maintained political equilibrium by balancing out or neutralising the political factions, while preserving unquestioned ascendancy over all her ministers. Then, in complete contrast, the 1590s saw a decline in the Queen's popularity and the growth of political instability which provided an ominous precedent for the earlier Stuarts. The end of the domination of politics by reliable ministers meant that more volatile influences like that of Essex were exerted on Elizabeth. Faced with this sort of decline the regime was actually fortunate to survive at all.

The revisionist approach has been to establish a greater degree of continuity between the phases of the reign. The earlier period was not quite as positive as was once implied and the later period less negative. The argument has now been put that the role of the Queen in ensuring the stability of the early years may have been exaggerated. The premise here is that she did not inherit a crisis from Mary; nor was she as much in control of the political situation and her ministers as was once thought. The corollary is that the 1590s were less disastrous for the regime than the traditional view suggests. The depression and bad harvests were insufficient to cause major opposition and were, in any case, no worse than they had been during the reign of Mary. As for the Essex revolt, it was no greater than some of the earlier threats, and Elizabeth showed no diminution in her ability to deal with it.

Perhaps the balance has gone too far the other way. Instead of, on the one hand, a contrast between success for most of the reign and failure at its end and, on the other, a record of more consistent – but less remarkable – achievement, there is a third possibility. This is alternation within the reign between periods of relative stability and periods of crisis. It therefore makes sense to divide the reign into four phases. The first, between 1558 and 1562, was one of adjustment after the reign of Mary. During this period Elizabeth established her ascendancy, introduced a new religious settlement as the most pressing priority (see Chapter 3) and settled on the balance of her ministerial team. There was, indeed, a considerable change in personnel between 1558 and 1559. Mary's main advisers, including Paget, were dismissed and the Privy Council, which was still the main governing institution, contained far fewer Catholics. Only Winchester, Arundel, Derby and Shrewsbury were included – and none was still in place in 1572. Instead, places were filled by Protestants, some moderate, others, like Bedford and Knollys, more radical. Undoubtedly the greatest influence of the period was William Cecil, who became Lord Burghley in 1571.

During the second period, between 1562 and 1570, this initial stability was threatened. The influence of Cecil was diluted by Lord Robert Dudley, the Earl of Leicester, from 1564 onwards, and the arrival of the Earl of Sussex on the Privy Council in 1565. The result was considerable rivalry, to an extent which has been seen as destabilising. Leicester pursued his own interests, attempting to undermine the position of Cecil. The cohesion of the Privy Council suffered and there were even threats to a harmonious succession. Sussex and Leicester, for example, tried to secure a marriage between Norfolk and Mary Queen of Scots. Should Elizabeth not have children of her own, any issue from this marriage would succeed. In the meantime, Cecil – arguably the real target of this plot – would be replaced by more openly Catholic advisers. The Northern Earls would, if necessary, enforce all this by military intervention. This is often seen as a dire threat to the Elizabethan government and could perhaps have succeeded had it been fully pressed. But the scheme was never carried out. Leicester and Sussex pulled out, the rising of the Northern Earls melted away after their forces had reached Durham, and Norfolk was forced into abject submission. The outcome of this potentially dangerous period was very satisfactory for the Elizabethan regime. The conservative element lost their chance to secure a Catholic settlement, which meant that the pendulum swung towards the Protestants, while stability was assured by the consolidation of Cecil's power.

Once the problems of the second phase had been resolved, England entered a more stable period during the 1570s and 1580s. Several factors made the difference. One was the administrative stability provided by the closer collaboration between Cecil, who harboured no grudge, and Leicester, who seems to have learned his lesson. To this were added the talents of Sir Christopher Hatton and Sir Francis Walsingham. Between them, the four statesmen dominated the third period – the 1570s and 1580s – giving rise to what has been seen as an era of moderation, consensus and stability. It was also, of course, the phase of the reign in which England overcame its most serious threat from Spain.

The fourth period, from the early 1590s to the end of the reign in 1603, saw a number of problems. One was the end of the continuity provided by Elizabeth's most famous ministers. Of the quartet which had dominated the era of stability, Leicester died in 1588, Walsingham in 1590 and Hatton in 1591. Although Cecil survived until 1598, his role was greatly reduced through illness. Another problem was economic depression in the second half of the decade, accelerated by three bad harvests in a row in 1594, 1595 and 1596. A third was the reduced effectiveness in the pursuit of the war with Spain, after the high point of the defeat of the Armada in 1588. Finally, there was an apparent increase in internal dissent, expressed particularly by Parliament, and a renewed threat to the Queen's security posed by the Essex rebellion. The reign therefore ended on a note of uncertainty.

Questions

1. 'A great queen, a glorious reign.' 'A reign which left more problems than it solved.' Have historians reflected these views?
2. Which is the more convincing perspective: 'a reign in parts' or 'a reign continuous'?

SOURCES

1. ELIZABETH AND THE TASK OF MONARCHY

Source 1.1: An extract from *Mirror for Magistrates* (1559).

> Full little know we wretches what we do
> When we presume our princes to resist.
> We war with God against His glory too,
> That placeth in His office whom He list.

Source 1.2: Edward Rishton's assessment of Elizabeth's policy towards Catholics, first published in Cologne in 1585.

In the midst of this cruelty exercised upon all Catholics of every rank, in order to conceal at times in some measure from foreign princes, and even the Pope himself, the severity of the persecution, and gain for themselves the reputation of being moderate and merciful, they show their mercy so fraudulently, that while they are harassing, torturing, and killing one, the royal indulgence is often extended to another. Thus when there is a lucid interval or rest from the slaughter of innocent people in London, the fury of the persecution breaks out in the country with greater violence, and while they seem to allow greater freedom to some, they at the same time harass others in the most cruel way. And in order that this their cunning may the better subserve their end, they keep certain persons in the courts of princes whose business it is to insist upon, set forth, and enhance this dishonest and delusive mercy in the presence of those who are unacquainted with our affairs, and at the same time to lessen or excuse the dreadful deeds of their unmeasurable cruelty, or to explain them in a sense contrary to the faith.

Source 1.3: Elizabeth's speech to her army at Tilbury, 8 August 1588.

My loving people, we have been persuaded by some that are careful of our safety, to take heed how we commit ourselves to armed multitudes, for fear of treachery. But I assure you, I do not desire to live to distrust my faithful and loving people. Let tyrants fear. I have always so behaved myself that, under God, I have placed my chiefest strength and safeguard in the loyal hearts and good will of my subjects; and therefore I am come amongst you, as you see, at this time, not for my recreation and disport, but being resolved, in the midst and heat of the battle, to live or die amongst you all, to lay down for my God, and for my kingdom, and for my people, my honour and my blood, even in the dust. I know I have the body of a weak and feeble woman, but I have the heart and stomach of a king, and of a king of England too, and think foul scorn that Parma or Spain, or any prince of Europe should dare to invade the borders of my realm; to which, rather than any dishonour shall grow by me, I myself will take up arms, I myself will be your general, judge, and rewarder of every one of your virtues in the field. I know, already for your forwardness you have deserved rewards and crowns; and we do assure you, in the word of a prince, they shall be duly paid you.

Source 1.4: Elizabeth's speech to Parliament in 1601.

I know the title of a King is a glorious title; but assure yourself that the shining glory of princely authority hath not so dazzled the eyes of our understanding, but that we well know and remember that we also are to yield an account of our actions before the great Judge.

To be a king and wear a crown is a thing more glorious to them that see it, than it is pleasant to them that bear it. For myself, I was never so much enticed with the glorious name of a king or royal authority of a queen, as delighted that God hath made me His instrument to maintain His truth and glory, and to defend this Kingdom (as I said) from peril, dishonour, tyranny and oppression. There will never queen sit in my seat with more zeal to my country, care to my subjects, and that will sooner with willingness venture her life for your good and safety, than myself. For it is not my desire to live nor reign longer than my life and reign shall be for your good. And though you have had and may have many princes more mighty and wise sitting in this seat, yet you never had or shall have any that will be more careful and loving.

Questions

1. What light do Sources 1.3 and 1.4 throw on Elizabeth's attitude to her royal responsibilities?
2. To what extent do Sources 1.1, 1.3 and 1.4 provide an answer to the charges made in Source 1.2?
3. 'As near fitted to the task of monarchy as it is possible to envisage.' Do these sources, and your own knowledge, support this view?

Worked answer: What light do Sources 1.3 and 1.4 throw on Elizabeth's attitude to her royal responsibilities?

[Advice: This question asks for a direct answer, based on the words 'attitudes' and 'responsibilities', which should be clearly identified. Avoid merely summarising Sources 1.3 and 1.4 separately. Instead, deduce the main issues from the sources and then develop them in your answer, in the process taking examples from both 1.3 and 1.4. Quotations should consist of short phrases only, within the context of

your own sentence structure. 'What light' obviously means what is revealed directly. But it could also allow for one or two indirect inferences – perhaps following the more detailed points.]

Several common features appear in both sources. One is that Elizabeth saw in her authority the proper fulfilment of a trust delegated from God, as indicated by the extracts 'under God' (Source 1.3) and 'God hath made me His instrument' (Source 1.4). This was to be exercised in devotion to her people, reigning 'more for your good and safety, than myself' (1.4); in return she expected – and accepted – 'the loyal hearts and good will' of her subjects (1.3). Protection of her realm was another key responsibility. In a time of peril from abroad 'I am come amongst you ... in the midst and heat of battle' (1.3); similarly, she expressed her intention to Parliament 'to defend this Kingdom ... from peril', while also extending this to preventing 'dishonour, tyranny and oppression' (1.4). In the process, she would act as 'judge and rewarder' (1.3) in the same way that she, as monarch, would 'yield an account of our actions before the great Judge' (1.4). Both sources indicate that she was aware that being a woman was a possible shortcoming in her power – but that she was determined to turn this into a strength. Hence although she had 'the body of a weak and feeble woman' she had 'the heart and stomach of a king' (1.3) and, although there may have been princes 'more mighty and wise', there would never be one 'more careful and loving' (1.4).

The two sources also show Elizabeth's ability to fit her perception of royal responsibilities to the occasion. Although their key components were very similar, their overall tone was different, indicating that the Queen had the duty both to inspire (Source 1.3) and to reassure (Source 1.4). The speech at Tilbury was a monarch's exhortation to victory over 'invaders of my realm', while the speech to Parliament was more a reminder that she had authority and a reassurance that she would use it wisely. Both, therefore, show the importance she attributed to statecraft.

2. HISTORIANS ON ELIZABETH'S LEGACY

Source 2.1: From J. Lingard, *A History of England from the First Invasion by the Romans to the Accession of William and Mary in 1688*, published in 1855.

The historians, who celebrate the golden days of Elizabeth, have described with a glowing pencil the happiness of the people under her sway. To them might be opposed the dismal picture of national misery, drawn by the Catholic writers of the same period. But both have taken too contracted a view of the subject. Religious dissension had divided the nation into opposite parties, of almost equal numbers, the oppressors and the oppressed. . . .

It is evident that neither Elizabeth nor her ministers understood the benefits of civil and religious liberty. The prerogatives which she so highly prized, have long since withered away; the bloody code which she enacted against the rights of conscience, has ceased to stain the pages of the statute book; and the result has proved, that the abolition of despotism and intolerance adds no less to the stability of the throne, than to the happiness of the people.

Source 2.2: From J.A. Froude, *History of England from the Fall of Wolsey to the Defeat of the Spanish Armada*, published in 1904.

The greatest achievement in English history, the 'breaking the bonds of Rome' and the establishment of spiritual independence, was completed without bloodshed under Elizabeth's auspices, and Elizabeth may have the glory of the work. Many problems growing out of it were left unsettled. Some were disposed of on the scaffold at Whitehall, some in the revolution of 1688; some yet survive to test the courage and the ingenuity of modern politicians.

Source 2.3: From J. Hurstfield: *The Elizabethan Nation*, first published in 1964.

She tried hard to heal the wounds and divisions of the England she inherited, and she met with a large measure of success. She was a divided person, torn between the individual, private interests of a highly intelligent, vigorous woman and the public tasks which denied her the full enjoyment and expression of her private being. In her public tasks she succeeded admirably during the first thirty years of her reign in healing the wounds and binding the nation to her own purposes; but she failed significantly during the last fifteen. Delay, ambiguity, the elevation of monarchy to raise the aims and unify the purpose of the Elizabethan people were no longer enough. In one sense, her reign was both too long and too short. If she had lived ten years less she might have gone down to history as the most successful monarch to sit on the English throne.

Source 2.4: From J.P. Kenyon, *The Stuarts*, published in 1958.

Elizabeth I was a great woman and a great queen, but in the decade straddling her death her popularity was at its nadir. The reign closed in an atmosphere of depression, with war abroad, pestilence and rising prices at home, the government wracked by faction and bitterly unpopular, and parliament sunk in discontented apathy. The Tudor polity was running down, and men awaited the first king to sit on the English throne for half a century in expectation of some decisive change.

Source 2.5: From C. Haigh's Introduction to *The Reign of Elizabeth I* (published in 1984), a collection of articles re-examining various aspects of Elizabeth's reign.

One of the foundations of Elizabeth's reputation among modern historians has been her apparent success in holding in check those movements which were to bring civil war forty years after her death. But one of the most obvious (if controversial) developments in the recent historiography of early-modern England has been the attempt to shorten the causal sequence leading to the Civil War. Conrad Russell has reinterpreted the parliamentary difficulties of the years 1604–29 and denied that there was any emerging constitutional crisis resulting from parliamentary pretensions ... and Anthony Fletcher has sought the origins of the war in the political misunderstandings and suspicions of 1640–2. If historians of early-Stuart England have abolished the long-term causes of the Civil War, wherein lies the greatness of Elizabeth I?

Questions

1. In what ways, and for what reasons, do Sources 2.2 and 2.5 differ in their approaches to Elizabeth's longer-term impact on England?
2. 'Historians have tended to praise Elizabeth's legacy to England.' Do these sources, and your own knowledge, support this view?

2

ELIZABETH AND PARLIAMENT

BACKGROUND

Altogether, Parliament met during twenty-six years of the reign of Elizabeth (1559, 1563–67, 1571, 1572–81, 1584–85, 1586–87, 1589, 1593, 1597–98 and 1601). It dealt with religious issues, especially the settlement of 1559, subsequent demands for modifying the settlement, financial needs for campaigns against Scotland and France, several rebellions, the attainder of Mary Queen of Scots, the increasing crisis involving Spain, and a variety of social issues, including the Poor Law. This was an extensive involvement, even if constitutionally less momentous than it had been during the reign of Henry VIII.

Analysis 1 considers the extensive reinterpretations: here it would be no exaggeration to say that former arguments have been stood on their heads. Analysis 2 examines the main changes made to Parliament during the reign, while Analysis 3 deals with the relations between Parliament on the one hand and the Queen and her government on the other.

ANALYSIS 1: HOW HAVE THE VIEWS OF HISTORIANS CHANGED ON ELIZABETH'S PARLIAMENTS?

Views depend on the perspectives of a particular period: inevitably the 'new view' of one period will become the 'old view' of the next. Elizabethan Parliaments have seen three clearly identifiable phases of interpretation. The first of these lasted from the nineteenth century until the 1940s, with major reinterpretations following in the 1950s. These, in turn, were widely accepted until the 1980s when they were summarily inverted.

The emphasis of nineteenth-century historians such as J. Lingard[1] was very much on the despotism of the Tudors, against which Parliament was relatively helpless (see Source 2.1 below). Parliament was considered to have played little part in the centralisation of government and administration under Henry VIII. The mid-sixteenth century saw no real change as the House of Commons was of little importance to Somerset, Northumberland and Mary, while Elizabeth continued the process of using Parliament to rubber-stamp constitutional and religious changes which were essentially executive decisions. There is here an overall pattern. Parliament had been far more important during the Middle Ages, especially during the Lancastrian period. It had begun its decline under the Yorkists and experienced a long period of subservience, even repression, under the Tudors, before reviving and challenging the royal prerogatives of the Stuarts. The Tudor period, including the reign of Elizabeth, was therefore seen as an interruption in the long-term process of parliamentary evolution.

This view was virtually reversed by two of the great historians of the first half of the twentieth century, A.F. Pollard[2] and J.E. Neale.[3] They put forward a very different perspective. Parliament had never really developed during the Middle Ages. Under the Tudors it gradually evolved until it reached maturity during the reign of Elizabeth. Its members were becoming more involved and self-assertive, willing to challenge the government and the decisions of the Privy Council. The core of the new resistance was the Puritan element. Neale deduced from a contemporary pamphlet, which referred to the 'Puritan Choir', that this was sustained and substantial. The Puritans maintained a consistent opposition campaign to Elizabeth and her government. It forced her to accept a more radical settlement in 1559, criticised her failure to marry and thereby guarantee an heir, placed incessant pressure on her government to provide further religious reforms, and pressed for the execution of Mary Queen of Scots. They also demanded the suspension of financial grants until these points had been satisfactorily addressed. Leadership was provided by Peter Wentworth, who was so outspoken in his criticism that he was imprisoned in the Tower, where he died in 1597. All this seemed to foreshadow the conflict between the House of Commons and the Stuart kings. The origins of the English Civil War can therefore be traced back to the opposition developing within Parliament during the reign of Elizabeth. Far from interrupting the evolution of

Parliament, therefore, the Tudor period – and especially the reign of Elizabeth – was a vital part of it.

This interpretation became strongly entrenched as the orthodox view on the subject. A new wave was bound to come sooner or later. But in this case it has been particularly spectacular: the Neale thesis of the Puritan core in Parliament providing a preview to the challenge to the Stuarts has been all but demolished. Considerable work was done in this area by G.R. Elton[4] and M.A.R. Graves.[5] The new argument stressed that far too much has been read into the existence of the Puritan Choir: it was much looser than Neale had suggested and the opposition alleged to have been orchestrated by the Puritans was just as likely to have been stirred up, on specific issues, by members of the Queen's own Council. In other words, the Queen's executive servants used the legislature as part of a strategy to get round her obstinacy. Several new dimensions were added to this reinterpretation of Elizabeth's Parliaments. One was the questioning of the use of long-term perspectives. Putting the reign of Elizabeth within the context of the origins of the Civil War was seen as too retrospective and as allowing a 'Whig' interpretation of history to dominate analysis. Hence, according to Graves, Pollard, Neale and others 'fell into the trap of trying to explain seventeenth-century upheavals, instead of studying Tudor parliaments in their own light and not as mere prologue'.[6] Second, G.W.O. Woodward had already added an important additional perspective to this by emphasising that we should not necessarily be looking for conflict between the crown and Parliament. 'Just as the king sometimes acts in and through his council, so on other occasions he acts in and through that greater council, his Parliament. . . . Never has there been a simple and clear division between the monarch and the two houses.' Hence there is no inherent need for conflict: 'because the Houses of Parliament are not necessarily to be found in conflict with their sovereign there is nothing inherently improbable about Parliament enjoying an increase in power and prestige at the same time as the Crown. There is in fact no paradox to explain away.'[7]

Yet the 'revisionist' approach has not been entirely accepted. Although he had helped demolish Neale's arguments about the development of concerted and long-term opposition within the Commons, Graves was not convinced that the preoccupations of MPs were entirely 'parochial' and that all was harmony 'between the Crown and governing class'. Instead, there were some grounds for genuine disagreement and the 'Lords and Commons were willing and able to challenge both the Queen and each other' (see Source 2.4 below). This is broadly the line taken in the next two Analyses. The overall picture is therefore of an institution which was changing but not in any radical sense. The process did not go beyond the normal pattern of evolution which one would expect over a forty-year period. This much is now generally accepted and the Neale thesis that the Elizabethan House of Commons was moving into incipient opposition to the Crown no longer holds water. On the other hand, it is possible to swing too far in the other direction and to underestimate the capacity of the Commons to follow specific issues which it considered important. Parliament may not have developed under Elizabeth into an oppositional institution. But it was quite capable of showing opposition on specific issues. The Neale thesis has been largely discredited without, as yet, a major alternative being established. Hence there remains something of a vacuum – until further research can fill it. Until then, there is a legitimate doubt that the pendulum may have swung too far the other way. There is a danger in segmenting interpretation which is potentially as great as that of linking the segments to obtain an interpretation. It is all very well to cut the Elizabethan Parliaments out of the long-term origins of the Civil War, but how far do we have to go to be confident about the causes of this conflict? Elton rightly maintained that 'all this still needs a lot of working out'.[8]

Questions

1. On what grounds did Pollard and Neale question the original view of Elizabeth and her Parliaments?
2. With what justification was Neale's interpretation subsequently challenged?

ANALYSIS 2: DID THE POWER AND ROLE OF PARLIAMENT CHANGE DURING THE REIGN OF ELIZABETH?

The controversy over the power of the opposition within Parliament inevitably affects interpretations as to its role. There are two quite distinct theories about this.

Neale summarised the main development as follows. 'At the opening of the sixteenth century Parliament was essentially a legislative and taxing body, its meetings intermittent. Even at the end of the century the same description might be formally applied to it; but in the meantime it had become a political force with which the Crown and government had to reckon.' The development of opposition meant the emergence of a group within Parliament with a distinctive alternative programme. This was bound to lead to a fundamental questioning of the power of the crown. Not so, argued Elton. Parliament achieved more during the reign of Henry VIII than under Elizabeth, underpinning the major political changes of the 1530s. But this was largely because Parliament was led in that direction by the King and his Council. Under Elizabeth there was no real change in Parliament – only in the attitude of the monarch. 'In the reign of Henry VIII, politics achieved their aim because the monarch, proprietor of Parliaments, took the lead. In the reign of Elizabeth, political debates in Parliament and especially in the Commons never achieved anything because the monarch was entirely free to ignore them and usually did so.' Hence the power of Parliament 'never changed in its fundamental characteristics'.[9]

Which of these views reflects more accurately the role of Parliament? Did it increase in importance by changing its role? Or did it remain essentially the same?

There would be a strong argument that at the beginning of Elizabeth's reign Parliament was well placed. This was the result of a gradual process comprising several major components. First, Parliament's prestige had been greatly increased since the 1520s. During the reign of Henry VIII the emphasis had been very much on the involvement of Parliament in all stages of constitutional change and the gradual emergence of the supremacy of statute law over all other forms. Contemporaries were certainly aware of the change in the importance of Parliament: during the 1560s Sir Thomas Smith wrote that 'the most high and absolute power of the realm of England consisteth in the Parliament'.[10] Second, the increase in the power of Parliament had been accompanied by a decrease in the power of the crown after the death of Henry VIII in 1547. Although we have already seen that the term 'mid-Tudor crisis' is highly contentious, there was nevertheless an inevitable decrease in the prerogative power of Edward VI, a boy king, and Mary, the first woman on the throne of England. Third, the religious swings during the period 1547–58 had been accomplished through Parliament – whether in the form of the acceleration of Protestantism under Northumberland, or the reversion to Catholicism under Mary. Religious settlements therefore entrenched the changed relationship between crown and Parliament. What had been considered a privilege during the 1530s had become habit and convention by the 1550s. Finally, the size of the House of Commons was increasing rapidly during the course of the sixteenth century: it had risen to 400 in 1559 and continued during Elizabeth's reign to the eventual figure of 462.

We can establish therefore that there was no going back to the position before the 1530s. Parliament was now a permanent component in the government of England and in the establishment of religious settlements, clearly the most important ideological issue of the day.

On the other hand, there was still plenty of royal power left to ensure that Parliament did not assume its own momentum of growth. This is perhaps where the main part of Neale's interpretation can be challenged. Parliament was, for example, still dependent on the crown for its summons and for its duration. The number of its sessions scarcely warrants the view that it had increased in importance. During her reign, Elizabeth called ten Parliaments, in 1559, 1563–67, 1571, 1572–81, 1584–85, 1586–87, 1589, 1593, 1597–98 and 1601. Altogether, these sat for a total of about thirty-six months during the forty-five years of her reign: each session lasted fewer than ten weeks. The majority of these sessions were not taken up with momentous constitutional issues – a clear departure from the developments of previous reigns. It is true that the first few years of Elizabeth's reign saw further legislation of major constitutional importance, but this did not set a precedent for further developments during the reign. After the initial settlement, subsequent Parliaments were summoned very much for specific purposes or to carry out the normal business of government. They were not called to bring about a major change. Specific reasons for calling Parliament included dealing with crises like the Northern rebellion of 1569–70 or the problem surrounding Mary Queen of Scots and the plots hatched on her behalf, together with the increase in Catholic activity in England in the 1580s.

Similarly, any fundamental growth in the power of Parliament would suggest that there was a quid pro quo for any co-operation with the crown. This did exist, but not in a way which would suggest the growing power of the House of Commons in relation *to* the crown. The positive side was that the House of Commons sometimes took it upon itself to initiate business, trying to make provision for the succession during the Queen's bout of smallpox in 1563 or persuading her to marry and provide an heir. On the other hand, there were two developments which would normally be associated with the political advance of Parliament which did not occur during Elizabeth's reign. One was the distancing of Parliament from the government. The other was the question of financial supply: Parliament did not yet make the supply of revenue conditional upon the redress of grievances or influence on policy.

Nor did Parliament alter its methods to enhance its power. According to Graves, 'Records, procedures and privileges existed and were refined in order to facilitate the transaction of humdrum legislative business, rather than to strengthen the Commons in its confrontations with the Queen.'[11] In any case, the House of Commons showed an inability to tidy up several areas where it was deficient. One of these was the matter of its attendance. Absenteeism was a major problem in most sessions of the House of Commons. Perhaps this has led to over-estimating the numerical importance of the Queen's critics: it was not so much that they were gaining in numbers compared with her supporters, but rather that the latter were unreliable in turning up and pressure had to be put upon them by the Council or by their patrons in the Lords. The fact that the Privy Council was concerned to maximise membership indicates that Parliament normally functioned in co-operation with the government. Any problems which emerged were likely to be associated with an irregular minority who were given temporary and disproportionate influence by the unpredictable patterns of attendance of the rest. This does not add up to an institutional challenge to the power of the crown. The problem was that there were few successful remedies during the Elizabethan period. Roll-calls were uncommon, excuses and evasions covered every conceivable eventuality. Bills were introduced to enforce attendance; they failed to get through. Fines were imposed from time to time, but not in a way which became systematic. The pattern of attendance, of course, worked both ways. On the one hand, it deprived the House of Commons of a corporate identity which would enable it to challenge the power of the crown. This meant that Elizabeth's prerogatives were never under any threat – or potential threat. On the other hand, absenteeism did give a disproportionate voice to the vociferous minority on occasions, which has possibly led to this being identified as an opposition.

What of the role of Parliament in legislation? Neale argued that the role of the House of Commons in legislation increased during the reign of Elizabeth and that this was evinced by the existence of a journal for the Commons from 1547.[12] Graves, however, challenged this on two grounds. First, records had been kept long before then and any improvements or refinements in the process were of institutional rather than political significance: they should not be seen as 'signs of the political maturation or rise of the Lower House'.[13] It has been argued that, far from making further progress in controlling the issue of legislation, Parliament actually regressed during the reign of Elizabeth from the higher points reached under Henry VIII and even under Edward VI and Mary. What seems to have happened is a refinement of the legislative process – especially the process of the first, second and third readings of Bills – without any real enhancement of parliamentary initiative in the introduction of those bills.

Finally, it is not even possible to say that the lower chamber had made much progress in relation to the upper. The House of Lords was still more efficient than the House of Commons and had just as much to do with legislation. It also had a strong influence over the Commons through a network of social connections and patronage. These provided for a considerable degree of continuity, as it was unlikely that those members whose seats depended on the favour of the Lords would seek to assert the independence of the Commons. The composition of the Lords also underwent little change – at least after the first year of Elizabeth's reign, when most of the bishops were replaced because of their objection to the nature of the religious settlement. Thereafter the membership remained constant at twenty-six bishops and between fifty-five and sixty-two lay peers. It has been estimated that up to one-third of the latter owed their titles directly to the Queen. More than ever, therefore, they were a force for conservatism and tradition, which suited the Queen admirably.

Questions

1. In what areas did the power of the House of Commons change during the reign of Elizabeth?
2. Was Parliament more efficient in 1603 than it had been in 1558?

ANALYSIS 3: HOW SUCCESSFULLY DID ELIZABETH AND HER GOVERNMENT MANAGE PARLIAMENT?

Looked at from the perspective of the beginning of her reign, the prospects for Elizabeth holding her own against Parliament, let alone dominating it, must have appeared remote. She was only the second woman to come to the throne; she inherited a nation divided along religious lines; and she ruled a country which had just been humiliated by the loss of Calais to France and was now threatened by the candidature of Mary Queen of Scots to the throne. There was plenty of material here for potential conflict between crown and Parliament.

We should not allow revisionist arguments which reduce the importance of Parliament under Elizabeth to imply that there were no conflicts at all. There were, in fact, several very important altercations. One concerned the religious settlement of 1559. Opposition was articulated by most of the Catholic bishops in the House of Lords, who as a consequence were removed from their posts. In the Commons, the 'Puritan Choir' tried to move the Church of England further in the direction of Calvinism. During the 1570s a more radical core emerged, led by members such as Cartwright, Field, Travers and Wilcox. In 1584, in particular, a campaign was launched to replace the Prayer Book by the Form of Prayers which was then being used in Geneva. Another Bill introduced two years later attempted to abolish the episcopal structure and establish the consistory preferred by Presbyterians. Further conflict developed over the Queen's reluctance to marry and thereby guarantee a Tudor heir to the throne. In 1563 and again between 1566 and 1567 a substantial part of the Commons – not just the Puritan Choir – attempted to put pressure on her to fulfil her duty to the dynasty. Third, there were occasions when the Commons objected to the Queen's insistence that they should discuss only issues sanctioned by her government. Peter and Paul Wentworth challenged her right to do this when she ordered that there should be no further discussion over her marriage in 1566. 'Here', according to Neale, 'was something fundamental: an innovation in parliamentary tactics': indeed, it was the 'dawn of a new age' and a 'harbinger of Stuart conflicts'.[14]

And yet, by and large, all the pessimistic prognostications about the ability of Elizabeth to handle these problems proved unfounded. She and her government were able on most occasions to face down the opposition they experienced. We need, however, to distinguish between the two constraints exerted on the House of Commons. One was by the Queen herself, and might be considered subjective. This showed the extent of her prerogative and the extent to which she was prepared to use it. It also demonstrates her skills in handling periodic opposition from factions within the Lords and Commons. The other constraint was longer term and objective: the way in which various parts of the constitution interacted, together with the influence of social factors.

The Queen's approach to Parliament showed respect, caution and firmness – even obstinacy. Her respect was shown in her response to the Petition for Privileges made by the House of Commons in 1559, conveyed by the Lord Keeper: 'To these petitions the Queen's Majesty hath commanded me to say unto you that her Highness is right well contented to grant them unto you as largely as amply and as liberally as ever they were granted by any of her noble progenitors; and to confirm the same with great authority.'[15] At the same time, she had a certain reluctance to make any more use of Parliament than was absolutely necessary. According to the Lord Keeper in 1593, 'Her Majesty hath evermore been most loth to call for the assembly of the people in her parliament and hath done the same but rarely.'[16] There were also times when she was determined to keep the House of Commons under the strictest control. On occasion she rejected the criticism of the House, as an entry in the Commons' Journals shows for 9 November 1566:

'Mr Vice-Chamberlain declared the Queen's Majesty's express com-mandment to this House, that they should no further proceed in their suit, but to satisfy themselves with her Highness' promise of marriage . . .'[17] Elizabeth also expressed her displeasure at Puritan bills in 1566, 1571, 1572, 1586, 1587 and 1593. As a final resort she dealt summar-ily with recalcitrant members, ordering, for example, the arrest of Cope in 1596.

There were several ways in which the House of Commons could be controlled as an institution rather than by the Queen's own express command. It has been argued that the increase in the size of the House of Commons during Elizabeth's reign could be seen as a potential threat to the power of the crown. In fact, it was quite the reverse. The majority of the new members were royal nominees and the enfranchisement of new areas was usually the result of direct requests to the Queen from reliable members of the aristocracy with strong influence over them. For example, many of the new seats were in Cornwall, Lancashire and the Isle of Wight, all of which had large royal duchies. The new blocs of seats in the House of Commons were not, therefore, connected with the emergence of a challenge to the crown, but were rather a means whereby the crown could ensure the continu-ation of its own influence. The members who filled them depended upon patrons who were likely to be courtiers and therefore dependent on the Queen's favour. As such, these members could be relied upon to support the Queen at all times. This must significantly have increased her confidence when she had to issue reprimands to the Commons or to confront them on contentious issues.

There was also a clearly defined channel whereby the legislature could be influenced, even controlled, by the executive powers. It has now been established that leading members of the Puritan Choir were, in fact, closely connected to the officials of the Privy Council and were used by the latter to put pressure on the Queen over specific issues such as her marriage and the execution of Mary Queen of Scots. These included Councillors such as William Cecil, Francis Walsingham and the Earls of Leicester, Sussex and Bedford. As members of 'a pre-dominantly Protestant governing class',[18] they were determined that a means should be found to make the Queen give way on what they saw as the key issues: a guaranteed Protestant succession and measures against the perceived Catholic threat, especially against Mary Queen of Scots. Far from developing as a core of opposition to the Queen and her government, members like Fleetwood and Norton were actually being used by the government and carrying out the orders of men such as Burghley. In fact, as Elton pointed out, no fewer than a dozen members of the Puritan Choir were actually *in* the Privy Council. He argues that ' "Opposition" is the wrong term to employ, and "Puritan opposition" an even more misleading concept.'[19] It seems that we should be looking instead at the Queen's government making use of Parliament to put across its own views on policy. Although this has disposed of the interpretative trend for 'parliamentary opposition', it may have opened up one for 'responsible government'.

Questions

1. How much scope did Parliament have to express its views on the Queen and her government?
2. How much parliamentary opposition was there during the reign of Elizabeth?

SOURCES

1. THE QUEEN AND THE HOUSE OF COMMONS

Source 1.1: Sir Thomas Smith, *De Republica Anglorum*, 1565.

The most high and absolute power of the realm of England consisteth in the Parliament. For as in war, where the King himself in person, the nobility, the rest of the gentility and the yeomanry are, is the force and power of England: so in peace and consultation where the prince is to give life and the last and highest commandment, the barony for the nobility and higher, the knights, esquires, gentlemen and commons for the lower part of the commonwealth, consult and show what is good and necessary for the commonwealth. . . . That is the prince's and whole realm's deed; whereupon justly no man can complain but must accommodate himself to find it good and obey it. That which is done by this consent . . . is taken for law. . . . For every Englishman is intended to be there present, either in person or by procuration and attorneys, of what pre-eminence, state, dignity or quality soever he be, from the prince (be he king or queen) to the lowest person in England. And the consent of the Parliament is taken to be every man's consent.

Source 1.2: From a speech by Peter Wentworth in the Commons, 8 February 1576.

Amongst other, Mr Speaker, two things do great hurt in this place, of the which I do mean to speak. The one is a rumour which runs about the House, and this it is:

'take heed what you do: the Queen's Majesty likes not such a matter; whosoever prefers it, she will be offended with him'. The other: sometimes a message is brought into the House, either of commanding or inhibiting, very injurious to the freedom of speech and consultation. I would to God, Mr Speaker, that these two were buried in hell. I mean rumours and messages, for wicked undoubtedly they are; the reason is the devil was the first author of them, from whom proceeds nothing but wickedness....

Now the other was a message Mr Speaker brought the last sessions into the House, that we should not deal in any matters of religion but first to receive from the bishops. Surely this was a doleful message, for it was as much as to say, Sirs, ye shall not deal in God's causes, no, ye shall in no wise seek to advance His glory.... It is a dangerous thing in a prince unkindly to abuse his or her nobility and people and it is a dangerous thing in a prince to oppose or bend herself against her nobility and people.... And how could any prince more unkindly entreat, abuse, oppose herself against her nobility and people than her Majesty did the last Parliament? ... And will not this her Majesty's handling, think you, Mr Speaker, make cold dealing in any other Majesty's; subjects toward her again? I fear it will.... And I beseech God to endue her Majesty with His wisdom, whereby she may discern faithful advice from traitorous, sugared speeches, and send her Majesty a melting, yielding heart unto sound counsel, that will may not stand for a reason; and then her Majesty will stand when her enemies are fallen, for no estate can stand where the prince will not be governed by advice....

Source 1.3: From the speech of the Lord Keeper to the Commons in 1592.

Her Majesty granteth you liberal but not licentious speech, liberty therefore but with due limitation. For even as there can be no good consultation where all freedom of advice is barred, so will there be no good conclusion where every man may speak what he listeth, without fit observation of persons, matters, times, places and other needful circumstances.... For liberty of speech her Majesty commandeth me to tell you that to say yea or nay to bills, God forbid that any man should be restrained or afraid to answer according to his best liking, with some short declaration of his reason therein, and therein to have a free voice, which is the very true liberty of the House: not, as some suppose, to speak there of all causes as him listeth [as he pleases], and to frame a form of religion or a state of government as to their idle brains shall seem the meetest [the most fitting]. She sayeth no king fit for his state will suffer such absurdities, and ... she hopeth that no man here longeth so much for his ruin that he mindeth to make such a peril to his own safety.

Questions

1. Explain the circumstances behind the views expressed in Sources 1.2 and 1.3.
2. To what extent does Source 1.3 answer the concerns expressed in Source 1.2?
3. 'Elizabeth managed to steer a course between offending the House of Commons and surrendering her own authority over it.' Do these sources and your own knowledge support this view?

Worked answer: How effectively does Source 1.3 address the concerns expressed in Source 1.2?

[Advice: The answer to this question requires a direct comparison between the two sources. This should be fully integrated, not based on end-on summaries of each source. After reading the sources carefully, select criteria based on the 'concerns' in Source 1.2. Then apply these criteria, one by one, as they are 'answered' in Source 1.3. If preferred, the order could be reversed (1.3 against 1.2). To answer the question fully, it is important to consider 'to what extent?' To make something of this, avoid possible extremes of 'not at all' or 'completely', neither of which is very likely anyway. Instead, go for 'to an extent but not entirely'.]

Source 1.3 provides effective responses to three concerns raised in Source 1.2 by Peter Wentworth, albeit sixteen years later. Wentworth had complained of messages to the House which were 'injurious to the freedom of speech and consultation'. The Lord Keeper's instructions were that the House enjoyed 'liberal but not licentious speech' or liberty 'with due limitation'. Second, to the accusation that care had to be taken not to offend the Queen ('take heed what you do: the Queen's Majesty likes not such a matter'), the Lord Keeper replied that no man 'should be restrained or afraid to answer' – but that this should relate 'to bills' and not to 'all causes as him listeth'. Third, Wentworth particularly disliked the constraints on dealing with 'matters of religion' except on the authority of the bishops. The official justification for this was that such control was necessary to prevent individuals framing 'a religion' which 'their idle brains' saw as most fitting. The answers provided by the Lord Keeper were clearly intended to reassure the House that, far from its powers were being threatened, they were actually being clarified.

Yet there are clearly concerns which were not addressed. If anything, the lapse of time had enabled the Queen and her government to set the boundaries more clearly than Wentworth and many of his fellow members would have wanted. There was, for example, no concession on 'liberty of speech' *beyond* the directives laid down by the Queen. Nor was there any concession made by the Queen to 'discerning faithful advice' from 'sugared speeches'. As for Wentworth's view that 'no estate can stand where the prince will not be governed by advice', the official response was a threat rather than an answer – that such attitudes pursued by individuals could lead to their own 'ruin' and be a 'peril' to their own 'safety'. It was clear that, by the 1590s, Elizabeth dealt with Parliament with measured care, but that she retained the right to enforce her will when necessary. This is not what Wentworth originally had in mind.

2. INTERPRETATIONS OF ELIZABETHAN PARLIAMENTS

Source 2.1: From J. Lingard, *A History of England from the First Invasion by the Romans to the Accession of William and Mary in 1688*, published in 1855.

Elizabeth firmly believed, and zealously upheld the principles of government, established by her father, the exercise of absolute authority by the sovereign, and the duty of passive obedience in the subject. The doctrine, with which the lord keeper Bacon opened her first parliament, was indefatigably inculcated by all his successors during her reign, that, if the queen consulted the two houses it was through choice, not through necessity, to the end that her laws might be more satisfactory to her people, not that they might derive any force from their assent. She possessed by her prerogative whatever was requisite for the government of the realm. She could, at her pleasure, suspend the operation of existing statutes, or issue proclamations which should have the force of law. In her opinion the chief use of parliaments was to vote money, to regulate the minutiae of trade, and to legislate for individual and local interests. To the lower house she granted, indeed, freedom of debate: but it was to be a decent freedom, the liberty of 'saying ay or no'; and those that transgressed that decency were liable . . . to feel the weight of the royal displeasure.

Source 2.2: From J.E. Neale, *Elizabeth I and her Parliaments, 1584–1601*, published in 1957.

From the constitutional point of view, the most important theme in our story is the relationship of the Puritan Movement to parliamentary development. . . . By 1584, with the formation of their Classical organization, we are presented with a case-study in revolution. Though we now know that the Puritan Presbyterian party was by no means so restricted or unrepresentative as was once thought and that these clergymen enjoyed considerable support among the gentry, nevertheless they were a minority group. But present-day experience has taught us that it is not numbers – it is organization and a fanatical purpose that count in subversive conspiracies. Expert as our own age is in the technique of revolution, we cannot but marvel at the precocious efficiency of the Elizabethan Classical Movement. Thanks to the inflexible determination of the Queen and the rigid character of Whitgift, their projects failed; but by skilful exploitation of propitious circumstances they were able to shake Crown, Church, Council and Parliament. In pursuit of their aims, they taught the House of Commons methods of concerted action and propaganda. Indeed, the art of opposition, which might be considered the outstanding contribution of the Elizabethan period to parliamentary history, was largely learnt from them or inspired by them.

Source 2.3: G.R. Elton, 'Parliament in the Reign of Elizabeth I' published in 1995.

Neale thus presented a coherent story of loyalty and conflict expressed in the workings of an institution which both offered opportunity for opposition and, in turn, learned through opposition to develop claims and machinery to make it effective. Neale's Parliament – or, rather, his House of Commons – fitted neatly into the received story of a growth from the supposedly acquiescent assemblies of Henry VIII's reign to the supposedly recalcitrant assemblies of the early seventeenth century....

The Elizabethan Parliament was a working institution engaged in the manufacture of legislation by agreement and in the sorting out of such matters as might cause disagreement. It was dominated by the Queen-in-Council, who guided business in both Houses and only rarely lost control; apparent loss of control either hid covert Council activity against the queen or resulted from factional divisions among those she expected to act in unison. 'Opposition' is the wrong term to employ, and 'Puritan opposition' an even more misleading concept.

Source 2.4: From M.A.R. Graves, *Elizabethan Parliaments 1559–1601*, published in 1987.

On the other hand there is an inherent danger in the revisionist approach: that concentration on the parochial nature of much parliamentary business and the emphasis on harmony between the Crown and governing class could sweep serious political disputes behind the door or under the carpet, as if they did not exist. Friction was seldom absent, whether it was between the Crown and members of the two houses or between competing economic, local or sectional lobbies. But this must be seen in its right perspective. Two of the functions of Elizabethan parliaments were communication between Queen and governing class and the fulfilment of parochial expectations. If these were sometimes expressed in a fractious way, that was not necessarily harmful and could be beneficial, because parliaments were also a safety-valve, a chance to let off steam. Nevertheless, genuine political conflicts should not be explained away as occasional aberrations in an otherwise harmonious relationship, without acknowledging their true significance. The Catholics in the Upper House stoutly resisted the Elizabethan Settlement in 1559; Lords and Commons worked together in 1563–66/7 in an attempt to extract a royal declaration on the succession; the Lower House protested volubly at William Strickland's sequestration in 1571; Presbyterians campaigned for ecclesiastical reform in the 1580s; the Lords confronted the Commons with a demand for increased taxation in 1593; and the Lower House was outspoken in its condemnation of harmful monopolies in 1601. The simple fact is that the Elizabethan Lords and Commons were willing and able to challenge both the Queen and each other. To this extent the political historians were right.

Questions

1. Compare the arguments in Sources 2.1 and 2.2 about the relationship between Queen and Parliament.
2. 'During the reign of Elizabeth, Parliament learned how to oppose.' Comment on the validity of this view, using Sources 2.1 to 2.4 and your own knowledge.

3

THE 1559 RELIGIOUS SETTLEMENT

BACKGROUND

When Elizabeth came to the throne in 1558, one of the key decisions to be taken concerned the future of the church. Should the Catholic trend of Mary's reign be continued? And if not, how many of the earlier features of the Reformation should be restored? Should steps be retraced to the predominantly Protestant settlement of the reign of Edward VI, or still further back to the doctrinally conservative measures of Henry VIII? There was a great deal of political diplomacy and constitutional see-sawing before a settlement finally emerged in 1559. Three Bills were drawn up by the administration, led by William Cecil, the Queen's Secretary. The first, the Bill of Supremacy, was intended to cut the connection which Mary had restored with Rome and to confer upon Elizabeth the title that both Henry VIII and Edward VI had held – 'Supreme Head' of the church. The other two were the Bills of Uniformity which aimed to restore the forms of worship set out in the 1552 Prayer Book of Edward VI. Had these measures gone through there would have been a straight return to the situation before 1553.

But they did not. Although they passed through the House of Commons, they were twice rejected in the Lords. The main opposition came from the core of bishops who had been appointed during Mary's reign. Elizabeth's government therefore had a struggle on its hands and had to produce a settlement which *would* be acceptable. This was achieved partly by breaking the control of the Marian bishops within the House of Lords. Some were removed after a disputation between the

Lord Keeper, Bacon, and certain bishops who were arrested for their reluctance to accept Elizabeth's authority. The other approach was to modify the Bills so that they took on the form more of a compromise.

The new measures were passed after the Easter recess of 1559 as the Act of Supremacy and the Act of Uniformity. The former provided for the organisation of the church leadership: Elizabeth now became 'Supreme Governor' of the Church of England. Under the same Act, members of the clergy and lay officials were forced to take an oath of loyalty or lose their office. In addition, a Commission for Ecclesiastical Causes was set up and the laws of heresy, passed during the reign of Mary, were repealed and freedom of worship was permitted for Protestants. By the Act of Uniformity the 1552 Prayer Book was reinforced and attendance at church was required, on pain of a fine of twelve pence. The form of the Eucharist was also redefined: communion in both kinds was allowed, thus reversing the changes made here under Mary. As for vestments and ornaments, which had been brought back under Mary, the regulations enforced were to be those of the second year of Edward VI's reign – before the more radical measures of Somerset and Northumberland.

The legislative settlement was followed by an administrative one. This was carried out largely by Injunctions which provided a more detailed interpretation of the Acts of Supremacy and Uniformity, in very much the same way that legislation today is given effect by regulations or statutory instruments. The Royal Supremacy was to be upheld fully by the clergy and a variety of Catholic observances, including certain processions and pilgrimages, was pruned. Preaching was to be conducted only by clergy with a Master's degree. Clergy were permitted to marry, but only with the permission of two justices of the peace and their bishop. The Injunctions were to be enforced by commissioners who were to investigate the state of the church, including the morality of the clergy and their use of the Prayer Book.

Doctrine was further defined by the Eleven Articles, drawn up by the bishops in 1561 and based on Edward VI's Forty-Two Articles of 1553. These were relatively mild and tried to avoid controversy. The Thirty-Nine Articles, however, contained a more explicit statement of the Protestantism of Edward VI's reign, together with a direct denunciation of certain Catholic doctrines like transubstantiation. Nevertheless, the Elizabethan church remained strongly episcopalian, despite the attempts of radical Protestants to move it more towards the consistorial form of organisation of Geneva. This meant that the bishops and two archbishops retained their full importance and were expected to play their part in implementing the changes.

ANALYSIS 1: HOW FAR, ACCORDING TO HISTORIANS, DID THE 1559 SETTLEMENT REPRESENT A 'COMPROMISE'?

There has always been a tendency to see the 1559 religious settlement as one based on moderation – the result of a compromise put together in difficult conditions and changing somewhat between its inception and its completion. Even so, there is plenty of scope for controversy as to the key influences behind and ingredients of the settlement. There is, for example, disagreement over the extent of the personal influence of the Queen herself, or over the prevailing influence of ideology at the time, or over the entrenched power of institutions such as the House of Commons and the House of Lords. Or, if the settlement is seen as a combination of all three, what are their relative proportions: was it a balanced or a lopsided combination? Also important are the broader perspectives on Tudor religious change. Was the 1559 settlement a resumption of the more moderate doctrinal trends of Henry VIII after interruptions from the more radical changes of Edward VI and Mary? Alternatively, was Elizabeth more in line with Edward VI, restoring Protestantism after Mary's attempts to destroy it? Or perhaps the 1559 settlement made concessions to both radicals and conservatives, restoring Protestantism while acknowledging that this had at least been diluted by the reign of Mary.

Sometimes historiographical changes are strikingly different in their evolution. In this particular case, however, interpretations have developed in a subtler way.

During the late nineteenth century, and indeed for the first half of the twentieth, there was a broad consensus that the Elizabethan religious settlement constituted a middle way – a 'via media' – between more radical alternatives. The moderate nature of the settlement was taken for granted, although there was some disagreement about exactly why common sense should at last have prevailed and the extremes have been pushed to their rightful place at the periphery.

One possibility is that the time was right for a compromise between a new Protestant monarch and the conservative remnants of the previous reign. Elizabeth's own views were distinctively Protestant, a legacy from her mother, Anne Boleyn, and from the Boleyn faction at court. They were reinforced by her upbringing and education organised by Catherine Parr, Henry VIII's last wife. It would seem, then, she had a closer affinity with the religion of her half-brother, Edward VI, than with that of her half-sister, Mary, or her father, Henry VIII. Wherever possible, therefore, Elizabeth held out for a Protestant settlement – but not for one which would incite resistance from the traditionalists.

In other words she was a reforming force trying to pull back the initiative lost to the conservatives during the reign of Mary. The result was bound to be a compromise. An alternative slant to the traditional view presents Catholic influence in a more positive light. This originates very much from the long Catholic tradition within England and was reinforced by the influence of the Oxford Movement in the nineteenth century, which saw the conversion of a number of prominent Anglicans to Catholicism. The emphasis is very much on Elizabeth recognising the constructive features of Catholicism and the achievements of the reign of Mary; Elizabeth therefore saw the sense of preserving at least some of them. A third view – again very different – is that Elizabeth had no religious commitments at all. She was, according to A.F. Pollard, 'sceptical or indifferent in religion',[1] while J.R. Green considered her 'almost wholly destitute of spiritual emotion', untouched by 'theological beliefs and controversies' and seeing everything in 'a purely political light'.[2] The 'via media' was therefore a retreat from ideology and doctrine altogether.

But, although these views differ in respect of the Queen's views on religion, they are of one accord over her personal role in drawing up the settlement. Quite simply, she was in firm control of the whole process and acted deliberately to redraw the balance. Each of the above assessments of her religious attitudes can accommodate this. Elizabeth the Protestant clearly intended to restore some of the Edwardian changes without irrevocably losing Catholic support. Alternatively, the daughter of Henry VIII was now deliberately drawing the line against radical Protestantism and allowing the sort of Catholic influence which had existed before 1547. Or Elizabeth the pragmatist showed impatience with both extremes and pulled Protestants and Catholics into a new balance least likely to threaten the political security of England.

The main problem with the traditional theory of the 'via media' – in whatever form – is that it is lopsided. In attributing so much to the personal influence of the Queen, it does not take proper account of the strong pressures coming from the Protestants, especially the radicals, who had been encouraged by Northumberland and then suddenly denied during the reign of Mary. Surely they exerted some pull on the settlement? This was certainly the view of J.E. Neale, who developed a new perspective during the 1950s. He saw the compromise as being not between a Protestant Queen and conservative influences, but rather between a conservative Queen and Protestant influences. According to Neale, the all-important role in shaping the settlement was played by Parliament. The Commons favoured a more Protestant approach and a well-organised faction, the 'Puritan Choir',[3] put considerable pressure on the Queen to favour a settlement which moved as far away from Catholicism as possible and closer to Calvinism. The main source of this pressure was the returning Protestant exiles, who had a strong representation in the House of Commons. There is here an overlap with one wing of the traditional view, except that for Neale the Catholic influences on Elizabeth came from the reign of Henry VIII, not as a reluctant admission of the achievements of Mary. Neale's theories about the Puritan Choir have since been challenged (see Chapter 2), but other historians have followed in resetting the balance of religious influences. P. McGrath, for example, called the settlement 'the highest common denominator among the various Protestant groups'.[4] W.P. Haugaard added a foreign policy dimension to the influence of Protestantism. In March 1559 England received news of the Treaty of Cateau Cambrésis between the Habsburgs and France. This enabled some of her Council to advise the Queen to play for safety in a compromise with a Parliament which was already mobilised and scenting victory.[5]

There has therefore been a swing from a consciously imposed 'via media' to a settlement resulting from the intrusion of radical influences. More recently, however, it appears that there may have been a resolution between the two approaches. The idea of moderation has reappeared, but with it the notion of external influences finding a new level. According to W.L. Sheils, 'The settlement did not result from compromise with any one group, but was a delicate operation to balance a variety of forces.'[6] This 'balance of forces' is highly appropriate since it involves, not only a compromise between Catholicism and Protestantism, but also one between the different Protestant groups. D. MacCulloch added another dimension by restoring the Catholic influence. As important as the Protestant pressures in the House of Commons were the Catholic influences in the House of Lords. 'They combined to wreck the government's first attempt to pass a Settlement in February 1559, and refused even to repeal the Marian laws against heresy; it was only after the key bishops had been removed from the political scene by arrest that the Acts of Supremacy and Uniformity were passed by the Lords after Easter 1559.'[7] This was initially as significant as the Protestant influence within the Commons and the impact on this of the returning exiles has been exaggerated: 'they were not a particularly numerous or important group'.[8]

This view also involves a reassessment of the role of the administration: recent interpretation tends to stress that the Queen's ministers were in control. According to MacCulloch, the settlement was 'an operation planned with great skill for the Queen by Cecil [the Queen's Principal Secretary] and his associates, taking into account the delicate diplomatic and political situation which they faced'.[9] The Queen also played her part with some skill. Contrary to the first two views, she kept her own ideas under wraps, so that it is often difficult to judge what they really were. There were some issues on which she took a stand, such as her preference for the formal altar, cross and candlesticks. But at other times she was prepared to be flexible, to take advice and to bend with the wind. Nevertheless, she played a far more important role in the construction of the settlement than has previously been acknowledged. An essential part of the most recent developments in interpretation is therefore the revived influence of the Queen herself. N.L. Jones put this into a more general context and pointed out the vital importance of the period 1558–59 as the foundation of the Elizabethan regime. 'By the middle of her second regnal year Elizabeth could congratulate herself on having safely navigated the dangerous shoals of governmental transition, religious change and international reorientation, laying a course that she was to sail for years to come.'[10]

There is much to be said for this 'balance of forces' approach. It can be seen at work in all the legislative components of the Elizabethan settlement. The concessions to Protestantism involved restoring the official situation as at the end of Edward VI's reign but, at the same time, there were attempts to placate conservative and Catholic opinion. There are three examples of this. First, the title 'Supreme Governor' as an alternative to 'Supreme Head' was intended to satisfy both Catholics *and* radical Protestants, neither of whom relished the idea of headship vested in Elizabeth: Catholics still regarded the Pope as the spiritual head of the church, while radical Protestants were averse to the original title of 'head' being conferred on a woman. Second, the reintroduction of communion in both kinds reflected the doctrinal developments of the reign of Edward VI, thus satisfying most Protestants, while the wording of the communion allowed for a flexible interpretation of transubstantiation and hence a residue of traditional doctrine for the Catholics. This wording combined the formula of 1549 with that of 1552: 'The body of our Lord Jesus Christ which was given for thee, preserve thy body and soul unto everlasting life: and take and eat this, in remembrance that Christ died for thee, and feed on him in thine heart by faith with thanksgiving.'[11] This was aimed especially at ganing the support of the House of Lords which contained a larger number of pro-Catholic traditionalists than the House of Commons. Third, policies on the wearing of vestments and the use of ornaments can be seen as an attempt at a compromise by returning to the position before Northumberland's iconoclasm and Mary's attempted full-scale restoration of the Catholic regalia. This was received with more relief by Catholics than by radical Protestants, but the latter were partly appeased by the supplementary injunctions of what should be worn: a surplice for ordinary services and a white alb with a vestment for the communion. Other materials should remain within the church but did not necessarily have to be used. Overall, there was something in the settlement and its follow-up to satisfy – and irritate – all religious groups.

The differences of opinion shown in this Analysis may, at times, seem marginal, using overlapping terms such as 'middle way' and 'balance of forces'. Historiography does, however, involve shades as well as colours, with subtlety playing an important role in reinterpretation.

Questions

1. Was the 1559 settlement imposed by the Queen – or upon the Queen?
2. To what extent have historians differed in their views of the 1559 settlement?

ANALYSIS 2: HOW EFFECTIVELY WAS THE SETTLEMENT IMPLEMENTED BY THE QUEEN AND THE CLERGY?

Drawing up the settlement was, of course, only part of the process of Elizabethan religious change. The other was interpreting and implementing it – or, to be more negative, simply living with it. Like most compromises, it was inherently flawed. It was to experience numerous difficulties and challenges but – despite these – it survived. In the view of W.R.D. Jones, 'it glossed over tensions which were never to be completely resolved, and established an equilibrium which at the time must have appeared both provisional and precarious. Yet it was to endure as the permanent basis of the English Church.'[12]

Historians tend to agree on the importance of Elizabeth's role in all this. According to P. Williams, 'The Queen was central both to the settlement itself and to its execution.'[13] This accords very much with contemporary views. The Bishop of Winchester wrote in 1571: 'Our excellent Queen, as you know, holds the helm, and directs it hitherto according to her pleasure.'[14] Elizabeth's objectives and influence were crucial for the development of the religious establishment in England.

She was determined to abide by the 1559 settlement, in which she took a proprietary interest. She also applied the brake to the two forces which threatened it – conservative Catholicism and radical Protestantism. She blocked the former by removing much of the doctrinal influence of the Marian church and returning to the stated doctrine of Edward VI's reign. But she frustrated the radicals by insisting on an episcopalian structure, or the retention of a hierarchy of authority headed by bishops and the two archbishops.

In some respects Elizabeth's influence and intervention were entirely logical. She was clearly concerned throughout her reign for the security of her own position. To her it made sense to preserve the middle way or the equilibrium and her overall objectives were therefore quite clear. The church must be preserved within the pattern prescribed for it by the legislation of the beginning of the reign and reinforced by royal Injunctions. She should there for receive considerable personal credit for any long-term stability. There were also examples of her influence in upholding and enforcing the settlement. The Injunctions bore the hallmark of her views. One is the intrusion of her own particular religious beliefs where she thought these could be accommodated without upsetting the settlement as a whole. She jealously guarded her right to interpret specific issues. Her distaste for clerical marriage was the reason for the restrictions imposed by the authorities: she did not want to make the process easy or to give the impression that it should become the norm; instead, it should be seen as an exception, covered by special conditions. On the other hand, she avoided the provocation which would have resulted from banning clerical marriages altogether. Similarly, the restriction on preaching was almost certainly due to her belief that it would not take much for radical Protestantism to spread through the parishes, quite possibly providing conflict with more traditional parishioners and therefore provoking civil unrest. To her it therefore made sense to confine words from the pulpit to those members of the clergy who had been trained within the moderate traditions of the Church of England.

Conversely, there was an apparently illogical and unpredictable element to Elizabeth's actions. She was inclined to intervene personally in ways which could be inconsistent or undermining. Alternatively, she might withhold support when it was requested. For example, she refused to back Archbishop Parker, failing to endorse his Advertisements over the vestiarian issue. There were times, too, when she seemed to deny the role of Parliament in underpinning doctrine. She would not, for example, enshrine the Thirty-Nine Articles in statute (by contrast with Henry VIII's Act of Six Articles) – and this was despite the establishment of the earlier Elizabethan settlement by statute. This can, however, be explained as intervention against any action which she considered incompatible with her own interests, irrespective of whether or not they were in the interests of the church. Her attitude towards the upper clergy was especially ambivalent. Ultimately she applied a political criterion. In the case of Parker, support for the Advertisements would be seen as agreeing to the undermining of the letter of the 1559 settlement and, furthermore, giving her Privy Council a greater degree of involvement in church issues. Who could anticipate where this might lead? Grindal, too, was showing too, much initiative which might possibly lead to a questioning of her authority. As for the limiting of the parliamentary role, Elizabeth had already encountered considerable opposition from that source in drawing up the original settlement of 1559. There were therefore strong political reasons for not engaging in polemics again.

It is true, therefore, that Elizabeth had a thoroughly one-sided view of the interests of the church: that she intervened or refused to provide support where this accorded with her own interests. This has been well put by J. Warren: 'It is hard to avoid the conclusion that the Queen seldom acted as the "nursing mother of the Church". At best, she was a very selfish parent, concerned with her own needs and authority and rarely responding to the needs of her offspring.'[15] And yet there was somewhere a sense of hard-headed realism and balance which the Queen appeared to possess more than any of her advisers or clerical officials. She seemed to know how to weigh up the secular and ecclesiastical priorities. If she were to support Archbishop Parker in the vestiarian controversy, she would be opening the door to further movements towards Protestantism, a process which would have been greatly accelerated by any support for Grindal. Similarly, to have the Thirty-Nine Articles ratified by Parliament would have the effect of ratifying a substantial amount of strongly anti-Catholic rhetoric. In each case the effect would be to upset the fine balance achieved in 1559. It would make it more difficult to win over Catholics through the gradual corrosion of their religion through disuse. The last thing she wanted to do was to antagonise them needlessly by developments which went beyond the 1559 settlement.

The enforcement of the settlement by the upper clergy met with a mixed success. The three archbishops most directly involved were Matthew Parker, Edmund Grindal and John Whitgift. Their experience was on the whole neither happy nor consistent. It showed several major swings, from the centre, to radicalism, to conservatism. The first of these was Archbishop Parker, who attempted in his Advertisements in

1566 to clarify the details of what was officially required over the administration of the sacraments and the acceptable form of clerical dress. The latter was defined as a simple surplice for parish services but more elaborate vestments for cathedral services. This provoked a heated debate with the Puritans, which is analysed in Chapter 5. Parker was also out of step with many of the bishops who, being Marian exiles, had a more forceful Protestant slant. Hence he became increasingly isolated, conscious of a 'deep, devilish traitorous dissimulation' and a 'horrible conspiracy'.[16] The swing to the radicals occurred when he was succeeded by Edmund Grindal. The latter came into deep conflict with the Queen over the issue of 'prophesyings', something to which Elizabeth took strong exception. It actually meant clergy gathering to listen to sermons together with a lay audience, followed by discussions among the clergy alone. He was effectively removed from office for holding out for this and was formally replaced on his death in 1583 by Whitgift, who was a Protestant but made it his business to impose discipline upon the upper clergy rather than to put the focus on reform. The latter half of the reign therefore saw a less problematic relationship between the Queen and Canterbury, coinciding with the deterioration in the Catholic situation (see Chapter 4).

If the experience of the upper clergy was ambivalent, how effectively did the lower clergy fit into the settlement? Elizabeth combined concessions with strict enforcement; for example, she confirmed that clergy were permitted to marry while, at the same time, she appointed official visitors to ensure that they fully accepted royal supremacy. The proportion of refusals is hard to assess overall, but records show that it ran at about 9 per cent in northern parishes. Since this was an area with Catholic pockets, the rate of refusals in the south-east was probably lower. According to Williams, 'it is evident that the lower clergy, unlike the bishops, were willing to conform even if their attachment to the new order was at best superficial and often reluctant'.[17] There were, however, remaining problems. One of the features of the Elizabethan Reformation was its emphasis on *educated* clergy. At the beginning of Elizabeth's reign the majority did not fit this description. Only a small proportion consisted of graduates (19 per cent in Worcester and none at all in Gloucester in 1570). As a result it was necessary to compromise on quality; according to Parker in 1560: 'occasioned by the great want of ministers, we and you both [Grindal], for tolerable supply thereof, have heretofore admitted into the ministry sundry artificers and others, not traded and brought up in learning, and, as it happened in a multitude, some that were of base occupations'.[18] Nevertheless, the numbers of suitably qualified incumbents did gradually increase by the end of Elizabeth's reign, attracted by a rise in incomes and educated in larger numbers at the two universities.

The full implementation of the settlement depended on the co-operation – active or tacit – of the majority of the clergy – upper and lower. We have covered the experience of the church itself, but there is another dimension: the treatment of those who refused directly to accept the settlement and those who wanted to subject it to further reforms. This is dealt with in Chapters 4 and 5.

Question

1.   How well was Elizabeth served by her archbishops of Canterbury in:
      i.   enforcing the 1559 settlement and
      ii. controlling the rest of the clergy?

SOURCES

1. THE RELIGIOUS SETTLEMENT OF 1559

Source 1.1: An extract from the Act of Supremacy of 1559.

To the intent that all usurped and foreign power and authority spiritual and temporal may for ever be clearly extinguished and never be used nor obeyed within this realm or any other your Majesty's dominions or countries: may it please your Highness that it may be further enacted, by the authority aforesaid, that no foreign prince, person, prelate, state or potentate spiritual or temporal shall at any time after the last day of this session of parliament use, enjoy or exercise any manner of power, jurisdiction, superiority, authority, pre-eminence or privilege spiritual or ecclesiastical within this realm.

Source 1.2: An extract from the Act of Uniformity of 1559.

From and after the said feast of the Nativity of St John Baptist next coming, all and every person and persons inhabiting within this realm or any other the Queen's Majesty's dominions, shall diligently and faithfully, having no lawful or reasonable excuse to be absent, endeavour themselves to resort to their parish church or chapel accustomed, or upon reasonable let thereof to some usual place where common prayer and such service of God shall be used in such time of let, upon every Sunday and other days ordained and used to be kept as holy days, and then and there to abide orderly and soberly during the time of the common prayer, preachings or other service of God there to be used and ministered; upon pain of punishment by the censures of the church, and also upon pain that every person so offending shall forfeit for every such offence twelve pence, to be levied by the churchwardens of the parish where such offence shall be done, to the use of the poor of the same parish, of the goods, lands and tenements of such offender by way of distress.

Source 1.3: An extract from William Camden's *Annales* or the *History of the Most Renowned and victorious Princess Elizabeth, Late Queen of England*, published in 1615. During the reign of Elizabeth, Camden was an Oxford scholar, travelled extensively through England and became headmaster of Westminster School. The spelling of the following extract has been modernised.

In the first beginning of her Reign, she applied her first care (howbeit with but a few and those her inwardest Counsellors) to the restoring of the Protestant Religion, which both by her instruction from her tender years, and by her own judgement, she verily persuaded herself to be the truest, and most consonant to the sacred Scriptures, and the sincerity of the primitive Church; and to restore the same she had with a settled and constant resolution determined in her mind.

Source 1.4: An extract from William Allen, *A True, Sincere, and Modest Defence of English Catholiques*, published in 1584. Allen was a Catholic, who founded an English college at Douai to train priests to convert England to Catholicism. He was made a cardinal by Pope Sixtus V in 1587. The spelling of the following extract has been modernised.

The truth is, that in the first year and Parliament of the Queen's reign, when they abolished the Pope's authority, and would have yielded the same authority with the title of Supreme head to the Queen as it was given before to her Father and Brother: [some] specially moved by Minister Calvin's writing, liked not the term, and therefore procured that some other equivalent but less offensive, might be used. Upon which formality, it was enacted that she was *the Chief governor as well in causes ecclesiastical or spiritual, as civil and temporal*. And another of the same was conceived accordingly, to be tendered at their pleasures to all the spiritual and temporal officers in the Realm, by which every one must swear that in conscience he taketh and believeth her so to be: and that no Priest or other borne out of the realm, can have or ought to have any manner of power in spiritual matters over her subjects. Which oath is counted the very torment of all English consciences, not the protestants, themselves believing it to be true: and of all true catholics, as before it was deemed in her Father a lay man, and in her Brother a child very ridiculous: so now in herself, being a woman, is it accounted a thing most monstrous and unnatural, and the very gappe to bring any Realm to the thralldom of all sects, Heresy, Paganism, Turkism or Atheism. . . .

Questions

1. Explain the reference in Source 1.1 to 'all usurped and foreign power and authority spiritual and temporal'.
2. Compare the approaches of William Camden (Source 1.3) and William Allen (Source 1.4) to the role of Elizabeth in the 1559 settlement.
3. Using Sources 1.1 to 1.4, and your own knowledge, assess the main purposes of the Acts of Supremacy and Uniformity.

2. INTERPRETATIONS OF INFLUENCES BEHIND THE 1559 RELIGIOUS SETTLEMENT

Source 2.1: From J.R. Green, *A Short History of the English People*, first published in 1874.

The young Queen was not without a sense of religion. But she was almost wholly destitute of spiritual emotion, or of any consciousness of the vast questions with which theology strove to deal. While the world around her was being swayed more and more by theological beliefs and controversies, Elizabeth was absolutely untouched by them. She was a child of the Italian Renascence rather than of the New Learning of Colet or Erasmus. . . . Her mind was unruffled by the spiritual problems which were vexing the minds around her; to Elizabeth indeed they were not only unintelligible, they were a little ridiculous. She had the same intellectual contempt for the superstition of the Romanist as for the bigotry of the Protestant . . . If Elizabeth won the Protestants by an Act of Uniformity which restored the English Prayer-book and enforced its use on the clergy on pain of deprivation, the alterations she made in its language showed her wish to conciliate the Catholics as far as possible. She had no mind merely to restore the system of the Protectorate.

Source 2.2: From S. Doran, *Elizabeth I and Religion*, published in 1994.

As soon as she was proclaimed queen, Elizabeth made it clear to her subjects that she intended to introduce a Protestant Church Settlement. Her new streamlined Privy Council had a decidedly Protestant complexion, and her most important minister, Secretary William Cecil, had previously withdrawn from public life in 1553 rather than publicly endorse Catholicism. Before the end of 1558, Protestants who had been deprived of their livings or had gone into exile under Mary were invited to preach on public occasions, while Catholic preachers were harassed or arrested. For example, on the Sunday after her accession Elizabeth allowed Dr William Bill, a Protestant who had been ejected from Cambridge during the previous reign, to preach at St Paul's Cross, yet she arrested the bishop of Chichester for preaching a rejoinder the following Sunday. Even before her first parliament met, liturgical changes were introduced, first in her chapel and then in the realm. Proclamations of 27 and 28 December ordered the use of the Epistles, Gospels, Lord's Prayer, Creed and Litany in English until parliament decided on 'matters and ceremonies of religion'. On Christmas Day Elizabeth displayed her disbelief in the doctrine of transubstantiation when she walked out of her chapel service after the officiant.

Source 2.3: From D. Loades, *Revolution in Religion: The English Reformation, 1530–1570*, published in 1992.

For some years Elizabeth's government proceeded gently with the enforcement of conformity, and many catholic and quasi-catholic practices continued with a minimum of concealment. Such tolerance was political rather than principled, and rapidly disappeared after the papacy launched its offensive against the queen in 1570. However, Elizabeth lived long enough, and pursued a sufficiently consistent policy, for the settlement of 1559 to take root and to become generally perceived as 'the face of an English church'. The only thing that had not changed throughout the turbulent years of the mid century was the structure of dioceses and parishes, archdeaconries and deaneries. The church courts continued to function throughout, tithes were collected (or litigated about), and churchwardens administered the consequences of each turn of the liturgical wheel. By 1570 the parishes were if anything more important than they had ever been, because they had also started to become the basic units of secular administration, and by the end of the century churchwardens were administering the poor relief which Elizabeth had accepted the responsibility to provide by statute.

Source 2.4: From P. Williams, *The Later Tudors*, published in 1995.

The Queen was the key figure: she proposed the original measures and without her consent the final settlement could never have been reached. But others played a significant role. The dominant group in the Commons ... pressed for an unequivocal Protestantism. The Marian bishops and the conservative peers obstructed proposals for change and compelled Elizabeth to look for support to the Protestants in the Commons and to ministers returning from exile. She could hardly consent to the supremacy bill as amended by the Lords without antagonizing Protestants and she would not gain Catholic support by such a compromise. Hence, probably, her change of policy on 2 March, when she adjourned Parliament without giving assent to any bill. From that moment she was committed to a Protestant solution, not because she was forced to it by a pressure-group from the Commons, but because she needed Commons support against the Lords.

Questions

1. Compare the interpretations advanced in Sources 2.1 to 2.4 about the Queen's attitudes to religious belief and to the Protestant–Catholic issue.
2. 'The 1559 settlement was arrived at as a result of pressures from outside rather than as a result of deliberate government policy.' Consider this view in the light of Sources 2.1 to 2.4 and your own knowledge.

Worked answer: Compare the interpretations advanced in Sources 2.1 to 2.4 about the Queen's attitudes to religious belief and to the Protestant–Catholic issue.

[Advice: 'Compare' means establishing similarities and differences. These should be integrated and should consist of specific references within the context of your own structured argument. All four passages should be referred to where possible. The structure of the question suggests two concise paragraphs.]

The Queen's religious attitudes are dealt with directly in Sources 2.1 to 2.3, although not in 2.4. There is some common ground between Green's statement that, although 'not without a sense of religion', she was 'destitute of spiritual emotion' and the belief of Loades that her tolerance 'was political rather than principled'. Both stressed the overriding importance of her pragmatism. Doran, however, emphasised Elizabeth's personal involvement in religious controversies (in contrast to Green's view that she 'was absolutely untouched by them'). Doran also provided specific examples of this, particularly the Queen's attitude to 'the doctrine of transubstantiation'.

Similarly, there is much in common between the approaches of Green and Loades over Elizabeth's attempt to introduce a new Protestant settlement without alienating the Catholics. Green argued that she 'won the Protestants by an Act of Uniformity' while trying also 'to conciliate the Catholics'; according to Loades, the government 'proceeded gently with the enforcement of conformity' which meant the continuation of many 'quasi-catholic practices' – at least until 1570.

Doran's emphasis is rather different. Elizabeth 'made it clear' that she intended 'to introduce a Protestant Church Settlement' and made personal interventions against former influences and practices; in this she had the support of a Privy Council with 'a decidedly Protestant complexion'. Like Doran, Williams (Source 2.4) emphasised her awareness of the Catholic–Protestant divide, in contrast to Green and Loades, who preferred to downplay it. There is, however, a difference of emphasis between Sources 2.2 and 2.4. Doran implied that the Protestant drive came partly from Elizabeth's own inclinations, whereas Williams suggested that she had to rely on the support of the 'Protestants in the Commons' against the mainly Catholic 'Marian bishops and conservative peers' in the Lords. This was above all a *political* choice.

4

CATHOLICISM AND THE CATHOLIC 'THREAT'

BACKGROUND

Elizabeth's reign followed a period in which the Reformation of Henry VIII and Edward VI had been reversed and the Roman Catholic Church fully restored. In the 1559 settlement the pendulum swung back towards Protestantism, although the final defeat of Catholicism was by no means inevitable. Analysis 1 examines the methods used after 1559 to enforce the compliance of Catholics to the new order and considers whether they were either justified or effective. Analysis 2 covers the historiographical debate on the reasons for Catholic decline during the period 1559–1603, with a particular focus on the significance of the seminary priests after 1570.

ANALYSIS 1: EXAMINE THE TREATMENT OF CATHOLICS BY ELIZABETH'S GOVERNMENT.

Elizabeth was faced with a choice at the beginning of her reign of either maintaining the Catholic restoration of Mary or returning to the Protestantism of Edward. The 1559 settlement was based on the latter. But this posed a second problem. How should the Catholic population now be made to comply? The government adopted a variety of measures, which were something of a contrast with each other. This raises the issue of whether the government was inconsistent – and sometimes unjustified – in its approach, or whether it was responding with flexibility to the particular circumstances in England and Europe.

Elizabeth and her government could have opted at the outset for draconian measures to try to stamp out Catholicism altogether. This, however, was not pursued for several reasons. It would have been a daunting task since the majority of the population at this stage was probably still Catholic. There were also insufficient Protestant clergy to replace all their Catholic counterparts immediately. Third, Elizabeth's own views favoured clemency and mercy – up to a point. Memories were still fresh of persecution from the previous reign and any repetition was to be avoided if possible.

Elizabeth's government decided instead to put long-term pressure on Catholicism. The settlement of 1559 built up Protestantism and was intended to undermine Catholicism so that it would eventually wither away. Under the Acts of Supremacy and Uniformity efforts were made to starve Catholicism. Refusal to take the oath of allegiance resulted in the loss of office and failure to attend an Anglican service meant a fine. Celebrating the Catholic mass could be punished by the death sentence, but this was not applied before 1577. The usual penalty for this in the meantime was imprisonment.

How effective was this policy? Subsequent events showed a variety of Catholic responses to such measures. During the first decade and a half of the reign Catholicism posed comparatively little direct threat to the crown. It seems that the majority of Catholics, many of whom were members of the nobility and justices of the peace, preferred not to become recusants but rather to pay lip-service to the settlement while doing what they could to continue their Catholic devotions in private. This was tolerated by the government partly because it posed no direct challenge and partly because it was difficult to enforce the law fully and secure convictions. Whether or not this could have continued depends on the interpretation as to whether Catholicism really *was* being subsumed, a debate considered in Analysis 2 below.

As it happened, it was never given that chance because, from the mid-1570s, significant changes occurred, in the form both of Catholic opposition and of the government's response. The catalyst was probably key developments abroad, which had the effect of pointing up the Catholic threat – either real or imagined. The ideological threat was politicised in 1570 with Pius V's Bull, *Regnans in Excelsis* (1570), which absolved English Catholics from obeying Elizabeth and ordered them to assist attempts to overthrow her. The Spanish connection occurred with the reconquest of the southern Netherlands by the Duke of Alva and its return to Spanish rule. This put Spain into the position of applying the sword of the Counter Reformation, which meant that for the first time that country came to be seen as an ideological enemy to England. All that was needed was a conduit for Spanish influence on English politics. This was provided by Mary Queen of Scots, who fled from Scotland to England and became the centre of Catholic hopes for the future. A series of plots followed. The rebellion of the Northern Earls had already collapsed in 1569. But more serious were those involving Mary Queen of Scots, with schemes to enthrone her with Spanish military and financial support. The first of these was the Ridolfi Plot (1571), which immediately provoked a government response in the form of the Treasons Act. Others followed – the Throckmorton Plot of 1583 and the Babington Plot of 1586.

Into this highly charged atmosphere entered another explosive ingredient: the Catholic 'mission'. Many of the priests who had initially held out against Elizabeth's settlement – the recusants – had either given up, been imprisoned or died. Hence there was an attempt from abroad to try to revive the impetus of Catholicism in England. The centre for this was a Catholic seminary at Douai in the southern Netherlands, founded by Cardinal William Allen in 1568. Its purpose was to train Catholic priests (mainly Jesuits) to preach in England and revive the traditional services which had lapsed. They were also prepared to follow the papal line on political activism against the Elizabethan government, which meant that some engaged in subversion. The government tried to limit the damage by deterring Catholics from receiving the missionaries such as Campion and Parsons. It became a treasonable offence to try to persuade English subjects to withdraw their allegiance from the Queen. A further measure followed in 1585 making it treason to become a Catholic priest or to help the missionaries, as some members of the nobility had been doing by concealing them in 'priest holes' in their houses. Altogether approximately 187 Catholics were executed during the reign, many suffering the dreadful death of being hanged, drawn and quartered, a fate which was experienced by Campion himself.

Could the more extreme measures taken by the government be justified? This is the most sensitive issue of the reign. The Elizabethan executions have always been used as a counter-argument to the charges against 'Bloody Mary'. They were deliberately conducted in the vilest manner, through the revival of the medieval punishment for treason. They were preceded by the use of torture to extract information and confessions; Elizabeth was fully aware of this and personally authorized it on two occasions. Some of the elements were particularly odious: for example, the use of informers and agents, who received commissions based on forfeitures or fines, and of professional interrogators like Richard Topcliffe, who had use of a private rack in his own cellar. In the words of Cardinal Allen's accusation: 'Nothing was there in those religious hearts but innocency and true religion.'[1]

On the other hand, normal penal legislation of the time was equally savage. 'If a woman poison her husband she is burned alive; if the servant kill his master, he is to be executed for petty treason; he that poisoneth a man is to be boiled to death in water or lead.'[2] In any case, practices were worse on the continent; according to Sir Thomas Smith: 'Heading, tormenting, demembering, either arm or leg, breaking upon the wheel, impaling and such cruel torments as be used in other nations by the order of their law, we have not: and yet as few murders committed as anywhere.'[3] A.L. Rowse represented the most common approach to the problem. He regretted 'the devotion, the spiritual energies, that went into sterile and futile conflict'; if only 'they had gone positively and constructively into making the Church and society better!' Yet, he added, 'what else could the government have done?' After all, 'The crucial question was the issue of allegiance.' The Queen had been excommunicated, 'her subjects encouraged to rebel' and 'invasion of the country promoted'.[4] Politicisation of the issue has therefore provided a form of justification – if tenuous – for extreme measures. The problem is both of the sixteenth century and timeless, as is shown by Black (see Source 1.1 below). The argument for defending a system based on an ideology by adopting extreme measures against those who threaten the system is, to this day, interpreted as an attack on alternative beliefs.

Irrespective of their justification, or otherwise, how effective were the measures taken to deal with the recusants? This, in turn, depends on whether the Douai missionaries revived Catholicism (see Analysis 2 below). In so far as they were supposed to act as a deterrent, the measures did not put off the missionaries, who were prepared for the fate they met. They did, however, make the majority of Catholics in England think twice before pursuing their faith into recusancy. They were most effective when applied selectively as a last-resort alternative to the earlier strategy of absorption. Measures used during the crisis were not uniformly applied; they were used flexibly as the occasion warranted, to be enforced with rigour or slackened in accordance with the government's perception of the *political* threat. Indeed, according to P. Johnson, 'by virtually excluding the Catholic gentry from the operations of her anti-Catholic legislation, Elizabeth effectively tamed Catholicism, at least for a time'.[5]

There is, finally, another perspective on the Elizabethan measures.

This concerns the impact of the reign on broader historical evolution. Did it have a positive or a negative impact on religious expression? In the late nineteenth century, J.R. Green's 'Whiggish' viewpoint was that a 'fresh impulse' was given to the 'growing current of opinion which was to bring England at last to recognize the right of every man to freedom both of conscience and of worship'.[6] A typical mid-twentieth-century approach was to lose the underlying acceptance of improvement, instead emphasising the dynamic of reaction, Hence, according to G.R. Elton, the recusants may have helped preserve the Catholic faith in England, but they failed to shake the Protestant state. Indeed, they 'assisted, by reaction, in the growth of a more ardent and uncompromising protestantism'.[7]

Questions

1. How different are the views of Green and Elton, provided in the final paragraph of Analysis 1?
2. Did Elizabeth's reign see a 'persecution' of Catholics?

ANALYSIS 2: HOW HAVE HISTORIANS INTERPRETED THE EXTENT AND INFLUENCE OF CATHOLICISM IN ENGLAND DURING THE REIGN OF ELIZABETH?

There is general agreement amongst historians that Catholicism was in a weaker state at the end of Elizabeth's reign than it had been at the beginning. The evidence makes this hard to contest. It has been estimated that, by 1603, the number of Catholics dwindled from more than 50 per cent to between 1 and 2 per cent of the population of England. Within these overall figures were two interacting trends. One was the contraction of the mass base of Catholicism, even though it was impossible to eradicate Catholic observance completely. The other was the disproportionate concentration of loyal Catholics in one particular class – the gentry. There were also examples of a serious rift between religious orders, such as the Jesuits, who still advocated the full re-establishment of Catholicism, and the secular clergy who hoped for compromise and a degree of toleration from the establishment.

Much more controversial is how this decline actually took place – and the way in which it related to the two main phases of Catholicism – before and after 1580. There are three possible arguments

The first is that the early part of the reign was marked by rapid Catholic decline; this was subsequently arrested by the Jesuit missionaries from Douai, whose activities ensured the survival of Catholicism, although at nothing like previous levels. The starting point of this approach is the emphasis on the drift into Protestant observance which was allowed by the 1559 settlement. A.G. Dickens, for example, maintained that 'an insignificant number' of Catholic clergy ventured 'to refuse the oath of Supremacy' and that 'little open defiance appeared'.[8] More recently, P. McGrath has stressed the importance of the slippage of Catholic observance by example: 'When the parish priest was ready to use the Book of Common Prayer and the squire publicly appeared at the new services, it was hardly surprising that the ordinary people followed the example of their social superiors.'[9] In desperate trouble by the late 1560s and early 1570s, therefore, Catholicism was rescued, according to McGrath, as 'the result of the work of the missionaries from Douai. The risks they took in saying the mass meant the survival of this essential feature of Catholicism, which might otherwise have faded away.'[10] They were protected by members of the gentry and the combination of the two ensured that Catholicism was able to remain in existence during the more tolerant era of the early Stuarts. This was also the view of J. Bossy, who argued that the strength of Catholicism was not so much its 'doctrinal affirmation' as its 'ingrained observances' which gave way to encroaching Anglicanism. The missionaries revived it but in more limited areas and in gentry households.[11] Finally, according to G.R. Elton, the missionaries arrested the decline of Catholicism and 'ended the government's hopes of destroying popery and drawing all Englishmen into the English Church'; they 'consolidated the catholic minority into a body able to survive persecution and erected a firm barrier between the Churches of Rome and Canterbury'.[12]

These historians, therefore, consider that internal factors were paramount in the decline of Catholicism – the external, however, serving to prevent its complete obliteration. The second approach is really the reverse of the first: the survival of Catholicism was not enhanced by the missionaries, either because the seeds for survival were already there, or because missionary activities alienated more than they converted. Catholicism survived, albeit in a weakened state, *despite* the activities of the missionaries.

The starting point of this argument is the initial survival of Catholicism, not its collapse. According to J. Guy, the recusant tradition was not 'forged by missionary priests in the face of widespread Catholic inertia before their arrival'; it was already there, nurtured by the 'ex-Marian clergy'.[13] Similarly, C. Haigh pointed to 'a substantial survival of conservative belief and practice in parishes served by ex-priests', and to the limitations of Protestant preaching which had left a 'reservoir of potential recruits for a separated Catholic Church'.[14] Both Guy and Haigh argued that the Douai missionaries had serious limitations, despite their efforts, which meant that they amounted to a 'heroic failure'. The number of seminary priests was not as large as has been maintained. They also concentrated their activity on the south and east, which contained only 20 per cent of the recusant population; this was largely because Essex, the Thames valley and London were most accessible to the entry ports of Dover and Rye. The north, with its greater concentrations of recusant Catholics, was largely neglected. There was also a disproportionate use of resources: the missionaries focused mainly on the gentry – partly because most seminary priests came from that class and partly because the gentry provided the most likely protection. As a result, Catholicism was remoulded socially. Haigh wrote of a 'seigneurially structured form',[15] which, according to Guy, 'existed until Catholic Emancipation in 1829'.[16] The result was the survival of Catholicism, but the dissipation of its mass base.

Which of these interpretations is correct? The answer depends very much on the intrinsic strength of Catholicism within England. Which was the greater threat: Elizabeth's deliberate policy of allowing it to fade away rather than trying to uproot it, or the Jesuit attempts to reinvigorate it?

A possible argument might run as follows. There were two distinct periods of Catholic reactions to the Elizabethan settlement. In the early years of the reign there was no major Catholic challenge for the same reason that there had been only sporadic and isolated upheavals in response to the religious changes made during the reigns of Henry VIII, Edward VI and Mary. Most people, whether Protestant or Catholic, preferred to follow a line of survival and not to draw attention to themselves. Hence there was unlikely to be a welling of dissent from the grass roots. Most of the initial opposition and recusancy came from the top of the Catholic hierarchy. The Catholic bishops fought the legislation of the 1559 settlement in the House of Lords and almost all of the bishops remaining from Mary's reign refused to take the Oath of Supremacy. In addition, some hundred academics went abroad rather than come under the influence of the new Protestant Church. But only a minority of the lower clergy, the parish priests, refused to conform to the new settlement and its regulations. Many paid lip-service to these, it is true, but the important point is that they did not actually defy the establishment. There was thus a low-profile adjustment with some surreptitious retention of traditional forms of worship. This weakened the formal structure of Catholicism but kept alive the basic commitment which many felt to the old faith. The government came to terms with this and the result was a stand-off.

During the second period the conflict between the government and Catholicism was politicised because of the intrusion of foreign policy and the Catholic mission. The result was certainly to sharpen Catholic resistance to the process of slow absorption. In this sense, a separate Catholic identity *was* retained. On the other hand, large numbers of Catholics were forced to abandon their beliefs and observances because they could no longer practise them in safety. In addition many were torn by conflicting loyalties to their faith and monarch and chose the latter. This crisis of conscience was the result of foreign threats, which enabled the government to claim legitimately that there was a threat to the internal security of the realm. It therefore took measures to put pressure on Catholics to choose between their loyalty to the Pope and their national allegiance. Most opted for the latter, especially during the period leading up to the Spanish Armada. Many Catholics were also highly suspicious of the activities of the missionaries, preferring to remain uninvolved either because they suspected treason or because they feared that they might themselves fall foul of a system which would exact a hideous revenge upon them.

Thus the effect of the Douai missionaries was paradoxical. The mission redefined the distinctive features of Catholicism which, after the initial resistance to the settlement, had been in danger of becoming blurred. Catholicism therefore retained a separate identity and did not simply disappear into the Church of England. But the process, because it was politicised, alienated almost all those who had once been Catholic. The more blurred the identity of the Catholic Church had been, the more adherents it had retained. The sharper the focus became, the more adherents the Catholic Church lost.

Questions

1. Who were the *real* recusants in Elizabethan England?
2. 'In 1603 Catholicism was sharper – but weaker – than it had been in 1558.' Do you agree?

SOURCES

1. CHURCH VS. STATE?

Source 1.1: From J.B. Black, *The Reign of Elizabeth, 1558–1603*, published in 1936.

Not only the reformation settlement in England but also the safety of the state was at stake. It was a life-and-death struggle, in which both parties – the medieval catholic church and the English government – were endeavouring to crush each other to powder. That being so, it was natural that the apologists for the state should represent the conflict as political. Those who suffered, said Burghley, did so, not because they believed in transubstantiation or upheld the Mass, but because they were traitors and sedition-mongers. But the catholic priests, on whom fell the burden and heat of the day, were just as convinced that they were martyrs for their faith. . . . Up to a point both were right; but when the whole sweep of the controversy is taken into account, it becomes clear that neither was wholly right. So long as loyalty to the state was interpreted in terms of loyalty to the anglican church, and loyalty to the Roman church involved acceptance of the papal bull, there could be no separation between politics and religion. Moreover, the confusion of religion and politics made it impossible for impartial justice to be administered.

Source 1.2: Extracts from the Act of Supremacy of 1559.

An act restoring to the crown the ancient jurisdiction over the state ecclesiastical and spiritual, and abolishing all foreign power repugnant to the same.
VII And to the intent that all usurped and foreign power and authority, spiritual and temporal, may for ever be clearly extinguished, and never to be used nor obeyed within this realm or any other of your majesty's dominions or countries; may it please your highness that it may be further enacted by the authority aforesaid, that no foreign prince, person, prelate, state or potentate, spiritual or temporal, shall at any time after the last day of this session of Parliament, use, enjoy or exercise any manner of power, jurisdiction, superiority, authority, preeminence of privilege, spiritual or ecclesiastical, within this realm or within any other your majesty's dominions or countries that now be or hereafter shall be, but from henceforth the same shall be clearly abolished out of this realm and all other your highness' dominions for ever . . .
VIII And that also it may likewise please your highness that it may be established and enacted by the authority aforesaid, that such jurisdictions, privileges, superiorities and preeminences, spiritual and ecclesiastical, as by any spiritual or ecclesiastical power or authority hath heretofore been or may lawfully be exercised

or used for the visitation of the ecclesiastical state and persons, and for reformation, order and correction of the same and of all manner of errors, heresies, schisms, abuses, offences, contempts and enormities, shall forever, by authority of this present Parliament, be united and annexed to the imperial crown of this realm; and that your highness, your heirs and successors, kings or queens of this realm, shall have full power and authority by virtue of this act, by letters patents under the great seal of England ... to visit, reform, redress, order, correct and amend all such errors, heresies, schisms, abuses, offences, contempts and enormities.

IX And for the better observation and maintenance of this act, may it please your highness that it may be further enacted by the authority aforesaid, that all and every archbishop, bishop and all and every other ecclesiastical person, and other ecclesiastical officer and minister, of what estate, dignity, preeminence or degree soever he or they be or shall be ... shall make, take and receive a corporal oath upon the Evangelist, before such person or persons as shall please your highness, your heirs or successors, under the great seal of England, to assign and name, to accept and take the same according to the tenor and effect hereafter following, that is to say: I, A. B. do utterly testify and declare in my conscience, that the queen's highness is the only supreme governor of this realm and of all other her highness' dominions and countries, as well in all spiritual or ecclesiastical things or causes as temporal, and that no foreign prince, person, prelate, state or potentate hath or ought to have any jurisdiction, power, superiority, preeminence or authority, ecclesiastical or spiritual, within this realm; and therefore I do utterly renounce and forsake all foreign jurisdictions, powers, superiorities and authorities, and do promise that from henceforth I shall bear faith and true allegiance to the queen's highness ... and defend all jurisdictions, preeminences, privileges and authorities granted or belonging to the queen's highness, her heirs and successors.

Source 1.3: The Bull of Denunciation 1570.

Elizabeth ... after she had gained the throne, usurped to herself monstrously the place of supreme head of the Church in all England and the principal authority and jurisdiction in it. ... She has taken away by a violent hand the use of true religion which had previously been overthrown by the apostate Henry VIII ... she has followed and embraced the errors of heretics. ... She has oppressed holders of the Catholic faith. ... She has abolished the sacrifice of the mass, prayers, fastings, choice of foods, celibacy, and Catholic rites; she has commanded books which contain manifest heresy to be spread through the whole kingdom; she has required services which are impious and instituted according to the prescriptions of Calvin to be accepted ... observed ... and acknowledged by her subjects. ...

She has compelled by an oath very many to agree to her wicked laws and to abjure the authority and obedience of the Roman pontiff, and to recognise her alone as mistress in temporal and spiritual affairs.... And so ... we declare the aforesaid Elizabeth a heretic and a favourer of heretics, and those who adhere to her in the aforesaid matter, to have incurred the sentence of anathema, and to be cut off from the unity of the body of Christ. Moreover she is deprived of her pretended right to the kingdom.... Likewise the nobles, subjects and people of the said kingdom ... (are) absolved perpetually for the future from all duty, fidelity and obedience due ... and we require and order ... all ... not to venture to obey her instructions, mandates, or laws.

Given at Rome, at St Peter's, in the year of the Lord's incarnation, 1570 (February) ... in the fifth year of our pontificate (Pius V).

Source 1.4: The 'Bloody Questions' administered to English Catholics.

1 Whether the bull of Pius V against the queen's Majesty be a lawful sentence, and ought to be obeyed by the subjects of England? ...

3 Whether the pope has, or had, power to authorize the earls of Northumberland, Westmorland, and others of her Majesty's subjects, to rebel, or take arms against her Majesty?

4 Whether the pope hath power to discharge any of her Highness' subjects ... from their allegiance .. to her Majesty ...?

6 If the pope do by his bull or sentence pronounce her Majesty to be deprived and no lawful queen, and her subjects to be discharged of their allegiance and obedience unto her, and, after the pope or any other of his appointment and authority do invade this realm, which part would you take, or which part ought a good subject of England to take?

Questions

1. Explain why Questions 4 and 6 were included in Source 1.4.
2. Compare Sources 1.2 and 1.3 as evidence for the Queen's *ecclesiastical* authority.
3. How well does Source 1.1 sum up the problems presented by Sources 1.2 to 1.4? Use all four sources and your own knowledge.

2. 'INTERNAL' AND 'EXTERNAL' OPPOSITION

Source 2.1: From A.G. Dickens, *The English Reformation*, published in 1964.

Of the external threats presented to the Settlement that of Catholicism remained insignificant for a decade. It then assumed menacing proportions between 1569 and 1588, yet was largely contained by the end of the reign. When in the summer of 1559 Elizabeth's commissioners toured the provinces they found an insignificant number of Catholic clergy venturing to refuse the oath of Supremacy.... Until the papal bull of 1570 excommunicated Elizabeth and urged her subjects to depose her, Catholic recusancy scarcely existed upon any measurable scale. English Catholicism was re-created during the last three decades of the reign by the adventurous labours of the Seminarists and Jesuits.... During the eighties and nineties under missionary influence the number of recusants grew apace in certain areas of England.

Source 2.2: From J. Guy, *Tudor England*, published in 1988.

Yet the dynamic change sprang from mortality. For the post-Reformation English Catholic community owed everything to Henrician and Marian survivalism, and relatively little to the missions of seminary priests and Jesuits after 1570. Although apologists have claimed that the recusant tradition was forged by missionary priests in the face of widespread Catholic inertia before their arrival, the truth is that the essential concept of a separated Catholic church existed before the seminarians and Jesuits landed; there was already a recusant priesthood providing sacraments for lay people who regarded themselves as Catholics; and it was the ex-Marian clergy who nurtured lay recusant Catholicism and established it before the missionaries could have had any significant effect. Over 225 Marian priests who saw themselves as Roman Catholics and who had separated from the Anglican Church were active in Yorkshire and Lancashire before 1571, supported by a fifth-column within the official church that remained willing to proselytize for Rome.

Source 2.3: S. Doran, *Elizabeth I and Religion*, published in 1994.

In conclusion, it was not the failure of the Catholic leadership in the 1560s that doomed Catholicism to decline under Elizabeth I; on the contrary, the Marian priests helped Catholicism to survive the first decade of the reign in reasonable shape. Nor was it the fault of the seminary priests that the Catholic community was reduced to a small minority sect by 1603; despite the weaknesses of their mission, it is difficult to see how without their input Catholicism could have survived into the next century as anything other than the superstitious rituals of backward communities. In reality, given the long reign of Elizabeth and the certainty of a Protestant successor after Mary, Queen of Scots' execution in 1587, the decline of Catholicism was a gradual but inevitable process. The long and remorseless governmental persecutions and the slow but sustained exposure to Protestantism weaned most Catholics from their faith.

Source 2.4: P. Johnson, *Elizabeth: a Study in Power and Intellect*, published in 1974.

By virtually excluding the Catholic gentry from the operations of her anti-Catholic legislation, Elizabeth effectively tamed Catholicism, at least for a time. Catholicism as a religious structure collapsed when state institutions withdrew their support in 1559. It survived in remote areas where private institutions, above all the landowning gentry, were the mainstay of society. Only large households could maintain the cyclical apparatus of Catholicism, the fasts and great feasts, the elaborate ceremonials of the liturgy. . . . The lords and squires thus became the effective government of English Catholicism, and the clergy merely household servants: it was a return to the old proprietory church of the Dark Ages. Since the gentry were in charge, Elizabeth could hold them responsible: and they repaid her toleration by their loyalty. She was quite happy with this situation, and so were the Catholic landowners and their tenants. . . .

The Counter-Reformation in England, as Elizabeth always insisted, was not therefore indigenous, but a foreign importation. The Catholic gentry deplored the papal Bull of 1570, and still more the violent manifesto of Cardinal Allen in 1588. They realized that the training of priests on the Continent was, in some ways, aimed at their status – a reassertion of the independence of the clerical order. The new priests, and especially the Jesuits, were not prepared to be treated as household servants. Moreover, since their seminary efforts needed finance, they accepted help and subsidies from the Catholic powers, above all Spain, and thus became involved in national and international politics. This, too, the Catholic gentry hated, for it upset the *status quo* and imperilled their lives and property.

Questions

1. Compare the argument in Source 2.1 with that in Source 2.2.
2. With which of Sources 2.1, 2.2 and 2.3 does the argument in Source 2.4 most agree?
3. Use Sources 2.1 to 2.4, and your own knowledge, to explain how and why historians have disagreed on the pattern of Catholic decline during the reign of Elizabeth.

Worked answer: Use Sources 2.1 to 2.4, and your own knowledge, to explain how and why historians have disagreed on the pattern of Catholic decline during the reign of Elizabeth.

[Advice: 'How' and 'why' both need to be addressed; the 'how' requires careful reference to all four sources to establish the ways in which historians 'have disagreed', and 'why' should have some historiographical explanation, although the focus should remain sharply on the sources.]

The way in which Catholic decline occurred during the reign of Elizabeth has been interpreted in almost every possible way, Sources 2.1 to 2.4 providing a good cross-section of the overall historiographical debate.

'Decline', 'revival' and 'survival' are the key concepts, although they have been used in different ways and combinations. Dickens (Source 2.1) approached the issue through the decline–revival–decline route. 'Catholicism remained insignificant for a decade', assuming 'menacing proportions between 1569 and 1588', which were 'largely contained by the end of the reign'. This is broadly in line with the view of the majority of historians, including McGrath, Bossy and Elton, who all stressed the importance of the Douai missionaries in the temporary recovery of Catholicism. The opposite scenario, survival–decline, was put by Guy (Source 2.2). Catholicism owed much to 'Henrician and Marian survivalism' and 'relatively little to the missions of seminary priests and Jesuits after 1570'. Guy was supported in this by Haigh, both placing the emphasis on the 'heroic failure' of those who tried to intervene from abroad. Doran (Source 2.3) argued instead for a steadier and longer-term development. Although there was initial agreement with the views of Haigh ('Marian priests helped Catholicism to survive the first decade of the reign'), Doran nevertheless maintained that 'the decline of Catholicism was a gradual but inevitable process'. In the extract included as Source 2.4, Johnson adopted a similar approach to that of Dickens (a decline), except that there was no revival during the 1570s. This was because the residue of Catholicism was salvaged by the gentry, although the latter were put off by 'the papal Bull of 1570'. The decline was not so much continuous, as suggested by Doran, as accelerated after 1570.

The only possibility not considered was that Catholicism was strengthened continuously during the reign: an unlikely survival–revival scenario. Nevertheless there is still the possibility of a contradictory development not covered in the Sources. The stronger the intervention from outside, the more distinct Catholicism remained. But the more distinct it was, the fewer it attracted. Revival of identity therefore resulted in a decline in popularity.

Most historical controversy is a matter of emphasis as well as judgement. In this case different weights were given to domestic and foreign influences. Dickens, Guy and Johnson all emphasised – in different ways – the importance of the Papal Bull of 1570 as a catalyst for the next stage, whether this was recovery or decline. Doran, on the other hand, focused more on domestic influences. Similarly, there might be a difference in the interpretation of Catholic decline which relates to the historian's broader approach to the English Reformation. Dickens argued that the spread of Protestantism was rapid, and from the grass roots as well as from above. Catholicism was bound to be in trouble – unless given a sudden stimulus from abroad. Guy, by contrast, maintained that it took a long time for Protestantism to supplant Catholicism – but that external interventions helped to discredit the latter. Johnson (Source 2.4) was providing a social dimension to the debate: 'The lords and squires thus became the effective government of English Catholicism, and the clergy merely household servants'; this is also part of the broader interpretation provided by Haigh.

Different emphases can also be reflected by historical dynamics – especially in terms of 'turning points', 'continuity' and 'change'. For Dickens 'change' revolved around a 'turning point' – the 'papal bull of 1570', before which 'Catholic recusancy scarcely existed upon any measurable scale'. Johnson used two 'turning points'. The first was the state institutions withdrawing 'their support in 1559', the second the reaction of the Catholic gentry against the Papal Bull of 1570; the first was compensated by the protection of the gentry – but this was cancelled out by the second. Other interpretations depend on 'continuity' rather than 'turning points'. Guy, for example, emphasised that the 'essential concept of a separated Catholic church existed before the seminarians and Jesuits landed'. Even that event had its precedents, as 'Roman Catholics . . . who had separated from the Anglican Church were active in Yorkshire and Lancashire before 1571'. Doran drew attention to the extended timescale involved: 'the long reign of Elizabeth and the certainty of a Protestant successor'.

Historians will always seek to establish alternative viewpoints and perspectives since this is the very essence of history writing.

5

PURITANISM AND THE PURITAN 'THREAT'

BACKGROUND

The term 'Puritan' was initially one of abuse and was not widely used during the sixteenth century. It was first applied to those who resisted the official doctrine and rubric in the 1559 Prayer Book. Those who came under the generic term preferred at the time to call themselves 'the Godly' or 'True Gospellers'. Analysis 1 considers the question of definition and how the views of historians have changed over the past century. Whether or not Puritanism was a 'threat' to the religious and political establishment is dealt with in Analysis 2; while the historiography of this issue is the subject of Analysis 3.

ANALYSIS 1: WHO WERE THE 'PURITANS'?

This has certainly been a slippery term to define. P. Williams maintained that there was no rigid body of doctrine that could be called 'Puritanism' – but that there were 'Puritans'.[1] The main characteristics included the influence of Calvin's ideas, especially of predestination, a desire to practise the precepts of Geneva's 'godly society' and an ordering of their moral behaviour strictly in accordance with the Bible. They were strongly anti-Catholic and emphasised the need for further Protestant reform of the Church of England; in particular, they wanted a simplification of clerical dress and they opposed 'popish' and 'superstitious' rituals such as making the sign of the cross and kneeling at communion. Their services also became renowned for the central role of preaching.

The main areas inhabited by Puritans were the south-west, especially Devon and Cornwall; the south-east, including Essex and Kent; East Anglia and Lincolnshire; parts of the Midlands; and southern Lancashire, especially Manchester – where they were seen as a counter-balance to the preponderance of Catholics elsewhere in the north-west. Some historians have argued that Puritans came primarily from the middle classes, especially from the more enterprising groups of skilled workers, shopkeepers and merchants. This appears to be borne out by the distribution of Puritanism, which was most widespread in towns, ports and other areas of more concentrated economic activity. But the explanations attributed to this need to be dealt with cautiously. On the one hand, it *is* possible to make a direct connection between religious affiliation and occupation on geographical lines: radical influences, for example, entered England from the continent along trade routes. It is also reasonable to argue that skilled occupational groups would be more likely to have sufficient education to be attracted by the need for self-thought and responsibility which Puritanism tended to promote. On the other hand, some arguments have gone too far. R.H. Tawney observed in 1926 that there was a close affinity between Puritanism and the rise of capitalism – 'Puritanism became a potent force in preparing the way for the commercial civilization' – and that opposition to restraints imposed by church and state on 'individual self-interest' appeared 'quite early in the reign of Elizabeth', eventually going on to influence the powerful movement which 'finally triumphed at the Revolution'.[2] This view can be criticised on the grounds that there was little sign of emerging 'capitalist' influences in sixteenth-century Puritan writings, that capitalism has also been equally strongly associated with Catholic states and entrepreneurs, and that significant numbers of Puritans also came from the non-commercial gentry and aristocracy.

It was once believed that Puritans were a distinct group who were identifiably different to the established church because of their religious views. The traditional argument is that Puritanism was separatist and largely antagonistic to the church, taking up its battle positions in the House of Commons. J.E. Neale, for example, saw a strong and distinct Puritan grouping within the Commons, identified as the 'Choir'. Historians frequently argued that Elizabeth's reign saw the second phase of the Protestant Reformation – a struggle between the established Anglican Church on the one hand and, on the other, Puritanism as a more radical form of Protestantism. Puritans were also considered to be a minority who, in reacting to various forms of discrimination against them, developed a coherent identity of their own. In 1931 E. Troeltsch veiwed Puritanism as one of the distinct opposition groups who, like the Calvinists in France and, at least initially, in the Netherlands, were 'minorities . . . forced out of public life and official positions in the State' and therefore 'obliged, in the main to go into business life'.[3] This, however, was to prove an oversimplified equation between Puritanism, dissent and commerce. Being a Puritan did not necessarily mean exclusion from the establishment: several of the Queen's ministers, including Walsingham, were of Puritan persuasion. Nor were the majority of Puritans likely to seek refuge in private enterprise; those individuals who did make a target of themselves were more likely to be found in the pulpit or in academia.

Such images of Puritanism have been strongly challenged. In 1983 P. Collinson maintained that 'It was not the name of a religion or denomination, still less of a political party or social class.'[4] It is no longer possible to say that Puritanism was the English version of Calvinism – opposing the 'Anglicanism' of the Church of England. The latter itself incorporated a great deal of Calvinism, and Puritans were identifiable more by the *extent* of their Calvinist beliefs than by the simple fact that they had any. But this should not imply any predisposition to open disagreement; Collinson argued that there was actually considerable concord and consensus within the Church of England, especially concerning Calvinist orthodoxy, Sabbath observance, preaching and anti-Catholicism.[5] According to S. Doran: 'It was only the intensity of their religious experience, their style of personal piety and their commitment to further religious reform that gave them a particular identity and earned them their pejorative nickname.'[6]

The revised approach, therefore, is to see Puritanism not as one movement but as a variety of tendencies, some within the church, others outside and in direct opposition to it. There were probably as many differences between these Puritan tendencies as there were between Puritanism and the church itself.

Most Puritans could be described as 'Conformists' or 'moderates'. These had probably been exiles during the Marian period, returning to England at the beginning of Elizabeth's reign, optimistic about achieving a radically Protestant settlement. After all, both the Puritans and the established church shared certain features of Calvinism, accepting the Calvinistic focal point of the concept of predestination. Calvin had maintained that 'all are not created in equal condition: rather, eternal life is fore-ordained for some, eternal damnation for others'. Salvation is a gift bestowed by the Grace of the Creator, who has 'the right to distribute this treasure to whom he pleases'.[7] But the Conformists sometimes went further in their emphasis. They attached more importance to the 'double predestination' of both the 'elect' *and* the 'reprobate', whereas the doctrine of the Church of England was based more heavily on the former. Conformist Puritans were also disappointed with what was put together in 1559 in the shape of the Acts of Supremacy and Uniformity. Nevertheless, they preferred to work from within the church in order to try to bring about modifications to the settlement. Some of the Conformists obtained high positions of authority: Grindal, for example, was a Puritan by doctrinal persuasion. In some ways, he was prepared to suppress his own religious views and take a political approach. But this foundered on the question of prophesyings, over which he clashed with the Queen – and was suspended for his pains. There were, however, several bishops who swallowed many of their own religious preferences in order to carry out the official policy of the church: they were therefore prepared to take a political rather than an ideological view. The argument of J. Warren represents current thought: 'It is essential to recognise that Puritanism and the Elizabethan Church of England were not necessarily mutually exclusive. It was possible to be a Puritan and to work within the Church. It was also possible to rise to the very top of the hierarchy, and yet to retain those central assumptions of Puritanism. But what was possible was not always easy.'[8]

This uneasy compromise may have been acceptable to some Puritans, but it was not to others. Those who could not bring themselves to operate within the church did so increasingly from *outside*. These subdivided into two further groups, the Presbyterians and the Separatists. The Presbyterians emerged in the 1570s, taking their stand very much on the question of the organisation of the church. They were strongly opposed to the episcopalian structure, preferring instead the Calvinist emphasis on congregations, ministers and lay elders; contacts between congregations would be maintained by synods. The Separatists went even further, denying any need for organisational connections between congregations. Instead, each congregation should have a unique identity and be permitted an individual interpretation of the scriptures. Of particular importance was the work of Thomas Cartwright, who argued for the end of all levels of the Church of England hierarchy: archdeacons, bishops and archbishops. He also believed that the election of ministers should replace the appointment of priests. Another influence was John Field, who reinforced Cartwright's attack on the system of bishops. His *A View of Popish Abuses yet remaining in the English Church* attacked the 1559 Prayer

Book as being 'culled and picked out of the popish dunghill, the Mass book full of all abominations'.[9] These views were, however, more acceptable on the fringes of Presbyterianism and Separatism than in their main parts or among the Conformists.

'Puritanism' therefore existed in a variety of shades and guises. What distinguished the type of 'Puritan' was the degree to which he or she felt that adaptations could be made to the Church of England as defined by the 1559 settlement or, to put it the other way round, the extent to which they demanded that that settlement had to be changed – by whatever means was necessary. Some Puritans did, therefore, occupy positions outside and hostile to the church. This is, however, a far cry from the large and distinct movement once seen to be a direct challenger to the Elizabethan settlement and for the soul of the later Reformation in England.

Questions

1. How useful is the term 'Puritan'?
2. What is the distinction between 'moderate' and 'radical' Puritanism?

ANALYSIS 2: EXAMINE THE TREATMENT OF PURITAN 'THREATS' BY ELIZABETH'S GOVERNMENT.

Almost all Puritans considered the 1559 religious settlement, defined by the Acts of Supremacy and Uniformity, as unsatisfactory. They therefore aimed to change these and thereby reform the Church of England, although the ways in which they went about this tended to define what type of Puritan they were. The reaction of Elizabeth, her government and the church varied in response to the nature of the threat; they encountered mixed success, although the balance sheet was generally in their favour by the end of the reign.

The first direct challenge was the Puritan attempt to modify the 1559 settlement through the Six Articles presented to the convocation of the church in 1563; these sought guarantees concerning the observance of the Sabbath, the positioning of the minister to face the congregation, changes to the ceremony of infant baptism, the end of kneeling at communion, the reduction of vestments and the removal of church organs. This was clearly more effectively organised and succeeded in its intention of focusing debate within the church. The Articles were, however, narrowly defeated in convocation and the church moved on to the offensive through Archbishop Parker's Advertisements, which enforced conformity on clerical dress and ceremonies. The Queen, shaken by the threat which seemed to have been posed to the internal unity of the church, had instructed Parker to impose his and her full authority. At this stage she tried to minimise any *appearance* of concern by claiming that the Puritans were raising questions which were *adiaphora* (or 'indifferent' to the salvation of the soul).

The next challenge was perceived as more serious. The House of Commons became involved as the reformers, defeated within the church, sought to gain their ends by Act of Parliament. The more radical Puritans promoted Bills to reform the church in 1566 and 1571. The rejection of these by the rest of the Commons provoked two 'Admonitions to the Parliament' in 1572; the first was the work of John Field and Thomas Wilcox, the second that of Thomas Cartwright. Between them, these warned that to achieve proper reforms there would have to be changes in the very structure of the Church of England. Instead of the 'popish' hierarchy, there should be a 'consistory', based on Calvin's Genevan structure and comprising equal ministers and 'godly' elders. This was to become the basis of the Presbyterian model, which began to develop outside the church. Although the proposals were defeated in Parliament, the Queen again expressed her severe displeasure with the presumption of the organisers. Field and Wilcox served a short time in Newgate prison and Cartwright fled abroad. This time she also saw a potential danger from within Parliament and made it clear that she did not want matters of religion to be discussed. This 'doleful message' was challenged by a Puritan member, Peter Wentworth; but he, too, was reprimanded and silenced. There was no evidence of the stirring of parliamentary opposition to an over-powerful monarch which would eventually culminate in a 'great rebellion'.

Silencing the more radical Puritans and sending a clear message to the Commons temporarily reduced the threat to the church – but it did not end the controversy. For both radical and moderate Puritans agreed on the fundamental importance of 'prophesyings', meetings which involved prayer, instruction on the Bible and preaching. Although many Church of England clergy sympathised with these meetings, the Queen herself disapproved of them and ordered Edmund Grindal, appointed Archbishop of Canterbury on the death of Parker in 1575, to suppress them altogether. Elizabeth's concern may well have been exaggerated; it was certainly personal. She disliked preaching, sermons and discussion. They allowed for departures from authorised services and she was convinced that some were directed specifically against her.

She objected, for example, to a sermon from Edward Dering, which accused her of tolerating lax standards within the church: 'And yet you, in the meanwhile that all these whoredoms are committed, you at whose hands God will require it, let men do as they list.'[10] Grindal tried to explain to Elizabeth in 1576 that prophesyings were an effective means of ensuring true doctrine and that their abuse by a few extremists should not result in action against all (see Source 1.1 below). The Queen was, however, determined to suppress such 'assemblies'; in a direct order to her bishops, which bypassed the archbishop, she explained that 'great numbers of our people, specially the vulgar sort . . . are . . . seduced and in a manner schismatically divided amongst themselves into variety of dangerous opinions' (Source 2.2 below). This was the essence of the issue: Grindal trusted the clergy to make positive and restrained use of open discussion, whereas the Queen did not. The latter got her way, as Grindal was suspended from his duties until his death in 1683.

Radical Puritans continued their appeals for fundamental reorganisation of the church. Some were already organising into a Presbyterian 'classis' structure, comprising ministers and elders from parishes who came together to maintain discipline and to elect representatives to local synods which, in turn, elected a national synod. Regular use was also made of Walter Travers's alternative to the Prayer Book, the *Full and Plain Declaration of Ecclesiastical Discipline*, published in 1574. Other radicals went even further. The 'Separatists', led by Robert Browne, Henry Barrow and John Greenwood, preferred independent congregations bound together by a 'covenant' but not subject to the authority of synods. Under Elizabeth's instigation the church stiffened its resistance to the radicals. John Whitgift, who succeeded Grindal as archbishop in 1583, issued Articles to enforce the 1559 settlement (Source 1.3 below), and made full and effective use of the High Commission to deal with radical dissidents. At first Whitgift targeted the 'Separatists'; two followers were hanged in 1583. The establishment was then confronted by Puritan measures within Parliament. In 1587 Anthony Cope's 'Bill and Book' was designed to impose the Presbyterian structure on the Church of England and to authorise regular use of the *Book of Discipline*. The Speaker of the House of Commons warned Cope against this, but a group of Puritans, led by Peter Wentworth, insisted on a reading. When the Bill was confiscated on the Queen's orders, Wentworth attacked royal interference, only to be imprisoned in the Tower for his efforts. This period, 1587–8, saw the establishment very much on top. As in the early 1570s, Puritanism had again failed to achieve its objectives in Parliament. Moderate Puritans were deterred from their own criticisms partly by the measures of Whitgift and partly by the threat to the nation posed by the Spanish Armada. Of the radicals, Greenwood and Barrow were pulled into prison in 1587, while Field died in 1588. This period also saw the death of three members of Elizabeth's Council who had shown any sympathy to the Puritans – Leicester, Walsingham and Mildmay.

Was Elizabeth exaggerating the 'threat' posed by the radicals, as Grindal had clearly thought she did over the 'prophesyings'? On this occasion there seems to be a case for saying that she may have been right in suspecting a danger. Whereas prophesyings never threatened the structure of the church – any more than the vestiarian controversy had – both the Presbyterian and Separatist proposals would have made the Church of England unrecognisable. The broad-based Calvinist consensus on doctrine would not have been sufficient to prevent the complete overturn, rather than reform, of the 1559 settlement. Nor was the Presbyterian structure a mere theory. It was a working model, which had already been applied successfully in Scotland and, according to Elton, was ready to impose itself on England.[11] Elizabeth was probably all too aware of this – and she was concerned about where this might lead next. Whitgift had warned her that 'In the end your Majesty will find that those which now impugn the ecclesiastical jurisdiction [will] endeavour also to impair the temporal, and to bring even kings and princes under their censure.'[12] Yet it could be argued that Whitgift was overstating the case in order to justify his measures. No less an authority than Lord Burghley protested to Whitgift that in a case involving two preachers, 'this kind of proceeding is too much savouring of the Roman inquisition, and is rather a device to seek for offenders than to reform any.'[13]

At all events the immediate danger had passed by 1588, no doubt helped greatly by the popular support for a regime under the threat of foreign invasion; the Spanish Armada drove back into the fold many of the moderate Puritans that Whitgift had alienated. By the 1590s Elizabeth and the church leadership were much more confident about their ability to contain the challenge of radical Puritanism. As is often the case, however, their measures intensified against a weakened opposition. Admittedly the provocation was more direct. Between 1588 and 1589 Penry and others printed and circulated the Marprelate Tracts satirising the establishment and launching personal and often scurrilous attacks on some of the bishops. The printers were highly elusive, moving from centre to centre, often with the help of local sympathisers. Elizabeth certainly regarded these as a direct insult. However, abusive satire is rarely more than annoying and Elizabeth was able to employ effective counter-measures. Whitgift was given a free hand. The Marprelate Tracts were countered in kind by John Lyly and Thomas Nash, who took the debate to a lower level and hence rendered it harmless. More draconian measures involved the arrest of those responsible for the Tracts and the execution of Barrow, Greenwood and Penry. Meanwhile, Parliament had been warned against a 'licentious' approach to discussion and was persuaded to pass an Act to 'retain the Queen's subjects in obedience'.

By the late 1590s Puritanism no longer posed a threat in any of its forms, although historians are divided as to whether this was a temporary or longer-term achievement. The reason had been Partly the lack of any united Puritan offensive, partly the measures – sometimes ruthless – to nip in the bud the aspirations of particular groups. Throughout the reign, however, the Church of England maintained the centrality of Calvinism to its doctrine, which prevented most Puritans from launching their criticisms from outside. There was often as much difference between the various Puritan sects as between Puritans and non-Puritans, which enabled the authorities to attack specific groups at particular times whilst seeking an overall conformity. At the very time that Whitgift was taking the ultimate measures against the Marprelate Tracts, he was also issuing the Lambeth Articles to affirm the crucial importance of Calvinist predestination to the official doctrine of the Church of England. Of greater weight were the five volumes of Richard Hooker's *Of the Laws of Ecclesiastical Polity*, which provided a scholarly and reasoned justification for the status quo; this had the effect of quietly reconciling the moderates – and of sending the radicals quietly on their way.

Questions

1. How much of a 'threat' were the Puritans to the Church of England during the reign of Elizabeth?
2. 'Effective and fully justified.' Is this an accurate description of the measures taken by Queen and church to deal with the Puritans between 1559 and 1603?

ANALYSIS 3: HOW HAVE HISTORIANS INTERPRETED THE 'THREAT' POSED BY THE PURITANS?

There are four quite distinct positions taken by historians on this issue.
The traditional approach to Elizabethan Puritanism is that there was

a very real threat which was well dealt with by the Queen, Whitgift and Parker. J.R. Green, for example, maintained that Elizabeth was provoked into taking firm and fully justified action. 'Her passion was for moderation, her aim was simply civil order.' She was confronted by 'clerical bigots', the worst of whom was Cartwright: 'No leader of a religious party ever deserved less of after sympathy than Cartwright. He was unquestionably learned and devout, but his bigotry was that of a mediaeval inquisitor.'[14] Half a century later, A.L. Rowse stated that containing the Puritan threat was one of Elizabeth's greatest achievements – in terms of the skill required and the service rendered. An alternative approach was taken by P. Johnson in 1974. There was indeed a threat – but it was one perceived by Elizabeth. She was so convinced that they were 'a threat to monarchical government' that she acted against them with 'an uncharacteristic lack of tolerance'[15]

A third possibility was suggested by G.R. Elton: the existence of a specific challenge from the Presbyterians. 'The classical movement continued to spread until there is reason to suppose that a very considerable part of the south, east, and middle of the country was riddled with presbyterian cells, all linked through personal contacts and occasional synods. If the signal had been given by the queen or Parliament, a presbyterian Church of England would have been virtually ready to step forth.'[16] Finally, some historians have argued that there was little or no threat. J. Guy, for example, brushed aside any notion of a subversive sect (see Source 2.2 below). 'The wider assumption of conventional historiography that mainstream puritanism was potentially anarchical, and therefore external to the Anglican Church, is misguided. Few puritans had "revolutionary" plans; the vast majority firmly disavowed separation.'[17] P. Lake made a similar point, although from a different angle. Paradoxically, the Puritans were too divided among themselves, and had too many links with the establishment, to endanger the status quo. 'We have evidence of a formal Calvinist consensus linking Whitgift and Bridges with Puritans (both moderate and presbyterian) like Cartwright, Fulke, William Whitaker and Laurence Chaderton. But we have within that consensus considerable differences of tone and emphasis, which were indicative of deep yet largely unstated disagreements about what true religion was and what the practical consequences of right doctrine were.'[18]

All of these arguments can still be advanced: Analysis 2 above steers between them. But one particular controversy seems to have been laid to rest. The Puritans were seen by J.E. Neale as a powerful House of Commons opposition group to the crown and government, providing a clear link with the eventual origins of the English Civil War.

But, as is discussed in Chapter 3, there is not much evidence for this. Most MPs put their social position and economic well-being before any radical religious views and therefore tended to play safe politically. It is therefore wrong to identify Parliament with Puritanism or even with a substantial Puritan minority. In addition, the Queen was well able to contain any minority signs of dissent. She could use her powers to prevent the discussion of specific religious issues. These were enough and she never had to resort to her prerogative powers to prorogue or dissolve Parliament. Yet we should not dismiss out of hand the notion of a threat within Parliament. The perception came from the Queen's government, which feared that religious dissension might translate into political opposition. Hence the arguments advanced by Neale and others may well be the way in which Elizabeth saw the process; but, like her perception, it was a distortion – or an exaggeration of reality. Did extremism threaten moderation? Or did moderates perceive an extremist threat and hence adopt immoderate measures to deal with it?

Another case was similarly overstated – with still less justification. Historians of the 1950s and early 1960s were inclined to draw parallels between the Elizabethan era and the twentieth century, especially in terms of ideological conflict. Rowse, for example, maintained that 'Puritanism started as a movement for reform and became, as such movements do, a campaign for power.'[19] He also made a direct comparison between 'the Protestant attachment to Predestination' and Marxism as 'deterministic creeds which create the greatest energy of will in their adherents' (see Source 2.4 below).[20] Neale and Hurstfield joined Rowse in praising Elizabeth's stand against incipient totalitarianism. According to Neale: 'Had it not been for her, the broad way of English life would have been narrowed and an experiment made with what we today term the ideological state.'[21] Hurstfield added: 'Elizabeth herself struck for liberty also: the ultimate liberty of the human conscience to be free from the dictates of the righteous' (Source 2.4 below).[22] Such analyses are now seen as flawed. Quite apart from assuming that Puritanism was more of a threat than it actually was, it reads into the Elizabethan period some of the values of the Cold War period, during which these historians wrote. The Cold War has been over for some time, and 'Marxism' is scarcely the threat it was perceived to be in 1960. Explaining the past by direct comparisons with the present may enlighten one generation – but it will confuse the next when, in the future, the present becomes part of the past. There is also the inherent danger of oversimplification. Comparing 'predestination' with 'Marxism' overlooks two key points. One is that predestination was officially sanctioned by the 1593 Lambeth Articles as part of the doctrine of the Church of England and should not, therefore, be seen as an alien ideology. The other is that Marxism took a variety of forms, only some of which were totalitarian; others managed to coexist with western liberal democracy. Such interpretations therefore become a superstructure which reveals much about the *historiography* of the period that is writing the *history* of another.

Had the Puritan 'threat' been contained permanently? Again, views have varied, usually in the light of the longer-term trends of the seventeenth century. One argument, pursued by J.R.H. Moorman – again in the 1950s – was that Puritanism remained strong, ready to be converted immediately into antagonism. During James I's reign 'the Puritan party was active, self-confident and aggressive', combining a continuing religious assault on 'the restrained conservatism of the Elizabethan Settlement' and a political alliance with those groups who were challenging 'the despotic power of the king'.[23] Other historians attribute greater success to Elizabeth by 1603, but with reservations about the future. According to Hurstfield, 'This is not to say that the queen solved the Puritan problem. Rather, as in other fields, she damped down the fires of opposition – and left them smouldering to her successor.'[24] Some historians have seen in the revival of Puritanism after Elizabeth a 'high road' to civil war. Although she recognised – and dealt with – the danger, James I and Charles I were less successful. In one of his earlier works, *England under the Tudors* (1953), G.R. Elton said that what Elizabeth could not foresee was that the Stuarts would provoke 'a vast revival of puritanism' through a distinctly more favourable policy towards Catholicism.[25] For Neale the development of Puritanism within the Elizabethan Parliament had huge implications for the future. There have also been arguments based more on socio-economic factors than upon politico-religious ones. C. Hill, for example, associated Puritan ideas with the development of capitalism, especially in the merchant class and among some members of the gentry.[26] Both developments were seen as culminating in internal revolution. In both cases the restraints imposed during the Elizabethan period were simply swept away during the first half of the seventeenth century.

The 'high road' approach has been significantly altered. The 'Marxist' analysis, based on the development of capitalism and subsequent class conflict, has been criticised for being over-prescriptive. The revision of the 'political' approach has been even more sweeping: C. Russell argued that the Civil War was less about long-term principles of law and liberty – whether or not inspired by Puritanism – and more about an immediate financial and structural crisis facing the monarchy;[27] K. Sharpe has also downplayed the longer-term Eliza-bethan parliamentary roots.[28] As for the religious component of the Civil War, it is no longer possible to generalise about Puritanism. Instead of a growing conflict between radical Puritanism and a Church of England partially re-Catholicised under Archbishop Laud, we now have several different possibilities. One is that there was no religious conflict at all. Another, advanced by N. Tyacke,[29] is that the Calvinist consensus with 'Puritanism' was fighting, as a conservative influence, against the more radical Arminianism. Such arguments reveal a series of twisting creeks rather than a 'high road' to war.

Changed perspectives on the conflict of the 1640s have several implications for any final assessment of Elizabethan Puritanism. If the Civil War is perceived to have had more immediate causes rather than being the result of a longer-term trend, perhaps the Elizabethan church was less threatened by Puritanism than was once thought. Elizabeth may well have dealt astutely with the problems which did occur, but the nature of these problems was possibly less severe. Hence the success of her government, depending on the perspective on the future, was either less striking in the short term or less completely undermined in the long term.

Questions

1. Why have historians disagreed so much on the nature of the Puritan 'threat' during the Elizabethan period and beyond?
2. Does the disagreement mean that some historians are 'right' and others 'wrong'?

SOURCES

1. THE ATTITUDES OF ELIZABETH AND HER ARCHBISHOPS TO 'PROPHESYINGS'.

Source 1.1: Extracts from a letter from Edmund Grindal, Archbishop of Canterbury (1576–83), to Queen Elizabeth, 20 December 1576. (These deal with 'exercises' or 'prophesyings'.)

... Now for the second point, which is concerning the learned exercise and conference amongst the ministers of the Church. I have consulted with divers of my brethren the bishops by letters, who think the same as I do, viz. – a thing profitable to the Church and therefore expedient to be continued. And I trust your

Majesty will think the like when your Highness shall be informed of the manner and order thereof; what authority it hath of the Scriptures; what commodity it bringeth with it; and what incommodities will follow if it be clear taken away. The authors of this exercise are the bishops of the dioceses where the same is used, who both by the law of God and by the canons and constitutions of the Church now in force have authority to appoint exercises to their inferior ministers for increase of learning and knowledge in the scriptures as to them seemeth most expedient....

These orders following are also observed in the said exercise: First, two or three of the gravest and best learned pastors are appointed of the bishop to moderate in every assembly. No man may speak unless he be first allowed by the bishop, with this proviso that no layman be suffered to speak at any time. No controversy of this present time and state shall be moved or dealt withal. If any attempt the contrary, he is put to silence by the moderator. None is suffered to glance openly or covertly at persons public or private, neither yet anyone to confute another. If any man utter a wrong sense of the Scripture, he is privately admonished thereof and better instructed by the moderators and other his fellow-ministers. If any man use immodest speech or irreverent gesture or behaviour, or otherwise be suspected in life, he is likewise admonished as before. If any wilfully do break these orders, he is presented to the bishop to be by him corrected....

Howsoever report hath been made to your Majesty concerning these exercises, yet I and others of your bishops ... as they have testified unto me by their letters, having found by experience that these profits and commodities following have ensued of them: 1. The ministers of the Church are more skilful and ready in the Scriptures, and apter to teach their flocks. 2. It withdraweth them from idleness, wandering, gaming, etc. 3. Some afore suspected in doctrine are brought hereby to open confession of the truth. 4. Ignorant ministers are driven to study, if not for conscience yet for shame and fear of discipline. 5. The opinion of laymen touching the idleness of the clergy is hereby removed.

... so as it is found by experience the best means to increase knowledge in the simple and to continue it in the learned. Only backward men in religion and contemners of learning in the countries abroad do fret against it; which in truth doth the more commend it. The dissolution of it would breed triumph to the adversaries, but great sorrow and grief unto the favours of religion.... And although some few have abused this good and necessary exercise, there is no reason that the malice of a few should prejudice all.

Source 1.2: Extracts from the Queen's letter to the bishops, ordering the suppression of prophesyings, 1577.

Right reverent father in God, we greet you well. We hear to our great grief that in sundry parts of our realm there are no small number of persons, presuming to be teachers and preachers of the Church though neither lawfully thereunto called nor yet fit for the same, which, contrary to our laws established for the public divine service of Almighty God and the administration of His holy sacraments within this Church of England, do daily devise, imagine, propound and put in execution sundry new rites and forms in the Church, as well by their preaching, reading and ministering the sacraments, as well by procuring unlawful assemblies of a great number of our people out of their ordinary parishes and from place far distant, and that also some of good calling (though therein not well advised) to be hearers of their disputations and new devised opinions upon points of divinity far and unmeet of unlearned people, which manner of invasions they in some places call prophesying and in some other places exercises; by which manner of assemblies great numbers of our people, specially the vulgar sort, meet to be otherwise occupied with honest labour for their living, are brought to idleness and seduced and in a manner schismatically divided amongst themselves into variety of dangerous opinions, not only in towns and parishes but even in some families, and manifestly thereby encouraged to the violation of our laws and to the breach of common order, and finally to the offence of all our quiet subjects that desire to serve God according to the uniform orders established in the Church, whereof the sequel cannot be but over dangerous to be suffered. Wherefore, considering it should be the duty of the bishops ... to see these dishonours against the honour of God and the quietness of the Church reformed, and that we see that ... great danger may ensue, even to the decay of the Christian faith, whereof we are by God appointed the defender, besides the other inconveniences to the disturbance of peaceable government; we therefore, according to authority we have, charge and command you ... to take order through your diocese ... that no manner of public and divine service, nor other form of the administration of the holy sacraments, nor any other rites or ceremonies, be in any sort used in the Church but directly according to the orders established by our laws. Neither that any manner of person be suffered within your diocese to preach, teach, read, or any wise exercise any function in the Church but such as shall be lawfully approved and licensed as persons able for their knowledge and conformable to the ministry in the rites and ceremonies of the Church of England. ...

... And in these things we charge you to be so careful and vigilant, as by your negligence, if we shall hear of any person attempting to offend in the premises without your correction or information to us, we be not forced to make some example or reformation of you, according to your deserts.

Given under our signet at our manor of Greenwich the 7th of May, 1577.

Source 1.3: An extract from the Articles of Archbishop Whitgift, 1583.

Sixthly, that none be permitted to preach, read, catechise, minister the sacraments, or to execute any other ecclesiastical function, by what authority so ever he be admitted thereunto, unless he first consent and subscribe to these articles following, before the ordinary of the diocese wherein he preacheth, readeth, catechiseth, or ministereth the sacraments: *viz.*

I. That her Majesty, under God, hath and ought to have the sovereignty and rule over all manner of persons born within her realms and dominions and countries, of what estate ecclesiastical or temporal so ever they be. And that none other foreign power, prelate, state or potentate hath or ought to have any jurisdiction, power, superiority, pre-eminence or authority ecclesiastical or temporal within her Majesty's said realms, dominions and countries.

II. That the Book of Common Prayer, and of ordering bishops, priests and deacons, containeth nothing in it contrary to the Word of God. And that the same may be lawfully used; and that he himself will use the form of the said book prescribed, in public prayer and administration of the sacraments, and none other.

III. That he alloweth the book of Articles of Religion, agreed upon by the archbishops and bishops in both provinces, and the whole clergy in the Convocation holden at London in the year of our Lord 1562, and set forth by her Majesty's authority. And that he believeth all the articles therein contained to be agreeable to the word of God.

Questions

1. Using Sources 1.1 and 1.2, and your own knowledge, briefly explain the term 'prophesying'.
2. Compare the arguments used in Sources 1.1 and 1.2 about 'prophesyings'. Why do they differ?
3. ' "Prophesyings" were a serious threat, effectively contained by the Queen and her Archbishops of Canterbury.' Using Sources 1.1 to 1.3, and your own knowledge, comment on this view.

Worked answer: ' "Prophesyings" were a serious threat, effectively contained by the Queen and her Archbishops of Canterbury.' Using Sources 1.1 to 1.3, and your own knowledge, comment on this view.

[Advice: Almost every word of this quotation needs to be addressed in the answer. 'Serious threat' is an assumption: is it justified – within and outside the sources? Was it 'effectively contained' – immediately or in the longer term? Did the measures taken actually work? As for the 'Queen and her Archbishops', were they working together – or were they in conflict? And in the context of all of these issues, can the sources be used at face value? What other information or 'own knowledge' might be needed at various stages of the answer? This should

be integrated into the answer, not be left for a separate section at the end.]

Contemporary documents and secondary works by modern historians have both differed as to the nature of any threat posed during Elizabeth's reign by 'prophesyings' (or 'exercises' based mainly on sermons and biblical discussion). Sources 1.1 and 1.2 show two strongly divergent positions, with 1.2 reinforced by 1.3. The starting point must clearly be whether there was a 'threat' at all, and if so – to what?

One possibility is that prophesyings posed a threat to the church and its doctrine and procedures established by the 1559 settlement. This was perceived by the Queen and some of her bishops – but strenuously denied by Archbishop Grindal in Source 1.1. After all, Grindal had ensured that all the proper procedures had been followed, enforced by 'two or three of the gravest and best learned pastors' appointed 'to moderate in every assembly'. Anyone misusing the scripture was 'privately admonished'. The advantages ('experience that these profits and commodities following have ensued of them') far outweighed any disadvantages, while abuse was limited to 'some few'. The Queen, by contrast, saw a more fundamental threat than admitted by Grindal: those involved were introducing 'sundry new rites and forms in the Church' (Source 1.2). The archbishop and the Queen represented different views about the future of the church: Grindal was sympathetic to the not inconsiderable number of moderate reformers, while the Queen intended to stand firm by the 1559 settlement. Her views were also coloured by her personal dislike for sermons and a preference for strictly controlled ritual. Her position was upheld by Whitgift in Source 1.3 – but there was some inevitability about this as Whitgift was the official replacement for Grindal.

Prophesyings might also be perceived as a challenge to the Queen's religious – and secular – authority. Although Grindal did not raise this issue directly, he did defend the practice as being within 'the canons and constitutions of the Church' (Source 1.1). Again, the Queen saw it differently, as likely to lead to the 'decay of the Christian faith' of which 'we are by God appointed the defender' and also to 'the disturbance of peaceable government' (Source 1.2). This explains the reference in Whitgift's Articles to 'her Majesty' having 'under God' the 'sovereignty and rule' over all within her realm 'of what estate ecclesiastical or temporal so ever they be' (Source 1.3).

The extent of any 'threat', whether religious or secular, has always been a matter of controversy. On the one hand, it could be argued that any group within the body of the church not following the prescriptions of the 1559 settlement could endanger the body as a whole, especially if its members had links with Presbyterians and Separatists. In this way, prophesyings could establish a link with those who aimed at nothing short of radical change to the entire church structure. On the other hand, this smacks of a 'slippery slope' and unjustifiably assumes that the large number of moderate Puritans actually wanted to take their prophesyings any further; recent historical research has certainly emphasised this point. It is clear that a threat was perceived – but it could well have been exaggerated, as Grindal implied.

Was it contained? In the shorter term, it seems not. Sources 1.1 and 1.2 point to a complete breakdown in communication on the issue between the head of the church and her primate. Grindal, for example, was 'informing' Her Majesty of the 'authority' that prophesying 'hath in the Scriptures' (Source 1.1), whereas the Queen stood firmly by 'our laws established for the public divine service' within 'this Church of England' (Source 1.2). The division was exacerbated by the Queen's decision to bypass the archbishop altogether and to make the suppression of prophesying 'the duty of the bishops' (Source 1.2). Many of these were known to be sympathetic to Grindal's position and were unlikely to be entirely co-operative. This was especially the case while Grindal was still officially archbishop: although Elizabeth suspended his effective powers in 1577, she was unable to remove him from office – which he continued to fill until his death in 1583. There was therefore a six-year period of uncertainty about the status of 'prophesying' which allowed it to continue – and possibly spread.

In the longer term, however, this uncertainty was removed. The appointment of Whitgift provided more convergence between the views of the Queen and her archbishop. Bishops and other members of the clergy had to 'consent and subscribe to' Whitgift's Articles (Source 1.3) and to 'use the form of' the Prayer 'in public prayer and administration of the sacraments, and none other' (1.3). This officially removed prophesyings from the options which had previously been open under Grindal. Whitgift also made it clear that he was prepared to enforce the Articles against all breaches, through use of the High Commission. Although the latter was generally reserved for cases of defiance more serious than the use of prophesyings, several members of the clergy did fall foul of the new procedures. Many moderate Puritans became increasingly cautious, especially during the period of the late 1580s when the church took the offensive against a perceived Catholic threat as well. To a large extent, therefore, any threat which had existed was largely removed by the 1590s. At the same time, even members of the

Queen's Council were moved to complain about the excessive nature of the counter-measures used.

2. HISTORIANS AND THE 'THREAT' OF THE PURITANS

Source 2.1: An extract from S.T. Bindoff, *Tudor England*, first published in 1950.

The enemy were already taking up new positions. The Puritan challenge of the eighties took two opposing forms. The 'classical' movement was an attempt to presbyterianize the Church from within. It takes its name from the 'classis' or local synod of Puritan clergy which did everything in its power to give the constitution of the Church a Presbyterian content and meaning. Candidates for the ministry were put forward for consecration after being elected by congregations, the Prayer Book was judiciously emended in use, the Scriptures expounded in a Puritan sense. These local efforts were supplemented and coordinated by those of district conferences and even by national conferences held in London.... The Presbyterians accepted the connexion between Church and State and were only concerned to make the Church pull the State instead of the State's pulling the Church. The 'separatist' movement determined to cut the connexion altogether. To the Separatist the only true Church was the congregation of believers, the 'two or three gathered together' in God's name and neither owing allegiance to, nor deriving authority from, any other power. Where the Presbyterian laboured to convert the magistrate, the Separatist founded his Church without tarrying for the magistrate. Ritual, ceremony, theological learning, these were but dross to men who more than made up for their lack of them by their emotional power and inspirational fervour. The Separatists were few but formidable.

   The Presbyterians strove to undermine episcopacy, the Separatists treated it as though it did not exist.

Source 2.2: An extract from J. Guy, *Tudor England*, first published in 1988.

Few puritans had 'revolutionary' plans; the vast majority firmly disavowed separation. Rather than puritanism being an external threat, the internalization of Protestantism within the Anglican Church was largely due to 'puritan' preachers and pulpit lecturers, as well as to the infectious enthusiasm of those who 'gadded' to sermons. 'Godly' preachers and lecturers, though socially isolated by virtue of their minority status, compensated for the inadequate provision of official Protestant teaching and did much to shift parish Anglicanism decisively towards the reformed faith by 1603. Whereas, too, it is often thought that the Elizabethan church was a rigid institution with a limited capacity to absorb autonomous movements, this fails to do justice to the value 'puritan' evangelism had in validating the national church in the eyes of committed Protestants. In fact, it was far from inevitable before Laud's ascendancy that mainstream puritanism would challenge the national and parochial church.

Source 2.3: An extract from J. Hurstfield, *Elizabeth I and the Unity of England*, first published in 1960.

That Peter Wentworth loved liberty is beyond dispute. . . . But the liberty he sought was, in the end, liberty for his minority faction to dictate the religion and the way of life of the whole nation. In those countries where it is not in power, a minority sometimes demands liberty of speech at the very time when its brothers-in-arms, already in control abroad, ruthlessly extinguish the last hopes of liberty. What the Puritans did when in power in Geneva under Calvin, and in England during the middle of the seventeenth century, taints the high zeal for liberty of men like Peter Wentworth. For, although he nobly suffered for liberty, he would never have extended that liberty to those who deviated from his own intolerant creed. No one can deny that, in defending and extending freedom of speech in the House of Commons, he won for himself an imperishable place in the history of democratic institutions. But the situation has its ironies. For, in thwarting Wentworth and the Puritans in these early battles, Elizabeth herself struck for liberty also: the ultimate liberty of the human conscience to be free from the dictates of the righteous.

Source 2.4: An extract from A.L. Rowse, *The England of Elizabeth*, first published in 1959.

Many have found it curious with regard to the Protestant attachment to Predestination, as they do today in the case of Marxist determinism, that it should be precisely these deterministic creeds which create the greatest energy of will in their adherents and drive them on to make the greatest efforts. It seems paradoxical in those who are at such pains to deny freedom of the will. The explanation can only be that to identify your desires and wishes with the march of events is the greatest assurance, comfort and reinforcement that human egoism can command. It stores up and releases untold energies. . . .

Questions

1. Compare the arguments of the authors of Sources 2.1 and 2.2. Which seems the more plausible?
2. 'Historians sometimes impose the values of the age in which they

live on to the age about which they write.' To what extent is this shown in Sources 2.3 and 2.4?

3. 'A serious threat, well contained by Elizabeth's government.' Comment on this view of the Puritans, using Sources 2.1 to 2.4 and your own knowledge.

6

FOREIGN POLICY

BACKGROUND

The reign of Elizabeth saw the reversal of most of the previous trends of foreign policy. With this came England's first prolonged conflict with a foreign power since the Hundred Years War.

Throughout the period, two areas were of vital importance for England. One, for strategic reasons, was Scotland. The other, commercially, was Burgundy. English foreign policy would have to focus on these and the strength of the threats to them would help determine who would be the major enemy to England at any one time.

Scotland was vital as the part of Great Britain which was open to foreign intervention against England. Throughout the sixteenth century it had provided an intermittent threat. The same applied to Ireland. These are more fully dealt with in Chapter 9. Burgundy, however, was a more continuous priority. The Burgundian connection was a counterpoise to the possible threat of French predominance in northern Europe. It also provided the outlet to much of England's woollen cloth trade, thereby underpinning the English economy generally. The crown obtained a substantial amount of its revenue from export duties: this was an essential component of its financial stability.

Logically, therefore, the reign should have seen a continuation of the sort of foreign policy which had broadly characterised the previous seventy years – occasional and opportunist intervention designed mainly to protect English interests. The most important objective had been the containment of France, which had, in turn, usually meant trying to maintain reasonable relations with Spain.

On Elizabeth's accession this approach seemed as appropriate as ever. France was still the main threat. In 1559 England formally lost Calais, its last foothold on the continent, and with it a presence in the vicinity of Burgundy. In addition, Francis II, who came to the throne in the same year, took assertive measures on behalf of his wife, Mary Queen of Scots. He sent French troops to Scotland, initially to secure Mary's position against Scottish rebels, but with the option also of installing her on the English throne should the opportunity arise. In the late 1550s and the 1560s, therefore, everything pointed to retaining cordial relations with Spain while focusing on France as the traditional enemy.

For a while this position was maintained. In 1560 English troops besieged a French stronghold at Leith. This was followed by the Treaty of Edinburgh which saw the withdrawal of English and French troops from Scotland. Elizabeth also became involved in intervention in France with an abortive attack on Le Havre in 1563. All this depended on the friendly neutrality of Spain. The process was actually assisted by Philip II's attempts to dissuade the Pope from excommunicating Elizabeth as a heretic, and by the benign influence of De Silva, Spanish ambassador at Elizabeth's court. After the Treaty of Troyes (1564) Elizabeth and her court continued to see France as a serious threat, both to Scotland and to Burgundy. French intervention on behalf of Mary Stuart seemed likely in 1569 and again in 1579, once again posing the danger of French action against England through the back door. On each occasion Elizabeth sent expeditions to the borders to put down any possibility of a general offensive and to discourage any direct French involvement.

Then, from 1568 onwards, the balance in foreign policy began to tilt. The major enemy to England ceased to be France and, for the rest of the reign, became Spain – to the point where open war prevailed on land from 1585 and at sea throughout the 1580s and 1590s. This was the result of a cumulative breakdown of relations between England and Spain and a gradual realisation that France was no longer the major threat. The process was not seamless and there were times when the older rivalries seemed as though they might reassert themselves. But the switch to Spanish enmity was the underlying trend.

A major reason for this breakdown in amity was a fundamental change in the relative strength of Europe's two major powers – Spain and France – and the way in which these were eventually perceived by England. For this the catalysts were the revolt in the Netherlands and the French Wars of Religion. The first brought Spanish troops into northern Europe and hence threatened English interests in Burgundy.

The second saw France become increasingly introverted and therefore less threatening than Spain.

England's dependence on trade with Burgundy required a stable political situation in the Low Countries. Under Charles V the area had been loosely connected by dynastic arrangements but had remained largely autonomous. Philip II, who inherited the area from Charles, along with the Spanish throne, tried to streamline and centralise his dominions. This precipitated a revolt in 1566, to which Philip responded by sending troops under the Duke of Alva.

This caused considerable concern to England. But the specific reason for Anglo-Spanish hostility was the advice of Philip II's ambassador to England, Don Guerau de Spes, to the governor general of the Netherlands, the Duke of Alva, to seize English merchants and goods in Burgundian ports to ensure the safe conduct of Spanish treasure shipments which had had to take refuge in English ports. The English, of course, retaliated by impounding Spanish property. One incident was insufficient in itself to destroy a century of Anglo-Spanish co-operation, even if this was set within the context of growing strains. But there were other factors too. For example, the hand of Philip of Spain, along with that of the papacy, was seen in the growing Catholic threat to Elizabeth's internal position. Hence Elizabeth sought alternatives to the Spanish connection. These included negotiations for alliances with the Lutheran German states in 1569 and marriage negotiations with the Duke of Anjou, one of the sons of Catherine de Medici. Although neither actually materialised, they were nevertheless part of a major change in English policy.

Meanwhile, hostility was also growing at sea as English activities threatened the Spanish monopoly in the Caribbean and the Americas. The three voyages made by John Hawkins in 1563, 1565 and 1567 were seen by Spain as a direct threat, especially as Elizabeth was one of the main shareholders in the third. There was an element of retaliation in all of these events and in Drake's subsequent attacks on Panama and Cartagena. At first there were also periods of reconciliation: for example, trading relations were reopened by the Convention of Nymegen in 1573.

During the 1580s, however, the conflict hardened. Elizabeth assisted Henry of Navarre with both men and subsidies against the Catholic League, which in the meantime was being supported by Philip of Spain. She also established links with the Netherlands, in revolt against Philip since 1566. Although she did not openly favour the rebellion of subjects against their sovereign, she allowed the movement of men and supplies from 1572 onwards and, from 1576, provided loans to the Dutch States

General. In 1585 she took the step of signing the Treaty of Nonsuch and sent the Earl of Leicester. By this stage England was involved in a war in both France and the Netherlands. In France she was assisting the King against the Catholic League; in the Netherlands she was assisting the rebels. In both cases the main enemy was now Spain. In 1588, and again in 1596 and 1597, England was threatened by a series of Armadas, seaborne invasions which were intended to inflict military defeat and impose a foreign occupation for the first time since 1066.

ANALYSIS 1: WHAT POLICY DID ELIZABETH PURSUE?

Historians have tended to agree more on the basic objectives of Elizabethan foreign policy than they have over domestic issues.

The original view was best expressed in 1936 by J.B. Black, who maintained that Elizabeth was 'a realist and an opportunist' who made 'interest the determining factor in all her political manoeuvres' and 'reason of state a sufficient justification for every act'.[1] An altogether different approach was advanced in 2005 by D.J.B. Trim, who strongly criticised the view that Elizabeth was largely uncaring about religious issues. 'It is time to look afresh at Elizabeth's foreign policy.' She was 'a genuinely committed Protestant', who was 'surrounded by zealous Protestant ministers, who, though by no means in total harmony over royal policy, had similar goals in mind'.[2] Hence 'confessional factors were ultimately of primary importance in determining Elizabethan foreign policy'.[3] This argument is, however, very much in the minority, most historians still following the approach of Black. D. Loades, for example, continued to stress that 'Elizabeth's strategy was always defensive',[4] while G.D. Ramsay went even further: 'To dignify the dealings of Elizabeth Tudor and her continental neighbours with the title of "foreign policy" perhaps suggests more than her often hesitant groping could substantiate.'[5]

The distinction between ideology and pragmatism can be over-stated: they did not have to be mutually exclusive then, any more than they do today. But it does seem unlikely that Elizabeth would have been *committed* to an ideological approach to furthering England's influence abroad. This would have involved the development of an international Protestant alliance designed to undermine the Counter Reformation. But it would not have made much sense for Elizabeth to have shown any underlying attachment to this, for three reasons. First, she was attempting to restore religious harmony within England. This would have been difficult to reconcile with the pursuit of religious policies abroad. Second, she was suspicious of some of the forms of Protestantism practised by England's allies, especially the militant Calvinism in the Netherlands. Third, this reservation was allied to a dislike she had for rebellion, even if there were mitigating circumstances in the revolt of the Netherlands against the Spanish crown. Hence, while Elizabeth could justify supporting the Protestants of northern Europe for pragmatic reasons, she was unwilling to commit herself totally to them in any fundamental ideological sense. She refused to be drawn into broader strategies or designs and was more inclined to be reactive than formative in her approach, especially in the first two decades of her reign. She did, however, have a clear image of the threats to England and was prepared to make whatever shifts and turns were necessary to try to neutralise them. Her intention was nearly always to apply the minimum amount of force and expenditure needed to achieve a specific objective. All this often gave the impression of indecision, inconsistency and less than total commitment.

This raises a related issue: how direct was Elizabeth's responsibility for the policies that were followed? Recent historiography suggests two broad approaches, each of which is open ended. First, did she impose her own will – or she was influenced into action? And, second, was she served by a Council which was divided and vacillating – or by one which was united in its views?

P. Williams favoured the view that her policy was an often equivocal response to a divided Council. 'Elizabeth's role, which must not be underestimated, lay in choosing, or often in refusing to choose, between policies drawn up and supported by councillors and others.' The latter, however, were usually divided between 'the protagonists of intervention' and 'the prophets of caution, like Burghley'.[6] J. Hurstfield's emphasis had been on a Queen determined to face up to a strong Council, although this sometimes made her seem indecisive in her policy. 'For Elizabeth it was a hard and thankless task to stand firm against her own idealists, to hold back when others said strike! It looked like lethargy, vacillation, lack of faith in the whole system upon which her monarchy was founded. Yet it was she, not the vigorous Protestant group, who was faithful to the interests of the monarchy and the unity of the nation.'[7] True to his vision of an emerging nation led by its greatest monarch, A.L. Rowse's version was a strong Queen over a united Council (see Source 2 below), while, most recently, D.J.B. Trim argued that the 'myth' of the fracturing of the 'Elizabethan body politic' by 'faction' has been exposed as 'false'. Instead, the focus should be on foreign policy as 'a function of government' rather than on 'the diversity of individual contributions'.[8] There is another possibility. Elizabeth's attitude was that the personal control of foreign policy was one of the essential royal prerogatives. This was real, even though she received strong advice from her Councillors and was expected to take this. On the other hand, it is clear that in most cases external influences and events dictated the overall direction she should take, even if she added her own refinements of emphasis.

One way in which the Queen *did* exert a direct influence on foreign policy concerned her wishes over marriage. Her refusal of the hand of Philip II of Spain has often been seen as the turning point in England's relations with Spain. It cannot be denied that what actually happened was very different from what might have been. It is difficult to imagine a dynastic link between Habsburg Spain and Tudor England being followed by open war between the two countries as occurred in the Netherlands and at sea. Nor was the choice inevitable. The previous marriage, between Philip II and Mary, had been slanted very much in England's favour to avoid the possibility of the country becoming a mere adjunct to Spain. Elizabeth's refusal to marry Philip undermined the prospect of continuing reconciliation. She had several motives for her action. One was her widely publicised desire to remain unmarried, a point over which Parliament frequently took her to task. Another was the need to distance herself from Catholicism following her attempt to undo the Marian policies and seek a 'middle way'. Being espoused to Philip would inevitably convey the impression that she was accepting the Counter Reformation. Later, her involvement in the marriage stakes was more positive in intention, although it actually came to nothing. Her negotiations for marriage with Anjou have been described by G.D. Ramsay as 'a personal contribution of the Queen's to the technique and substance of international relations'.[9] Elizabeth also directly influenced foreign policy by promoting certain patterns of commercial activity designed to break into the Spanish monopoly in the Caribbean. For example, she invested in two of the voyages of Hawkins and encouraged the privateering activities of Drake. Hence, according to Pollitt, 'there is a strong possibility that the trade was being used by the Crown as an instrument of its policies'.[10]

In the light of these debates on Elizabeth's role in policy formation, how should we see the shift from initial enmity with France to one of eventual conflict with Spain? The following might be an overall explanation.

Between 1558 and 1585 Elizabeth aimed to neutralise the long-term French threat to Scotland and the Netherlands while, at the same time, forcing Spain to withdraw from the brink of full-scale war. To do this she adopted measures which appeared sometimes to be anti-French, sometimes anti-Spanish. But the momentum towards growing confrontation with Spain became increasingly apparent towards the end of the 1570s. Hence the view that France was the main threat and that things must be patched up with Spain in order to deal with it gave way to another perception – that Spain had become the main threat and must be contained with help from any quarter, including France. The whole shift was gradual and reluctant. This approach gives more structure to a policy which otherwise seems broadly inconsistent. It emphasises the reactive nature of Elizabeth's policies – but then, this could hardly have been otherwise since the impetus for change came not from England but from the two great struggles taking place on the continent. Although these were obviously instances where Elizabeth deliberately pursued specific lines of policy, there were others in which she had to react to developments over which she had no real control. This does not mean that there was no creative element to her diplomacy: rather that she could not have the original initiative.

The rupture between England and Spain over Burgundy was certainly unsought by Elizabeth. But, given the growing confrontation between Spain and the Netherlands, what did Elizabeth hope to make of it? Three possibilities have been suggested. One is that Elizabeth wanted the Netherlands free of Spanish rule. This may have been either for religious reasons, or for pragmatic commercial reasons so as to guarantee England's trade in the future without the constant threat of intervention against it from a major power. This would explain the gradual increase in her support for the rebels and the sending of an army from 1585. Second, Elizabeth hoped for an amicable settlement with Spain. According to R.B. Wernham, 'She wanted to retain Spain as a counterpoise to France' and for the Netherlands, 'though restored to their ancient liberties', to remain under Spanish rule 'so that they would not become French'.[11] This would explain the way in which Elizabeth alternated between support and hostility for the rebel cause as a series of adjustments to promote their liberties but discourage the eventual autonomy. Or, third, Elizabeth was simply reacting to a complex sequence of events as they occurred. This is very much the line of C. Wilson, who considered her policy 'a bewildering series of expedients'.[12]

The line which makes most sense is that Elizabeth placed England's trading position in Burgundy first and foremost. This meant that she continued the broadly pragmatic policies of her predecessors. At first it seemed that the most likely outcome was a settlement with Spain and between Spain and the rebels. Hence she weaved between providing and withholding support. She also put pressure on Spain by tactical support for the rebels and by intervention in France. As it became clear that Spain could not resolve the situation, Elizabeth came down more and more clearly on the side of the rebels. None of this involved a conscious attempt to seek expansion into Europe, or to create a Protestant crusade. Basically she wanted, as Wernham suggested, the Netherlands to remain under Spanish rule. But the situation got so out of hand that she had to react increasingly against Spain.

There is a similar lack of clarity over Elizabeth's relations with France. Again, this is largely because she was having to respond to a situation she had not originally created or sought. Part of the reason why Elizabeth could not make up her mind about a firm policy towards the Netherlands was that she was afraid that if Spain lost the area, France might gain it. Initially, therefore her policies were more anti-French than anti-Spanish. There was also a certain amount of opportunism here, especially her desire to regain Calais in 1563 and with it England's foothold in France to ensure the safeguarding of English interests in the Netherlands.

But the Treaty of Troyes changed this to a more reactive stance as the Queen departed from the earlier policy of trying to regain lost English territory in France. Nevertheless, she could not ignore the dangers which were gathering from the Guise faction and she reacted accordingly. In the process, she took advantage of the civil strife within France, although this was as need arose and not as a proactive scheme. She was prepared to assist the Protestants whenever it appeared that the Catholic faction in France was becoming too powerful. Hence in 1570 Elizabeth provided the Huguenots of La Rochelle with a subsidy and in 1573 with supplies. She also sent money to Henry of Navarre in 1585. But these were essentially defensive measures rather than part of a broader scheme for domination in northern Europe.

After 1585 the interest of England became more obviously one of survival against the growing Spanish threat. But even here Elizabeth's objectives were limited. She kept the English presence in the Netherlands deliberately small: in the words of S. Doran, 'she viewed her troops as merely a relief expedition to halt the inexorable progress of Parma'.[13] This meant that the war aims of Elizabeth were essentially limited. They included a settlement of the Netherlands conflict and the restoration of some sort of power balance between France and Spain. It has been argued that Elizabeth expanded the scope of her policy as a result of the defeat of the Armada in 1588. She became more ambitious in two areas: the invasion of northern France and the Portugal expedition, both of 1589. Again, however, these were essentially limited and defensive in purpose. The Portugal expedition was intended primarily to destroy the remnants of the Armada as it sheltered in Spanish ports and to divert Spain by instigating a rebellion in Portugal. Overall, England lacked the infrastructure necessary to launch a systematic offensive against either France or Spain. This is particularly apparent if one considers the downturn in the English economy in the late 1590s. In this situation the overriding motive must have been survival – at best consolidation – rather than the pursuit of dominance.

Questions

1. Did Elizabeth have a 'foreign policy'?
2. Which was the more serious threat to England during the reign of Elizabeth: France or Spain?

ANALYSIS 2: HOW SUCCESSFUL WAS ELIZABETH'S FOREIGN POLICY BETWEEN 1558 AND 1603?

1558–85

We have seen in the Background and Analysis 1 that the main pre-occupations of English foreign policy were France and Spain. By 1585 Elizabeth had had some success in neutralising the French threat via Scotland, although she could not follow this up with the recovery of English lands lost to France. Relations with Spain were another matter. Although Elizabeth succeeded in delaying the conflict with Philip, the situation in Burgundy proved too complex for her to handle successfully. Successive attempts by England to mediate between the rebels and Spain failed, forcing Elizabeth to settle for more assertive measures by 1585.

Elizabeth's relations with France showed a combination of success and failure. Usually this related to the degree to which she sought to involve England. Defensive policies seemed to work more effectively than offensive ones: where the focus was on Scotland, there was more likelihood of success than where attempts were made to restore English territorial losses in France. There are examples of both.

In 1559 Elizabeth intervened in Scotland in a limited way to try to neutralise the French threat there. She wanted to be careful so as not to hand outright victory to the Scottish rebels, of whom she disapproved. Instead, she pursued a policy of phased confrontation to remove French support for Mary Stuart and the French military presence from Scotland. This involved first of all a naval blockade at Leith, followed by limited military action by Lord Grey. The campaign and pressure had their desired effect with the withdrawal of all troops and the signing of the Treaty of Edinburgh (1560). The timing proved excellent, as military intervention occurred at the time when the Guises in France were coming under pressure from the Huguenots. The reward was the neutralising of the French threat to Scotland at least for the time being. When this recurred in the late 1560s Elizabeth showed the same reluctance to become fully involved. She encountered the same success with a minimal degree of intervention. The supporters of Mary Stuart continued to expect help from the Guise faction, while the pro-English Protestants hoped for assistance from Elizabeth. The latter succeeded in doing just enough to safeguard England's position without increasing the threat from France. Hence the three expeditions to Scotland in 1569 eventually subdued the border lords and deprived the rebels of their backing. The French, clearly in a weaker position, decided against intervention. A similar moderation was shown ten years later. Elizabeth had no intention of absorbing Scotland, merely of keeping France at bay while she was dealing with the growing threat of Spain. In this she clearly succeeded.

But any attempt to follow this up with the recapture of English territory was a failure. The pragmatism of Elizabeth's efforts to regain Calais by taking advantage of the disunity of France was transparent even to the Huguenots whom she claimed to support. Hence the failure of English military intervention was due partly to the decision of the Huguenot leader, Condé, to do a deal with Catherine de Medici and temporarily to close ranks against the English invasion of Le Havre. The result was the humiliating Treaty of Troyes (1564). Neutralising French influence in Scotland could therefore not be used as a springboard for regaining English possessions in France.

Elizabeth also encountered mixed fortunes in dealing with the threat of French involvement in the Netherlands. The main problem was the possible intervention by Huguenots on the side of the rebels. Should the Huguenots also win the civil war in France the result would be permanent French control over the Netherlands and the realisation of England's worst long-term fears. Again Elizabeth refused to be pushed into precipitate action, despite strong recommendations, even pressure, from Burghley that England should intervene on the side of Spain against France in 1572. As it turned out the Queen was right to refuse, since a French force was defeated by the Spanish army.

A second French threat was also dealt with – again by Elizabeth's reluctance to be drawn into military conflict and her preference for other measures. When the Duke of Anjou undertook to send French troops to help the rebels, Elizabeth sought with him a marriage arrangement which would give England and France a close identity of interest, moderate French action and put pressure on Spain to come to an early agreement. Again, the French threat was neutralised – but not in the way Elizabeth had intended. Strong opposition within England forced her to abandon the marriage, for which she had shown some personal as well as diplomatic inclination. As the Spanish army increased its pressure on the rebels from 1579 Elizabeth finally came to the conclusion that the best method of dealing with Spain was by coming to an agreement with France. She therefore sent Walsingham to negotiate an Anglo-French League in 1581. But the King of France, Henry III, refused to be drawn into this without the marriage. Elizabeth therefore subsidised Anjou without the treaty. Anjou's intervention was, however, a disaster and he was forced to give up and return to France.

By the early 1580s, therefore, Elizabeth had seen the French threat contained – if not entirely by her own efforts. But she had not succeeded in forestalling the Spanish one. Although by this stage she had come to the conclusion that Spain was a more serious menace than France, she had not succeeded in counterbalancing the former with the latter. Her measures had been reactive and cautious. More often than not this caution had proved right in specific circumstances. But what it had not done was to anticipate the general trend of Spain's hostility and to build up a powerful counter-alliance to it.

This was because Elizabeth had always hoped for reconciliation with Spain as the best means of guaranteeing the integrity of England's trade. There were instances when this seemed to work. In 1573, for example, the Convention of Nymegen restored trading relations. It is possible that Philip II was concerned about the prospects of a marriage between Elizabeth and the French throne, and he was certainly worried about the Treaty of Blois with France. It could also be that he was feeling the pressure of English privateering activities. In other words, Elizabeth's policies of selective aggression were working at this stage. But the more the crisis in the Netherlands escalated, the more Elizabeth found herself entrapped and the harder it became to achieve what she really wanted. Her efforts at mediation between the two sides seemed to succeed with the Pacification of Ghent in 1576, which saw the Spanish withdrawal from the Netherlands. This, however, was only temporary and in any case had less to do with any negotiation by Elizabeth than with the mutiny of the Spanish army at Antwerp. Elizabeth was powerless to prevent the return of the Spaniards in 1577 or their victory over the rebels in the Battle of Gembloux in 1578.

At this stage Elizabeth's policy seemed thoroughly indecisive. Some of her advisers, including Walsingham, recommended intervention.

The latter wrote to Sussex in 1578: 'Truly, my Lord, if Her Majesty do not presently resolve to take an other course than I perceive (to my great grief) she is inclined to, I see apparently that this country will become French.'[14] But she was opposed to taking this course. Instead, she subsidised the use of German mercenaries from the Calvinist Palatinate.

By 1578 Elizabeth's policy had clearly been unsuccessful. She had not managed to bring about a conciliation between the rebels and Spain which would have been in England's best interests. Spain had been offended by her specific actions in seizing treasure ships, sponsoring privateers and aiding the Dutch Sea Beggars. The Dutch, on the other hand, were unconvinced that England was serious in wishing to uphold their interests in any way. If anything, the situation had deteriorated still further. There was an imminent prospect of Spanish victory. And Spain's power in relation to England actually increased, with Philip's acquisition of Portugal in 1580, together with a second colonial empire, access to enormously rich trade markets in the East Indies, and a considerable number of ships. By 1585, therefore, the balance had tilted firmly against England and it had clearly become necessary to consider further involvement in order to protect England's interests.

1585–1603

The result was the Treaty of Nonsuch (1585) and the despatch of five thousand troops and one thousand cavalry to the Netherlands. This was followed by Philip II's preparations for full-scale war and the launch of the Armada in 1588. How should we see England's performance in the greatest struggle seen in the Tudor period? Two distinct pictures emerge, relating to war on land and war at sea.

On land, Elizabeth's problem was that England was fighting not so much for military victory as for a political objective – to force Spain to come to terms with England. This meant less than total commitment and was bound to show up in a struggle with an opponent who attached the highest importance to victory in the Netherlands. Indeed, England's whole involvement was badly mishandled. There was almost immediate acrimony between Elizabeth and Leicester as the latter accepted the title of governor general in 1586. He also became involved in political dealing which served only to alienate various factions of the Dutch war effort. It is, of course, arguable that the involvement of England in the Netherlands at least prevented the rebels from agreeing to a negotiated settlement with Spain. This could well be true.

But there is no direct evidence that this would have been against England's true interests. After all, was this not what Elizabeth had consistently intended? And was she not, in any case, anxious to avoid the descent into open warfare between England and Spain? If anything, her despatch of troops to the Netherlands ran counter to everything she had so far tried to do. It perpetuated the war – without achieving any English military success. It also persuaded Philip II that he would have to take more direct measures to deal with the threat now posed by Elizabeth. He therefore prepared for the 'Enterprise of England', which included plans for the first full-scale invasion of England of the entire Tudor period. It is clear that Elizabeth recognised the new danger. She tried to pull back from the brink in 1587 by conducting negotiations for peace with Parma. This was, however, totally unsuccessful. Philip was now set upon the sort of projective policy which Elizabeth had always avoided, and would not now be deflected from his purpose. All Elizabeth succeeded in doing was to antagonise the Dutch Estates and to ensure that they did not contribute to the defence of England in its time of peril in 1588.

In contrast to the situation on land, England's seapower had made substantial gains. It had, for example, shown a capacity for self-defence against a larger power. According to Harding, 'this was the first occasion on which naval activity had a major impact on both the defensive and offensive strategies of England.'[15] There were several sides to this achievement. One was the mobilisation of sufficient warships at relatively short notice. This was accomplished by supplementing a limited number of warships with the merchant marine, something the crown had been promoting for many years. This was crucial in the defeat of the Armada. For example, Drake's preliminary attack on Cadiz in 1587, which delayed the sailing of the Armada, was accomplished by six warships and seventeen merchant vessels. As for the main campaign, the combination of warships and merchant ships meant that the English were far from outnumbered or overpowered in terms of weight.

Another positive achievement was the reforms of Hawkins, treasurer to the navy, which ensured that those warships which England did possess were fully operational and equipped: English vessels actually possessed 153 guns of long range to the Armada's 21. Tactical changes also occurred. Drake managed to persuade the Queen of the importance of an offensive strike to weaken the impact of the Armada. This was put into effect as the Armada sailed up the Channel. Howard and Drake used an early line-ahead formation and peppered the tightly packed Spanish crescents. The use of fireships in Calais caused these crescents to break up and expose themselves more openly to the superior artillery of the English.

The combination of these factors meant that England was self-consciously emerging as a naval power with incipient use of all the methods which were later to be essential components in the British naval arsenal, especially line-ahead tactics, rapid manoeuvrability and heavy artillery bombardment.

Also vitally important for the growth of English seapower was the contribution of privateering. It has been estimated that, altogether, Spain and Portugal lost something like a thousand ships to English privateers during the 1590s, which inflicted a major blow on the Spanish economy. This proved to be of greater significance than English contributions to the land war against Spain. A partnership was quickly established between the crown and groups of merchants, so that eventually the Tudor state built up an effective administrative system to combine official naval policy with mercantile private enterprise. Privateering had a further bonus. The profits acquired from this unorthodox activity were eventually to finance the development of the East India Company, founded in 1600, as well as those set up during the reign of James I – the Virginia Company in 1606 and the Newfoundland Company in 1610.

There were, however, negative features in the growth of English seapower. For one thing, the defeat of the Armada, usually seen as the greatest victory in English naval history, may have been given exaggerated significance. There are also certain myths – possibly inspired by nationalism – that need to be dispelled. The Armada was not defeated by a smaller force. Nor, arguably, was it defeated by the English at all. The English ships were able to inflict damage at close quarters but not to destroy the Spanish formation. It was really factors working against the Armada which decided the outcome. These included the lack of any provision for the collection of the Duke of Parma's invasion force from Flanders, since the coastline lacked a deep-water port to serve as an anchorage, and the onset of bad weather which did far more damage than the English ships ever could. The precise turning point was the use of fireships: this was crucial in breaking up the tight formations. But it was the Spanish decision to anchor in Calais which made this possible and the subsequent storms which completed the job.

It could also be argued that England lost the opportunity in 1589 to inflict a major blow against Spain. Portugal, annexed in 1580, was ripe for revolt against Spanish rule, the remnants of the Spanish Armada were scattered along the coast of northern Spain, and the Spanish treasure fleets were inadequately guarded. The purpose of the Portugal expedition of 1589, therefore, was to incite a rebellion, destroy the remaining ships and seize the *flotta* at the Azores – in that order. The enterprise, however, proved a disaster since the Portuguese revolt did not materialise, the ships were ignored and an attack was made on the Azores which proved abortive. Spanish historians consider this as great a failure as the Armada of 1588 – with some justification.

Nor will it do to overestimate England's strength in relation to Spain. The very nature of England's war with Spain showed the limitations of its military base. The struggle could only realistically be defensive or, if offensive, piecemeal. This meant that privateering was the only form of offensive action which was ever likely to have much effect. Nor did this activity prevent Spain from launching further Armadas in the 1590s. The fleet of 1596 was almost as large as that of 1588, showing that Spain's capacity to threaten England was no more than dented. Spain also succeeded in reorganising its defences in the Caribbean which meant that the impact of privateering was considerably reduced during the 1590s. In any case, the ultimate damage to the Spanish economy was done not by the gradual disintegration of the treasure supply through English privateering but, more insidiously, by overdependence upon it. Spain declined because of its addiction to the treasure of the New World, not because of England's disruption of its supply.

Finally, it would be false to assume an uninterrupted connection between developments during Elizabeth's reign and those of the future. It took another thirty years for English seapower to become a permanent base for English foreign policy. Under James I the navy stagnated, largely because of the more peaceful climate in Europe following the peace with Spain in 1604. For the next twenty years the connection between the crown and private enterprise was so weakened by the absence of opportunities for privateering that Charles I found considerable difficulty in reviving it when he attempted a more assertive policy against France and Spain in the late 1620s. The reign of James I also saw a deterioration in the maintenance of naval vessels and administration. The Elizabethan changes were important for the future – but not for the immediate future.

The balance sheet

What was the balance sheet for the reign?

On the positive side, Elizabeth had fended off successfully threats from two major powers, France under the Guises and Spain under the

Habsburgs. In the process, she had managed to avoid bankruptcy. England preserved at least some commercial contact with the Low Countries; although Philip II succeeded in retaining the Southern Netherlands, the northern section remained independent, owing at least in part to English assistance. Meanwhile, Europe had returned to the sort of equilibrium which was in England's best interest. France was revived as a counterfoil to Spain and the religious tension which had seemed likely to disrupt the Elizabethan religious settlement was partially resolved by the Edict of Nantes which provided toleration for the Huguenots. Spain would continue to keep France preoccupied from the south while, at the same time, being forced to recognise that it had itself been effectively contained in the north.

On the negative side, England was still no nearer to entering the great power stakes within Europe than she had been during the reign of Henry VII or Henry VIII. By the end of Elizabeth's reign England was still eclipsed by France, now healed and resurgent under Henry IV, and Spain, not yet in decline. And the cost had been considerable. Bankruptcy may have been avoided at the financial level, but the underlying economic trend was unfavourable, a depression emerging as a result of the interruption of trade with Spain and Burgundy. Even the independence of the Dutch Republic was a mixed blessing as, during the seventeenth century, its commercial and naval threat came to overshadow those of Spain and France. It is also strongly arguable that the successes of the reign were a result less of conscious policy than of favourable objective factors such as the inappropriate strategies pursued by the Armada or the diversion provided by the civil war in France.

And yet England had been more directly involved than before in a struggle for survival – and had succeeded. This more than anything else explains the patriotic element of Elizabethan history. The major achievement of the reign was to recover from mistakes in foreign policy to survive – making effective use of a limited infrastructure. Limited this may have been, but it was still an achievement.

Questions

1. Which was England's greater enemy during the reign of Elizabeth: France or Spain?
2. Would it be accurate to describe 1585 as a 'turning point' in Elizabethan foreign policy?

SOURCES: HISTORIAN'S VIEWS ON ELIZABETHAN FOREIGN POLICY

Source 1: From J.B. Black, *The Reign of Elizabeth, 1558–1603*, first published in 1936.

The chief object of her diplomacy . . . was to establish her throne and kingdom in a position of unassailable security and power. To attain this end she was prepared to use every instrument that gave promise of being serviceable, every ally that chance or necessity threw in her way, while at the same time avoiding commitments that might jeopardize her own freedom of action, or lessen the advantage she possessed as the ruler of an insular state. Both a realist and an opportunist, she made interest the determining factor in all her political manoeuvres and combinations, and reason of state a sufficient justification for every act. . . .

Continental protestants, oppressed by tyrannical governments or struggling for their lives against the superior might of catholic armies, beckoned her in vain to a crusade on behalf of the reformed faith. The fervent appeals of her own ministers, who believed that the protestant cause was also England's cause, struck no responsive chord in her cold and calculating brain. Her one thought was how she could use their respective idealisms for the furtherance of her own secular aims.

Source 2: From A.L. Rowse, *The Expansion of Elizabethan England*, published in 1955.

The revolt of the Netherlands became the prime problem of European diplomacy, an issue immensely complicated and confused . . . Philip would never grant freedom of conscience, which the rebels made a condition of peace – so the war had to go on. Elizabeth's government genuinely wanted peace between the combatants. English interests demanded that neither Spain nor France should subjugate the Netherlands: their independence was a prime objective of our policy. Elizabeth's calculation of our interests was exact, and her defence of them brilliant; but it went against the grain with her to have to support rebels against constituted authority, and she never liked the Dutch. . . . On the other hand, the sympathies of the Prince of Orange were pro-French – necessarily so: he was a *grand seigneur* in culture and outlook, his principality of Orange was at their mercy, and he did not believe that the Queen would ever bring herself to intervene. The rest of Europe did not think she would dare; but on the Prince's assassination – at Philip's orders – she had to, or see the Netherlands go under.

The year 1575, then, was taken up with complex negotiations. Requesens wanted to renew the alliance with England and to get the Queen to permit English exiles (rebels to her) to serve for him at sea . . . An embassy was sent to her, but she was not falling for that. At this, Orange sent an embassy asking her to undertake the protection of the Netherlands and their sovereignty. This hazardous offer of greatness was rejected.

Source 3: From an article by D.J.B. Trim, 'Seeking a Protestant Alliance and Liberty of Conscience on the Continent, 1558–85', published in 2005.

In sum, then, my argument is that from 1558 to 1585 there was a consensus within the Elizabethan regime that England was threatened by the Catholic powers of Europe (especially France and Spain) as part of a cosmic struggle; commercial and strategic factors informed government policy but confessional considerations took priority. There were differences between ministers, for sure, but they were over exactly what should be done in a given situation to make the policy work, not over the policy itself. The government sought to meet the Catholic threat by enlisting the support of, and giving assistance to, the other Protestant powers of Europe: and it especially hoped to establish Protestantism in the Netherlands and France, both to help co-religionists there obtain the right to worship God in a manner pleasing to Him, but also as a way of weakening the Catholic powers. These were viewed as a threat to Elizabeth personally and England as a commonwealth because of their faith, which in and of itself turned traditional friends into contemporary enemies. Yet the history of English relations with foreign states from 1558 to 1585 ... shows that the government was prepared to prioritise the defence of those who shared Reformed beliefs, *because* they shared those beliefs, over narrow national political advantage. This was not a policy of exclusivist English self-interest.

There is sufficient motivation, magnitude, continuity and government-direction about the assistance given to the Huguenots and Dutch (i.e. to the Protestants actually threatened by Catholic powers in this period), and sufficient intentionality about English foreign policy initiatives between 1558 and 1585, to characterise English foreign policy in that period as, effectively, a Protestant foreign policy. That is what many of Elizabeth's ministers and prominent members of the English body politic wanted it to be; it is what most foreign Catholic observers thought it was. It is time to take their opinions seriously.

Source 4: From D. Loades, *Elizabeth I*, published in 2003.

Elizabeth's strategy was always defensive; protective of her own position and of her country's autonomy. Her intervention in France in 1562 was not in the interests of promoting international Calvinism, or even to increase England's weight in the game of European power politics, but simply to recover a piece of land around Calais which everyone in England regarded as an integral part of the kingdom. Her intervention in Scotland was not intended to secure the ascendancy of

Protestantism, and certainly not to reassert English overlordship, but simply to prevent the French from using the northern kingdom as a base from which to attack her. Unlike her sister, she had no fixed preconceptions of where virtue and safety lay. This made her extremely pragmatic, and the council that she assembled shared that pragmatism. Before 1570 there was no question of England, with its fragile Protestant church and limited military resources, leading any kind of crusade against the Counter Reformation.

Questions

1. Comment on the use of 'our' in Source 2 (lines 4 and 5).
2. Examine the main differences between the arguments in Sources 1 and 3.
3. Sources 3 and 4 are more recent than Sources 1 and 2. Do they indicate that the debate on Elizabeth's foreign policy has opened up 'new territory'?

Worked answer: Comment on the use of 'our' in Source 2 (lines 4 and 5).

[Advice: This is an open question, designed to make you think. Since the sources are all secondary, the emphasis is likely to be historiographical. 'Comment on' means explaining the use of as well as giving an opinion on. 'Our' invites comments on the historian's use of a 'subjective' term – but you could go further by mentioning the priorities of the period in which the author wrote this particular book.]

The word 'our' involves personal or group ownership and is normally used more in a political than a historical setting; after all, politics is more about obtaining support for a particular identity. History does, however, make occasional use of 'our' in a national sense, although some historians prefer to avoid it in order to avoid appearing one-sided in their interpretation. A.L. Rowse departed from the norm because he was writing in a period of revived national consciousness, when he was celebrating the beginning of a new 'Elizabethan era' after the coronation of Elizabeth II in 1953 (which probably took place at the time he was actually writing *The Expansion of Elizabethan England*). The context in which the term is used shows that it was no Freudian slip. Rowse, and some of his contemporaries like Neale, made comparisons between the struggle of Protestant England with Catholic Spain, and the similarly ideological struggle of the Cold War between the West, including 'our' Britain, and the Soviet bloc. There is, however, a potential danger in this. Parallels between different periods rarely work successfully, and soon date once the second era is over. In any case, in making such parallels – and in reinforcing them with terms like 'our' – historians run the danger of 'colonising' the past as well as explaining it.

7

THE DEVELOPMENT OF
THE ECONOMY

BACKGROUND

This chapter adopts a more general focus by looking at economic issues across the broader Tudor period, although with the main emphasis on Elizabethan England. The themes to be addressed and explained are the growth of population, the pressures of inflation, and changes in agriculture, industry and trade.

ANALYSIS 1: EXPLAIN THE CHANGES IN POPULATION TRENDS IN TUDOR ENGLAND.

In the absence of contemporary census statistics it is impossible to provide any more than general estimates for the population of England in the sixteenth century. The overall picture, however, appears to be as follows.

The eleventh, twelfth and thirteenth centuries had seen a steady increase in the population of England and Wales to a total of about 6 million by 1300. The rate of increase has been estimated at something like 300 per cent during this period. Yet, by the middle of the fifteenth century the population stood at only 2.1 million and could have been as low as 1.5 million. By 1525 this had risen slowly to 2.3 million, accelerating more rapidly to 2.8 million by 1545 and 3 million by 1550. Thereafter it dropped below 3 million in the late 1550s, before gradually increasing every decade until the end of the century, by which time it had reached about 4.1 million. This was half as much again as that of Henry VII's England, but still only two-thirds of that of 1300. The overall increase therefore constituted a long-term recovery, but was held back from being the sort of population surge which occurred in the eighteenth and nineteenth centuries.

What were the main reasons for these changes? Strictly speaking, there can be only three determinants of population levels – the death rate, the birth rate and population movement. A likely overall explanation is that external factors affected the death rate, over which the population had very little control. As long as these operated, the birth rate was unlikely to offset them. On the other hand, a period of relief from a heavy mortality gave the longer-term and less obvious changes in fertility a chance to have an impact. Any movement of population was unlikely to have much impact on the overall figure, although it did lead to shifts of population distribution.

The death rate was heavily influenced by external factors which were unpredictable, even catastrophic. What were these? One can be largely discounted as having had much of an impact. This was war. At no time during the sixteenth century was England involved in a major war – with the single exception of the struggle with Spain. This, in any case, involved only a small-scale continental commitment and the casualties at sea were minimal. None of the expeditions during the reigns of Henry VII and Henry VIII had involved large-scale losses. England had certainly no equivalent to the losses incurred by the continental powers in the Italian wars or the Habsburg–Valois struggle.

A more significant disruptive and unpredictable factor was disease. There had been very few recorded epidemics during the three centuries of rapid population growth before 1300. Then occurred the Black Death, which, from its main impact in 1348–50 and residual impact down to the last quarter of the fourteenth century, reduced the population by well over half. The damage was also done by accompanying epidemics, often ignored, such as typhus, cholera and dysentery. During the fifteenth and sixteenth centuries there was a decline in the overall vulnerability of the population to epidemics, but there were, at the same time, sufficient patterns of recurrence to prevent anything more than a gradual drop in the mortality rate. The greatest single positive factor was the absence of the previous pandemic proportions of bubonic plague, certainly to the extent which had afflicted the population in the fourteenth century. On the other hand, there was sufficient recurrence of epidemics in urban areas like Norwich, Bristol and, above all, London, to prevent population growth from being anything but gradual. Since the spread of plague was greatly assisted by urban squalor, London was affected frequently during Elizabeth's reign – in 1563, 1578–79, 1582, 1592–93 and 1603; nearly one-quarter of its population died in 1563 and again in 1603. Further constraints on any population 'take-off' were the mysterious 'sweating sickness', especially between 1485 and 1528, and the influenza pandemic which swept through Europe and England between 1557 and 1558. At this time England suffered an overall population loss, but this was subsequently made up. The key reason was a regular rebalancing. Palliser argued that, although the 'larger towns generally suffered a surplus of deaths over births', the 'rural surplus' was sufficient 'to increase the numbers who remained on the land' and 'to more than make up the losses in the towns by migration'.[1]

Another factor which affected the death rate was the harvests. Under the Tudors there were frequently runs of good harvests as, for example, between 1537 and 1542 and 1546 to 1548. These coincided with the fastest rate of population growth – during the last decade of Henry VIII's reign. Other good periods were 1566–71, 1582–84, 1591–93 and 1601–06. On the other hand, there was always a braking mechanism – the likelihood of failure of harvests and the sudden incidence of famine, as, for example, occurred in 1549–51 and 1554–56. This might combine with disease or, alternatively, might be unrelated to it. For example, during Mary's reign, and the opening years of Elizabeth's, the two combined, as they did also between 1594 and 1598. In each case it has been estimated that the mortality rate was trebled. Why were there such violent fluctuations in the harvests? A crucial factor was the increasingly harsh climate to which England was subjected between the thirteenth and eighteenth centuries. This involved a series of wet summers and cold winters alternating with more favourable conditions. These would have had the effect of tipping already marginal subsistence levels into occasional – but recurrent – disaster.

A vital factor in upward population trends is an increase in the birth rate, or the growth of fertility at a faster rate than mortality. This was the case for much, although not all, of the Tudor period. Between 1575 and 1584, for example, a survey of four hundred parishes has shown that there were on average three births for every two deaths. Again, however, there was no reason for any sudden increase in fertility. It was once argued that a fall in the average age of marriage for women to sixteen extended their childbearing span. This has been refuted by Palliser and others who maintained that, between 1550 and 1599, the average age of marriage was twenty-five, rising to twenty-six after 1600. It has also been argued that there was an increase in the number of births outside marriage during the Tudor period. Figures, however, show that these were minimal (a survey of the records of ninety-eight parishes showed that illegitimate births constituted 2.8 per cent of all live births in the 1580s and 3.1 per cent in 1590s). Hence the overall increase in population (or the birth rate compared with the death rate) was the relatively modest one of 0.5 per cent per annum, compared with 1.3 per cent per annum in the early nineteenth century.

The third possible determinant of population levels was population movement. Most important was the impact of movements on local variations in population growth. There was unquestionably greater mobility during the sixteenth century. Some of this was positive, in the sense that it contributed to the growth of towns and industries. Some of it was negative, exacerbating the problem of vagrancy. Tudor England, therefore, saw a tendency for population pockets to develop as part of the more general process of population increase. The towns attracted migrants on an unprecedented scale: by 1600 some 10 per cent of the population lived in towns, compared with 5 per cent at the beginning of the century, London particularly benefiting. The density of population in the countryside varied considerably, with the south-east being more heavily populated than the north and west. Immigration from outside Britain occurred in two main waves as religious refugees fled from the continent between 1553 and 1585. About 50,000 passed through London before dispersing elsewhere, although the capital continued to have 10,000 immigrants at any one time – up to 10 per cent of its total population. Yet the overall impact of immigration was relatively small in terms of total numbers. Nor would emigration have amounted to any significant loss. This did not really occur until the nineteenth century, when the developing overseas empire and the United States both exerted a pull. During the Tudor period the empire was only in its infancy and any overseas settlement had to be promoted to make the small number of new colonies viable.

All these factors would often interact, making it difficult to single any out as a primary cause for the rate of population growth. For example, a bad harvest might contribute to the death rate directly through starvation, or reduce the birth rate through forcing the postponement of a significant number of marriages until bad times had passed. Similarly a poorly fed population would be that much more vulnerable to the effects of disease, whether epidemic or endemic. At any time there would be incentives – whether positive or negative – to move to other areas, thereby causing regional variations and adjustments.

How significant were these changes for the economy? There is bound to be some difference in overall emphasis. Demographic historians tend to focus primarily on the impact of the change in numbers on the economic and social fabric. Marxist historians, by contrast, see developments occurring more in terms of the replacement of feudal relations by capitalist structures based upon wages and class exploitation. An alternative to both of these approaches is to see the population increase as a catalyst speeding up other processes which may or may not have been directly related to it. This is apparent in Analyses 2 and 3.

Questions

1. Why did Elizabeth have more subjects than Henry VII?
2. Why did she not have still more subjects?

ANALYSIS 2: EXAMINE THE CAUSES AND EFFECTS OF INFLATION BETWEEN 1500 AND 1600.

One of the most striking economic trends of the period between 1500 and 1600 was inflation. Source 2.2 below illustrates the main trends in agricultural and industrial prices. The former saw a steady rise until the mid-sixteenth century, followed by a slowing down in the 1560s and 1570s, then a rapid increase towards the end of the reign. The reasons given for this development can be categorised into 'monetary' and 'non-monetary' or 'real'.

Monetary influences can, in turn, be subdivided into the debasement of the coinage and the growth of the bullion supply. There was no doubt in the minds of many contemporaries as to the main culprit. According to a treatise by John Hales (published in 1581), 'immediately after the baseness of our coin in the time of King Henry the eight, the prices of all things generally among all sorts of people rose'.[2] Another example of this is the argument of Sir Thomas Gresham, founder of the Royal Exchange, that Henry VIII had caused the inflation by 'abasing his coin' (see Source 2.1 below).[3] Several specific instances can certainly be pointed to in the deliberate policy of debasing the coinage, to which Tudor monarchs resorted from time to time. Examples included Henry VIII's reduction of the bullion content in 1526, mainly to finance Wolsey's increasingly complex foreign policy. This resulted in the issue of smaller silver coins and gold coins which carried a greater face value. Other debasements followed in 1544 and 1551. In the latter some of the coins, such as the groat, were deprived of up to two-thirds of their previous silver content. These debasements adversely affected the purchasing power of the coinage and thereby acted as a catalyst for further increases in prices.

John Hales added: 'Another reason I conceive in this matter to be the great store and plenty of treasure which is walking in these parts of the world, far more in these our days than ever our forefathers have seen in times past.'[4] Similar arguments were being advanced on the continent where, for example, Bodin drew in 1568 a direct link between rising prices and the growth of the supply of bullion. In the nineteenth century – and the first half of the twentieth – historians continued to regard monetary influences as the most important. Some, however, focused on the debasement of the coinage, others like E.J. Hamilton (1928) and J.U. Nef (1941) preferring to attribute inflation to the impact of bullion from the New World, via the Spanish market, on Europe's economy. This is explained by the growing Spanish dependence on treasure shipments and the tendency to pay increasingly in cash for imports from England.

How convincing is all this? Certainly the combination of increased treasure and periodic debasements for a swift profit would have been inherently inflationary, as would the injection of precious metals from the dissolution of the monasteries. On the other hand, this would have produced periodic fluctuations. The worst debasements occurred in the first half of the century, whereas the amount of treasure being imported into England did not increase significantly until the second half. The impact of monetary change would certainly have been disruptive, but it is difficult to see how it could have sustained the upward pressure of inflation by itself. Other factors were of equal, perhaps greater, importance. These have been given greater emphasis by more recent historians since 1950, such as D.C. Coleman[5] and R.B. Outhwaite[6]: they consider that the monetary factors need to be seen within a broader perspective.

'Non-monetary' or 'real' factors include four additional explanations. First, a series of bad harvests (1549–51, 1554–56, 1594 and 1598) drove up food prices and these were often slow to return to former levels. Second, a period of more intensive warfare (especially after 1581) could disrupt the normal flow of the economy by driving up the cost of imports, and by increasing taxation levels. Those affected would try to pass on the impact by raising rents and reducing wages. A third factor was the increased investment in farming. The capital expenditure involved in enclosures would result in price increases for grain and meat, the two essential ingredients in the cost of living figures. Finally, the rate at which the population grew was a key factor. According to Outhwaite, 'population change was obviously not the sole determinant of the price level in Tudor and Stuart England but it looks to be by far the most important influence upon it'.[7] Coleman considered that, while it need not exclude other factors, the population-based theory had 'the advantage of providing rather better answers to questions posed by characteristic features of this Tudor and Stuart inflation'.[8] For example, even a modest increase in mouths to feed would exert pressure on agricultural production and would explain the faster rate of inflation in the agricultural sector than in the industrial. Increased production was more problematic in agriculture than in industry, which meant that food supply was 'inelastic', whereas the supply of manufactures was 'elastic'.[9]

Overall, we need to consider the *combination* of influences, as affecting different periods. Hence debasement would bring short-term and very sharp increases in general inflation. Bad harvests would result in higher food prices, which would soar well above the general rate. Trade might well be affected by shifts in foreign policy and there was, in the second half of the century, an undercurrent of inflation from the import of treasure which compounded the amount on the market after the dissolution of the monasteries. And underlying all these trends was the persistent pressure of the population growth which made a more continuous upward curve out of a series of oscillations.

Whatever its causes, the growth of inflation did not affect the population evenly. Amongst the least influenced were the small-scale subsistence farmers who provided for their own requirements and were not affected by monetary changes. By and large the more affluent members of society benefited from the inflationary trends, whereas the lower orders were more likely to suffer. This is the reverse of the situation which had occurred after the Black Death. Those who benefited most included the landed aristocracy, who were able to pass on price increases by raising rents. They also had the investment potential to make improvements in farming methods to consolidate their financial position within the context of the price rise. In this sense they were able to harness and ride the inflationary trend. The lesser gentry and yeomanry benefited in accordance with the terms of their rents. The most fortunate were freeholders and copyholders, who had protected terms. Others, such as leaseholders, were more likely to experience an increase in rents. Manufacturers benefited in so far as the differential could be maintained between higher prices and constant wages, provided that this gap was greater than that between raw materials and finished products. There was, therefore, bound to be increased diversity of success between one individual enterprise and another. Merchants too had diverse experiences, although in their case it is sometimes difficult to distinguish here between the effects of price rises and the impact of foreign policy; this is especially true of the reign of Elizabeth, which saw the disruption of normal markets as a result of the growing conflict with Spain. Again, however, the opportunities were considerable, as the growing connection between commerce and privateering shows.

Those who suffered included wage-earners or rent-payers not protected by agreement. This applied to the majority of the population. The landed labourers, in particular, were affected by the long-term growth of inflation and also by the short-term peaks brought about by poor harvests. Small craftsmen, unable to pass on the inflationary trend to others, also suffered. Small-scale farmers and squatters who managed to remain self-sufficient were more likely to survive intact. But they were greatly outnumbered by those who found marginal subsistence farming impossible and who drifted as vagrants into the towns. There was, therefore, a significant increase in poverty and a widening of the differential between rich and poor. The impact of this is examined separately in Chapter 8.

Questions

1. Why was currency of the same face value worth so much less in 1600 than it had been in 1500?
2. How much did this matter to the people of England?

ANALYSIS 3: EXAMINE THE CHANGES IN THE MAIN SECTORS OF THE ECONOMY.

Agriculture and the land

The growth of population and the rise of inflation both interacted with major changes during the Tudor period in the ownership, management and use of land. Of these, the two most important were the commercialisation of agriculture and the development of enclosures.

The previous pattern of self-sufficiency among the majority of farmers, based on smallholdings, gradually gave way to commercial agriculture, especially the market orientation of agricultural produce. This should not be seen as an entirely new development unique to the Tudor period, as there is evidence that it had already started after the mid-fourteenth century. But it undoubtedly speeded up under the Tudors. The main impetus was the demand of an ever-expanding market, brought about by the growth of population, and the prospect for higher prices, the result of inexorable inflation. This could not be satisfied by the existing pattern of relatively inefficient subsistence farming based on small plots producing a wide variety of different crops for domestic use. The growth in population put pressure on the availability of land and reduced the chance of allowing for the natural recovery of its fertility. Many small-scale holdings therefore became increasingly marginal in their productivity, a situation which could be exacerbated by a run of bad summers. It became increasingly common during the sixteenth century for gentry and yeomen farmers to consolidate smallholdings by accumulating the freehold, leasehold or copyhold on areas adjacent to their own. This tendency occurred more in the south than in the midlands or north, where more traditional patterns of ownership persisted.

The movement towards enclosures was increasingly considered a precondition for effective agricultural change, since it enabled a more rational approach to crop farming and reduced the chance of interference from outside. Another incentive to enclose land was to increase its value, making it possible to command higher rents from tenants.

How extensive were the changes in agriculture? Some historians have claimed that there was an agricultural revolution – which preceded that of the eighteenth century. E. Kerridge,[10] for example, maintained that the key components of this revolution were the transformation of production techniques and the more efficient use of a labour force. In addition, the 'up and down' method of crop rotation was a major advance on the previous open field rotation. The former method alternated for longer periods between pasturage and crop farming, providing a better chance of nutrient recovery than the three-field alternation with fallow. Other methods included the improvement of animal feed through clover and the fencing of cattle and sheep. These changes alone amount to a transformation well before the great changes of the eighteenth century. According to Kerridge, 'the agricultural revolution took place in England in the sixteenth and seventeenth centuries and not in the eighteenth and nineteenth'.[11]

On the other hand, these changes were not particularly widespread. They were confined largely to the south-east, and even there they were most likely to occur near towns where the main outlet would be found for the food. There is also the point that many enclosures were used not so much for arable farming as for animal husbandry, especially for sheep. Hence the increase in the production of wheat was less than it might have been, a problem exacerbated by the bad harvests. For these reasons, alternative views have been put by G.E. Mingay,[12]

A.G.R. Smith[13] and J. Thirsk.[14] Mingay argued that the development of modern farming 'can be seen as stretching back into the sixteenth and seventeenth centuries', but 'gathering pace in the later eighteenth and nineteenth centuries'.[15] Thirsk preferred to see the changes as part of a 'continuum', in which there were 'periods of more and less rapid change' – with pressures for change 'stronger at some periods than at others'.[16] Overall, it may be going too far to refer to agricultural changes as a 'revolution'. They were, nevertheless, substantial. The land under cultivation was increased in area, marginal land was brought under the plough, marshlands and fens were drained. New agricultural methods were used, and enclosures were implemented. In the words of Smith, 'We do not need, therefore, to accept the concept of an agricultural revolution in early modern England to agree that during the sixteenth and early seventeenth centuries English agriculture responded in notable ways to the challenges imposed on it by a rising population.'[17]

The impact of the changes on the population varied. On the one hand, when they were carried out to improve arable farming, enclosures assisted the increase in the supply of food which was essential for the sustenance of a growing population. In some areas there was also the prospect of more work as a result of increased productivity. This would have provided a more certain existence to many who had previously been on the breadline. Enclosures could, on the other hand, bring hardship, especially to those sectors of the population who had been geared up to subsistence and survival. Many people had depended on their right to use the commons for keeping an animal or for gathering firewood. The enclosure of common land was therefore an important contribution to vagrancy and was recognised as such by the government of the day.

To what extent did the increase in profits from agriculture affect the economy as a whole? Marxist historians see the commercialisation of agriculture as one of the key stages in the development of capitalism in England. The feudal structure, already undermined by the Black Death and the subsequent crisis of the fourteenth century, was followed by the emergence of an entrepreneurial class, comprising mainly the yeomanry and gentry, which consolidated their land at the expense of the smaller-scale peasantry. The latter moved from a position of self-sufficient subsistence farming to being exploited as wage labour. This provided the basis for the subsequent industrialisation of Britain from the eighteenth century onwards. Tudor England, therefore, saw a decisive shift in the overall economic structure.

But Marxist history is inherently structuralist and, as such, seeks relationships between developments within the overall perspective of a long-term continuum. This is usually oversimplified and deterministic in its approach. It is probably quite true that commercial farming moved the development of capitalism along more quickly; that a larger proportion of the population was involved in a wage structure; and that the control of agricultural production was concentrated in fewer hands as a result of the consolidation of estates. But the corollary to the wage structure in the development of the capitalist economy is the extent to which capitalism was underpinned by entrepreneurial investment. It is by no means certain that the profits generated were at this stage ploughed into industry. Many were soaked up by the increasing inflation or ploughed into maintaining social status. In this respect the eighteenth century, not the sixteenth, was still the real starting point of the connection between agriculture and the great changes.

Manufactures and industry

The changes we have seen so far in population, inflation and agriculture exerted a combined impact on the development of Tudor industry.

The increase in population created an increased demand for consumer items. At the same time, the higher prices, which drove many off the land, developed a larger labour pool. Some of this was soaked up by agriculture, the rest found employment in the smaller-scale industries which were traditionally closely related to the countryside – especially textiles. Some of the products went into the domestic market, especially to the wealthy sections of the population who had benefited from the rise in agricultural prices. The rest went abroad. Meanwhile, the improvement in agricultural methods, even if relatively modest, ensured that an expanding labour force was sustained.

The main change in industry was its diversification across town and countryside. Most industries expanded somewhat, whether coal, iron or shipbuilding. Coal extraction increased from 170,000 tons per annum to 2.5 million tons per annum between 1550 and 1650 – largely in the north-east around Tyneside and Durham. Iron production expanded over the same period from 5,000 tons per annum to 24,000 tons. The number of iron-smelting furnaces in Sussex increased from three in the 1530s to twenty-six by the 1560s. Other rapidly expanding industries included brewing, paper-making, window and bottle glass, dyeing and tanning, and shipbuilding. The building trade prospered as a result of the creation of large country homes.

But the main developments in industry during the Tudor period occurred in textiles. This was an acceleration of earlier trends which had started during the thirteenth century. The process which was particularly important was the diversification of the cloth industry, previously directed by master craftsmen in the towns, into the countryside as well. Increasingly, however, these clothiers were basing their activities in rural areas. This was to take advantage of the pool of labour created by the expanding population and to avoid the higher rate of inflation in the towns caused by rising food prices. Indeed, the domestic textile industry became during the Tudor period the largest single employer apart from agriculture. Between 1450 and 1650 the value of English textiles increased between five and six fold: this was a real increase, even taking account of the inflation of prices. Most of the produce was woollen cloth, but progress was also made with worsted yarns, linen and hosiery.

As in other areas of the economy, there has been some historiographical debate as to the extent of industrial change. Some, like Nef, maintained that there was an industrial revolution during the Tudor period which anticipated that of the eighteenth century – a parallel to the argument that there was also an earlier agricultural revolution. Nef based his argument on the rapid expansion of the coal and iron industries, which provide a base for a rapid general expansion.[18] Other historians have challenged the extent of the industrialisation, pointing out that much of the coal extracted, especially during the sixteenth century, was used in domestic consumption rather in industry. It is true that there were some increases in the scale of industrial production, but these were more apparent in consumer goods, which did not require a large-scale expansion in size. These included the stocking and pin-making industries, which could be accommodated more easily to the cottage industrial base. This means that there was little attempt to change the organisation or structure of industry. There were occasional experiments with grouping cottage workers, especially weavers, in larger units, thus anticipating the factory system – but these were few and far between, and were never taken up on any scale.

What about the Marxist argument that there were major changes in the methods of production which amounted to proto-capitalism? It has been asserted that the changes in the cloth industry, especially during the Tudor period, were vitally important for the eventual relationship between exploiter and exploited and an essential foundation for the Industrial Revolution. There is perhaps some mileage in the argument that capitalism was emerging through the tendency of weavers to work on materials purchased and supplied by clothiers, and that they therefore no longer owned the product on which they were working. But it was not yet sufficiently systematic or organised on a wide enough basis to be described as 'capitalism'. What actually seems to have occurred in the late sixteenth century was not a foretaste of the industrial revolution of the eighteenth century, which saw England forge ahead of its continental rivals, but rather a process of catching up with some of the leading continental competitors of the previous century. England, in other words, had experienced a phase of consolidation rather than the dramatic change which is best ascribed to a later period.

Trade

Internal trade expanded rapidly during the Tudor period. This was due primarily to the growing population which was bound to create an expanding internal market. It was also stimulated by the growth of wage labour, a result of the reduction of land ownership through the agricultural changes. There were also two major advantages. One was geographical – transportation of heavy cargoes was facilitated by England's extensive coastline and navigable river network. The other was a longstanding absence of internal customs barriers of the type which affected many continental countries and which were bound to drive up costs.

England's external trade has always received more attention than the internal. In fact, however, its total volume was probably much smaller. The main development in England's overseas trade was the rapid expansion of exports in woollen textiles, which amounted to about 80 per cent of England's total exports by the mid-sixteenth century. This increased steadily from about 1460, through the reign of Henry VII and into that of Henry VIII. During the 1540s it accelerated rapidly. This was due primarily to the relative fall in the value of the English currency as a direct result of the debasement of the coinage by Henry VIII: this made English cloth cheaper to foreign importers. On the other hand, England was also susceptible to trade slumps. The first occurred during the 1550s with the efforts made by Edward VI from 1551 to restore the currency to its former value. The problem of oversupply was exacerbated by the influx of new clothiers who had attempted to take advantage of the prospect of indefinite prosperity. The cloth trade did recover, but the rate of growth was slower in the second half of the century than it had been in the first.

The Elizabethan period, in particular, saw changes in the direction of overseas trade. During earlier periods the London–Antwerp connection had been predominant. During the second half of the sixteenth century, however, the scope of English commercial enterprise expanded rapidly. This was due largely to complications in foreign policy and the growing enmity with Spain which produced the crisis in the Netherlands dealt with in Chapter 6. As western Europe became increasingly destabilised, the attraction of the maritime trade became greater. This was strengthened initially by the privateering connection, which led to deliberate attempts to break into the Spanish and Portuguese overseas markets. Examples were the voyages of Hawkins in 1562, 1564 and 1567, Drake's raids on the Isthmus of Panama (1572–73) and Drake's circumnavigation (1577–80). The process was supplemented by attempts at colonisation in North America, such as Gilbert's voyage to Newfoundland in 1583 and Raleigh's efforts to establish Virginia in 1584.

Overseas trade saw major changes in organisation. The most important was the emergence of new chartered companies such as the Muscovy Company (1555), the Eastland Company (1579), the Levant Company (1581), the Barbary Company (1585) and the East India Company (1600). These were given monopolies in the trade with their particular areas. On the other hand, this was never fully effective and there was also a considerable, although unquantified, volume of trade carried out by individuals and small partnerships not actually connected to the great companies.

Finally, the expansion of overseas trade also led to an increase in English shipping. Shipbuilding more than doubled between the 1570s and 1620s, while the number of ships larger than 400 tons increased from 14 to 150 over the same period. This growth was accompanied by an important change in carriage as more and more goods came to be transported in English ships rather than in foreign, especially Hanse and Flemish, ships.

What was the importance of all this for the future? Again, it would be too much to talk of the Elizabethan period as having undergone a 'commercial revolution'. Many of the major advances in trade and shipbuilding which underlay the real commercial revolution of the eighteenth century occurred after 1650, not before 1600. Nevertheless, many future patterns had been set in motion during the Tudor period. One of the most important of these was the projection of English interest beyond Europe into a more maritime context. At this stage there was still insufficient investment to make this as profitable as internal trade, but at least the process of diversification had been started.

Questions

1. Which of the economic sectors saw the greatest expansion during the Elizabethan era by comparison with the period of her Tudor predecessors?

2. Did Tudor England experience an 'agricultural', 'industrial' or 'commercial' revolution?

SOURCES

1. STATISTICS ON ENGLISH POPULATION, 1500–1610

Source 1.1: Estimated population increase in England, 1541–1611 (in 000s).

1541	2,774	1581	3,598
1546	2,854	1586	3,806
1551	3,011	1591	3,899
1556	3,159	1596	4,012
1561	*2,985*	1601	4,110
1566	3,128	1606	4,253
1571	3,271	1611	4,416
1576	3,413		

Source 1.2: Estimated age structure in England, 1551–1601.

	Percentage of population aged:				
	0–4	*5–14*	*15–24*	*25–59*	*60+*
1551	14.7	21.5	17.9	37.5	8.4
1561	*10.2*	23.6	19.6	39.3	7.3
1571	13.3	*19.5*	19.8	40.1	7.3
1581	13.5	21.1	*16.4*	41.4	7.6
1591	12.4	22.3	17.9	*39.5*	7.9
1601	12.3	20.6	19.3	39.5	*8.3*

Source 1.3: Estimated populations of European countries in 1600 (millions).

Germany[a]	20.0
France	16.0
Italy[b]	13.0
Spain and Portugal[c]	10.0
Poland and Lithuania	8.0
European Turkey[d]	8.0
England and Wales	4.5
Scotland and Ireland	2.0
Scandinavia	1.4

Notes:
[a] I.e. the Holy Roman Empire, comprising hundreds of autonomous and rival political units.
[b] Comprising the different Italian states, some under foreign control (Spain, France).
[c] Spain and Portugal, including their overseas empires, were united under one crown between 1580 and 1640.
[d] Comprising about one-half of the Ottoman Empire.

Source 1.4: Estimated populations of Europe's leading cities in 1600.

100,000+	*200,000+*	*500,000+*
Amsterdam	Naples	Constantinople
Antwerp	Paris	
London		
Lisbon		
Milan		
Palermo		
Rome		
Seville		
Venice		

In other parts of Britain:
Edinburgh	10,000
Dublin	10,000
Cardiff	3,000

Questions

1. Explain the figures in italics in Sources 1.1 and 1.2.
2. Comment on the origins and reliability of figures like those in Sources 1.1 and 1.2.
3. 'England did not have the population base to be ranked among the great European powers in the late sixteenth century.' Do Sources 1.1 to 1.4, and your own knowledge, support this view?

Worked answer: Comment on the origins and reliability of figures like those in Sources 1.1 and 1.2.

The basic problem with early population data such as these is that there is no official overall figure from the period: the first national population census was not held until 1801. This means that figures for the sixteenth century are based on a combination of existing evidence, computation and informed conjecture. The result is likely to be controversial, since different methods will yield different totals, and the names of individual economic historians have been associated with specific estimates. The use of cross-checking and modern technology such as computers and databases has, however, increased the chances of accuracy.

The figures in both sources are the result of interpretation of a variety of data, cross-checked with each other where possible. The most obvious form is parish registers for baptisms, marriages and burials, which were ordered for each parish by Thomas Cromwell in 1538. There are, of course, problems related to these. Births were not included and an unknown number of infants would have died before being baptised; on the other hand, the very fear of this would have meant baptism as soon as possible, usually within a week. Similarly, a single parish might not be typical of others in its area; but this can be offset by calculations based on the aggregation of blocs of parishes.

Other figures can be derived from contemporary records on numbers and composition of households, kept by towns such as Coventry from 1523 and Poole from 1574. These can also be used to calculate the average family size and ages. 'Family reconstructions' can then be used for comparable locations to build up a broader picture. Lists of communicants have been added to the process: these are especially useful in an age when church attendance was compulsory, although the ages at which people were confirmed varied extensively within as well as between parishes.

Producing 'broad' figures also involves 'back-projection', working data from later periods back into periods where there are gaps. The basic skill of demographers covering the Tudor period is therefore the aggregation of what is bound to be fragmented information in order to achieve a rounded figure for the country as a whole. No better system has yet been devised.

2. THE PRICE RISE

Source 2.1: The explanation of inflation to Elizabeth I by Sir Thomas Gresham.

It may please your majesty to understand that the first occasion of the fall of the exchange did grow by the king's majesty, your late father, in abasing his coin from six ounces fine to three ounces fine. Whereupon the exchange fell from 25 shillings and 8 pence to 13 shillings and 4 pence, which was the occasion that all your fine gold was conveyed out of this your realm. Secondly, by reason of his wars, the king's majesty fell into great debt in Flanders. And for the payment thereof they had no other device but to pay it by exchange, and to carry over his fine gold for the payment of the same. Thirdly, the . . . granting of licence for the carrying of your wool and other commodities out of your realm . . . it may plainly appear to your highness as the exchange is the thing that eats out all princes, to the whole destruction of their common weal, if it be not substantially looked unto; so likewise the exchange is the chiefest and richest thing only above all other to restore your majesty and your realm to fine gold and silver, and is the means that makes all foreign commodities with all kinds of victuals good cheap, and likewise keeps your fine gold and silver within your realm . . .

Source 2.2: Index of prices, 1491–1610.

	Foodstuffs	Industrial products
1491–1500	100	97
1501–10	106	98
1511–20	116	102
1521–30	159	110
1531–40	161	110
1541–50	217	127
1551–60	315	186
1561–70	298	218
1571–80	341	223
1581–90	389	230

	Foodstuffs	Industrial products
1591–1600	530	238
1601–10	527	256

Source 2.3: Index of agricultural wages, 1491–1610.

1491–1500	101	1551–60	160
1501–10	101	1561–70	177
1511–20	101	1571–80	207
1521–30	106	1581–90	203
1531–40	110	1591–1600	219
1541–50	118	1601–10	219

Source 2.4: Total currency in circulation in England at various times between 1544 and 1603.

	£ million
1544	1.23
1546	1.45
1548	1.76
1549	1.92
1551 (July)	2.66
1551 (Aug)	1.38
1560	1.71
1561	1.45
1606	3.50

Questions

1. Examine the argument used by Gresham in Source 2.1.
2. Comment on and explain the different rates of growth:
   a. between agricultural and industrial prices (Source 2.2), and
   b. between agricultural prices (Source 2.2) and agricultural wages (Source 2.3).
3. 'The main reasons for inflation during the Tudor period were related to the coinage and the money supply.' Do Sources 2.1 to 2.4, and your own knowledge, support this view?

8

SOCIETY AND CULTURE

BACKGROUND

The economic changes analysed in the previous chapter led to a major social transformation. The main trend was for the expansion of the wealthy elite, which grew in size through opportunities and social and economic mobility, and a lower order which found subsistence more and more difficult. This is the theme of Analysis 1. To what extent was this social polarisation accompanied by a conceptual polarisation – the development of a dichotomy between 'respectability' and 'vulgarity'? This will be examined within two further contexts: the issue of law and order (Analysis 2) and culture (Analysis 3).

Taken together, the overall argument of this chapter is as follows. Between 1450 and 1603 there were extensive changes in England's social structure. At one end of the scale, the elite expanded to take in the gentry and the professional classes. At the other end, poverty affected a larger proportion of the population than ever before. There was therefore increasing polarisation between the two. This was reflected by alterations in the pattern of crime, the proportion committed by the marginalised sectors such as vagrants growing rapidly. As a result the attitudes of the elite became more intolerant – even repressive. It has been argued that culture provided temporary social cohesion, at least during the reign of Elizabeth. But any such cohesion was superficial, with deep cracks already opening up below the surface. These corresponded with the social polarisation as a general phenomenon.

ANALYSIS 1: WHAT SOCIAL CHANGES HAD OCCURRED BY THE END OF ELIZABETH'S REIGN?

According to William Harrison, a clergyman, in his *Description of England*, published in the 1570s, 'We in England divide our people commonly into four parts, as gentlemen, citizens or burgesses, yeomen, and artificers or labourers.'[1] This more or less defines the fundamental division of Tudor England into the social elite, or the 'gentlemen', and the rest of the population, graded into descending levels of social importance. Gentlemen comprised 'dukes, marquises, earls, viscounts, and barons', all of whom were 'of the greater sort' or 'lords and noble-men', next to whom were 'knights and esquires', who were 'simply called gentlemen'.[2] The main pattern of change in Tudor England was the expansion of the social elite to incorporate groups below the top level. But the lowest level became increasingly impoverished and at the bottom of it there developed a large and marginalised sector. According to Smith, 'The increasing prosperity of the richer groups in society and the pauperization of large numbers among the lower orders represented a striking economic polarization between the upper and bottom ranks of Englishmen.'[3]

The social elite grew larger because of reduction in the difference between the top few layers of society. In the first place, L. Stone has argued that the peerage lost a degree of its authority and status by comparison with its position in the fifteenth and early sixteenth centuries.[4] Although the extent of this decline has caused considerable controversy, it was certainly sufficient to narrow the gap between them and the social groups below them. Palliser puts a slightly different case – that there was 'less a decline of the nobility than an expansion of the gentry within which the nobles formed a smaller proportion'.[5] Along with the gentry, the merchants and professional classes increased considerably in status – especially lawyers. Equally, the opportunities in trade attracted growing numbers from the lower sections and the opportunity grew for self-made men. It is difficult to pinpoint the degree to which the yeomen managed to rise into the gentry, but it seems likely that the price rise (see Chapter 7) helped split this class, elevating some while depressing others.

The general pace of change was slow up to 1560, then accelerated increasingly during the reign of Elizabeth. By the end of the sixteenth century there had been no social revolution – instead, a surprising degree of continuity. Nevertheless, stratification had occurred between the rich and poor, with the main movement and change taking place into and within the elite at one end and into and out of the lower stratum. Instead of the four groups identified earlier in the century, by 1600 there were probably six. The top three comprised nobility, gentry and other elites. The next two corresponded broadly to the remaining original three. One was the lesser yeomanry together with shop-keepers, tradesmen and artisans. Below them came the labourers and any remaining self-sufficient cottagers. The unemployed and poor had by now emerged as a distinct and numerous subgroup.

Meanwhile, several categories of impoverishment had become apparent. Official statutes of the period differentiated between the dis-abled and the able-bodied poor. But another contrast was between the settled and vagrant poor.[6] The former were regarded as legitimate targets for any Poor Law policy or legislation, while the latter were considered outside its scope and frequently as a criminal sector. The settled poor usually comprised somewhere between a third and a fifth of the population of any particular area, of whom more than two-thirds were able-bodied – at least during the Elizabethan period. The vagrant poor were smaller in number, although it is difficult to establish even approximate totals. Calculations are also complicated by the overlap with groups who would make a living out of itinerary occupations, such as magicians, pedlars and entertainers. It has, however, been estab-lished that the majority of sedentary poor were women, while the vagrant poor were more likely to be young men.

There were several reasons for impoverishment. The usual starting point was personal misfortune, which could strike at any point and in any age. This might include bereavement, disablement or loss of liveli-hood due to the circumstances of the employer. But the combination of pressures was especially great during the period because of a number of factors entirely beyond the individual's control. One of these was the pattern of population growth, with the birth rate exceeding the death rate. The result was a distortion of the overall population balance and the predominance of younger age groups: as much as 40 per cent of the population and 45 per cent of the poor in the sixteenth century were children younger than ten. As such, large numbers were unable to pro-vide for themselves or were dependent on those who found it difficult to fend for their enlarged families.

A second factor in the growth of poverty was that the labour supply grew more rapidly than the demand. This meant two things: an increase in the level of unemployment and, for those who did find work, low levels of wages relative to the growth of inflation. In many instances, wages actually fell while prices of consumables were rising. Third, many of those who had previously aimed at self-sufficiency were caught up in the agrarian changes, which involved both enclosures and the consolidation of agricultural holdings. The process of 'engrossing', in particular, threw large numbers of small farmers out of the means of subsistence. Fourth, the ranks of the poor were swelled by the demobilisation of troops after continental campaigns, which had occurred especially during the first and last decades of the reign of Henry VIII and the second half of Elizabeth's. The habit of the Tudors was to draw a substantial portion of their troops from the criminal classes and vagabonds, which meant that the problem of reintegration into society was perpetuated.

Most of the poor remained in the place of their birth. But a substantial minority became vagrants, seeking improved prospects elsewhere. Some went to the towns, helping the urban population increase fourfold between 1500 and 1700 and London to expand from 50,000 in 1500 to 575,000 by 1700. The problems confronting them, however, meant that integration was in most cases impossible. This meant a further period of vagrancy or, alternatively, acceptance of alternative forms of subsistence through crime. In turn, the contemporary propaganda distorted the threats that this posed, in the process helping to solidify the social changes which had already occurred.

Question

1. How useful is the term 'social class' when applied to Elizabethan England?

ANALYSIS 2: EXAMINE THE PERCEPTIONS OF, AND MEASURES AGAINST, POVERTY AND CRIME DURING THE PERIOD.

Poverty

The Tudor period experienced a range of attitudes to poverty, ranging from charity at one end, through exploitation to fear and hostility at the other. In part these views were pragmatic responses to immediate situations in which people were involved with the poor; in part they were influenced by an undercurrent of religion and ideology.

The hierarchical approach to society carried the implication that the poor were a natural part of it. There was, however, a certain moral obligation by the rich to provide charity: indeed, this was seen as an opportunity for them to practise virtue through the exercise of charity. It has, however, been argued that the emphasis on unconditional charity was stronger at the beginning of the period than at the end.[7] Part of the reason for this was the increase in numbers and the bad reputation of the vagrant beggars. Henry Smith said in 1592 that 'to give unto such as we know of lewd behaviour, thereby to continue them in their wickedness, were very offensive'.[8] Under the Tudors, charity therefore became more and more selective. This was because of the growth of discrimination between worthy and unworthy poor – between those who became poor 'against their will', through sickness or misfortune, and those who were poor 'by their will': the latter could be categorised either as virtuous and unworldly, or as the 'sinful poor'.

Why did this discrimination develop? According to some historians, the ideological attitude to poverty derived partly from the Renaissance, partly from the Protestant Reformation. The distrust of the poor was reinforced by a variety of pamphlets produced during the course of the sixteenth century. There were also writers who accused the poor of undermining the cohesion of social hierarchy. Renaissance humanism stressed the importance of changing attitudes through education, and totally condemned those who chose to withdraw from worldly involvement or activity, whether through asceticism or idleness. A connection has also been established by some historians between Protestantism, hard work and capital accumulation. The corollary of this was that the work ethic was an essential ingredient in living a godly life, while the idle were damned since they displayed vices like shiftlessness instead of fortitude and hard work. This was particularly apparent in the vagrant poor since they were the most likely to be connected with crime. On the other hand, the accumulation of wealth, according to the Protestant ethic, should not be channelled into the pursuit of pleasure, which meant that there was a charitable outlet for those of the poor who were considered to be deserving of it. This applied almost always to members of the sedentary poor. At the same time, such charity would probably be accompanied by strong, even harsh, value judgements about the recipient's character and by stringent attempts to reform it.

The vagrant poor were a particular cause for concern – and often fear. They were regarded as criminals, partly because of their dependence on begging, burglary and theft to make ends meet. They were condemned as dirty, immoral and as purveyors of disease. They were also connected with the underworld, especially in Elizabethan London. As a result, official attitudes were much harsher to the vagrant than to the sedentary poor. This was reinforced by exceptions recommended to charity: the Bishop's Book (1537), for example, stated that anyone living 'by the graft of begging slothfully' should be excluded from charity.

The stereotyping of the poor into worthy and unworthy, or belonging to God or the Devil, provided the basic guidelines for the way in which they might be treated. The differentiation is clear in the most important statutes concerning poverty. During the reign of Henry VIII there were three: in 1531, 1536 and 1547. The most important was the Act of 1531 Concerning Punishment of Beggars and Vagabonds which provided for the licensing of begging for alms by the 'impotent' poor but for the whipping of vagrants and their forcible return to their place of origin. Edward VI added two more, in 1550 and 1552: the latter confirmed the measures against vagabonds and provided for the collection of arms for the impotent poor, which was intended to replace begging. Mary's reign saw the return of licensed begging in 1552, again for the impotent poor only, as designated by special badges. The reign of Elizabeth saw a series of statutes designed to tidy up measures for the two categories of poor: these were passed in 1563, 1572, 1576, 1598 and 1601. The difference between the deserving poor and vagrants was greater than ever. The former were registered under the 1572 Act, and Justices of the Peace (JPs) could assess the contributions to be made by 'all inhabitants' for their relief. The 1598 Act allowed JPs to tax some parishes to help others. Vagrants could be burned through the ear as well as whipped under the 1572 Act, and, by the 1598 Act, compulsorily moved on to the place of last dwelling, or committed to prison.

How effective were the measures dealing with the 'deserving' poor? For much of the period up to the 1570s they lacked co-ordination, before becoming progressively more organised and integrated. Initially much of the policy was left to local authorities, with periodic attempts to reduce the threat posed by vagrants. This was very much the emphasis, for example, of the 1531 Act, which was a direct response to the economic problems of the previous decade. At this stage no action was taken to provide assistance for the impotent poor, beyond the official licensing of begging. But this was not a long-term solution and provisions were introduced instead for the parish to become responsible for providing relief. This was not actually implemented until 1552, and even then it was repealed in 1555, with begging reintroduced. The basic reason was widespread opposition to the principle of compulsory payments rather than voluntary charity. Parliament and government both therefore hit obstacles. They tried, by the 1563 Act, to enforce payments by directing that there should be lists of non-contributors. But the Northern Rebellion of 1569 was the real impetus behind the imposition of compulsory weekly payments by the Acts of 1572 and 1576. The latter measure also provided an administrative structure through the appointment by JPs of collectors of assessment and over-seers of the poor. Again, however, it was difficult to apply this legislation and these methods systematically. Efforts were relaxed slightly as a result of a series of good harvests. Then came another round of legisla-tion, promoted by the run of poor harvests from the mid-1590s and incidents and riots associated with popular opposition to enclosures. The Act of 1598 confirmed and extended the measures of the 1572 Act. Landowners and householders could be taxed to provide for the impotent poor, while overseers were to be appointed by JPs to keep public accounts, and further measures were to be taken to build houses of correction, alms houses and hospitals. The 1601 Act confirmed these measures.

It therefore took some time for effective administrative and financial systems to come into operation. Each stage would lapse, and then be revived and added to as a result of a particular crisis. There was there-fore a gradual progression as a result of external stimulants to action. There was also competition between central government and local initiative. Parliament was often in the position of trying to catch up with and control what was happening in the localities. The latter often took the initiative. London local officials, for example, bought Bridewell and Bedlam and acquired Christ's hospital, along with St Bartholomew's and St Thomas's. The aim was to distribute between these the sick, the elderly, children, the insane and vagrants. Bridewell, in particular, became a model for other authorities, which established their own 'bridewells' for the able bodied in Norwich and York.

All this points to a mixed record by the end of the Tudor period. Overall, poverty had become more widespread but was at least being recognised as such by central government and local authorities. Responses were based on a fundamental distinction between deserv-ing and idle poor. The former were approached in an *ad hoc* way with the gradual establishment of an infrastructure which did eventually begin to cater for their needs. The vagrant poor were, by contrast, the target of ever more repressive legislation, and no progress was made during the period in coming to terms with the economic reasons for unemployment. Even so, the Tudor period, it is generally recognised, coped with a reasonable degree of success with a mounting problem. According to J. Pound, 'In normal circumstances both poverty and vagrancy were fairly well contained, and to say that either created a dangerous national situation would be to strain the evidence.'[9] P. Slack goes further, pointing to the beginnings of a 'machine of social welfare' which had further grown and 'become well established by the later seventeenth century'.[10] Nevertheless, there is also the possibility that the problem of poverty appeared to have been contained by the end of the Tudor period because the economic conditions which had contributed to it were being alleviated. By the last years of Elizabeth's reign the demand for food was being recognised as a possible source for profit, while the cloth trade had been disrupted by the wars with Spain. Both of these slowed – and then reversed – the swing from arable to pastoral agriculture. The move back to food production at the end of the sixteenth century therefore meant an increase in demand for employment, which began to check the problem of vagrancy. The economy and society were, by the end of Elizabeth's reign, beginning to move into closer harmony with each other, irrespective of government policy.

Crime

Criminal behaviour comprised a wide variety of offences. One category may be described as crimes against authority. Rebellion and treason were seen as particularly atrocious: in the words of Richard Taverner, 'Kings represent unto us the person even of God himself.'[11] Also considered subversive to authority was crime based on religion. Such offences were often involuntary – people being caught out by a change of regime or of policy. The Carthusian monks, for example, fell foul of Henry VIII's Act of Supremacy; Latimer, Hooper and Cranmer, along with three hundred other martyrs, were unable to accept the Marian changes; and the Catholic recusants were stigmatised and executed for so-called treasonable activities during the reign of Elizabeth. Third, witchcraft was proceeded against vigorously under legislation passed during the reigns of Henry VIII, Mary and Elizabeth. The main motive was to undermine any potential opposition to the various religious settlements and, for secular reasons, to eradicate any form of subversion and secret association. Apart from crimes against authority, the other main categories were crimes against the person and crimes against property. The former included homicide (which could, in turn, be subdivided into murder, manslaughter and infanticide), rape and assault, and physical violence. The most common of the crimes against property was theft, which included shoplifting, picking pockets and house burglary. Some property crimes were more relevant to rural areas, especially the theft of farm animals and poaching.

Did crime and disorder increase during the period? The authorities certainly seemed to think so. William Lambarde, a Kent JP, believed that 'sin of all sorts swarmeth'.[12] The figures which are available show an increase in the number of prosecutions. For example, these rose in Kent from 33 per annum in 1571–75 to 70 per annum between 1596 and 1600, with similar increases occurring in Surrey, Sussex, Hertfordshire and Essex.[13]

Within this overall increase, however, was the beginning of a polarisation. The crime committed by the upper levels of the social order were going down – certainly in Essex, Sussex and Hertfordshire, as has been shown by local studies undertaken by J.S. Cockburn.[14] The same probably applied over the country as a whole. At the same time, crimes committed by the lower orders were going up, especially in the period 1559–1625. Crimes of violence against the person (rape, homicide and assault) increased far more slowly than offences involving property, especially theft or burglary. There seems to be a direct correlation here between crimes against property and the growing hardship as a result of economic conditions. They were committed largely by vagrants and the peak periods coincided with rising food prices and bad harvests, especially between 1596 and 1598. There was also polarisation in violent crime. Public order offences were very much on the increase by the end of the sixteenth century. These were associated increasingly with the lower, especially the marginalised, orders. William Lambarde warned in 1582 against a multitude of beggars. 'We are touched in sorrow for the horrible uncleanness and other mischiefs that they commit amongst us.'[15]

Several measures were employed to try to reduce the incidence of crime. One was the religious and moral exhortation through the church, especially the pulpit. Most of the population were regular churchgoers – indeed they were obliged to be – and were therefore a ready target for sermons emphasising respect for the social hierarchy and the different levels of authority. There is no doubt that the social elite were largely exempted from the strictures of the church, except for the warnings about treason, which covered everyone. Another was the application of punishment. The motivation for this varied. Modern societies emphasise rehabilitation and restitution. Tudor punishment, however, focused on retribution and deterrence. Hence punishments were deliberately severe. For treason the penalty was hanging, drawing and quartering – or beheading for members of the aristocracy. Witchcraft was punished by hanging, not, as is commonly believed, by burning at the stake. Vagrancy was dealt with by a variety of expedients: the Act of 1572 stated that vagrants should be 'grievously whipped, and burnt through the gristle of the right ear with a hot iron of the compass of an inch about'. Homicide, whether preconceived or not, nearly always merited hanging, as did proven cases of rape. Women convicted of murdering their husbands could be burned. All forms of theft were punishable by death. For example, 'On 30 September 1579 the house of the Earl of Sussex at Boreham (New Hall) was broken into by John Crosfield. He removed a gilt bowl (worth £4), a silver bowl (30s), a silver combcase (£4), and two silver trencher plates (30s). Found guilty, he was hanged.' Or again, 'In 1597 Thomas Clarke, a Great Bardfield husbandman, was sent to the gallows for burglary involving only 12d in money.'[16]

Punishments, too, indicated social polarisation. For one thing, most punishable offences affected the lower orders. Burglary, theft, picking pockets, and poaching were hardly likely to be much in evidence among the aristocracy or gentry, or among the extended elite. There were also two fundamental approaches to homicide, allowing duelling at one end of society while dealing severely with brawling at the other end. The ultimate crime, treason, was more even in its participation: both the upper and lower orders were involved, as was shown in the Pilgrimage of Grace. Yet the different punishments meted out showed that the aristocracy were accorded a greater degree of respect owing to their rank, even though they may have threatened the throne. There was also the motive that the crown relied upon information from other members of the aristocracy about potential treason: would this have been forthcoming had the punishment been hanging, drawing and quartering?

To reduce crime the authorities also tried to control the use of weapons. Hence from 1514 a series of statutes controlled the use of firearms, and in 1562 Elizabeth prohibited the wearing of long swords. The government also criticised various authorities for not taking strong enough action against pistols; this implies that there was only a very limited success in the enforcement of firearms regulations. In 1600, for example, it was claimed that 'licentiousness hath grown so far as it is usual not only with common and ordinary persons travelling by the highways to carry pistols and other kinds of pieces, but that ruffians and other lewd and dissolute men . . . wheresoever they go ride in the highways or streets . . . do in secret manner go provided of such means to do mischief'.[17]

But all of these measures were limited in their effect. The main problem was always that the emphasis had to be on deterrence rather than on detection, on punishment rather than on apprehension. In the absence of a regular police force the apprehension rate was low – probably as little as 20 per cent. Even when caught, offenders went through a cumbersome trial system. The problem here was that cases before the Assizes or Quarter Sessions generally had to be initiated by the victim. It was also difficult to impanel juries, since this meant loss of earnings and the jurors, usually men of lower rank, could ill afford this. Proceedings were often hurried and the evidence not carefully presented or weighed. The process was also socially divisive. It was unlikely that acts of violence committed by the aristocracy or gentry would come before the Quarter Sessions. Most would be dropped or alternatively settled by a form of plea bargaining which might result in a fine. Overall, according to Williams, 'it is unlikely that Tudor law courts had much impact on the ordinary crime-rate'.[18]

Questions

1. To what extent was poverty seen as 'self-inflicted' during the Elizabethan period?
2. To what extent was 'crime' related to 'poverty' in Elizabethan England?

ANALYSIS 3: WHAT WAS TUDOR 'CULTURE'?

The Tudor period saw a combination of unprecedented cultural changes and considerable continuity. These might be seen as operating at two levels: popular and elite cultures. Most studies have traditionally focused on the cultural changes of the elite. But since the 1960s there has been a strong tendency by historians to study popular culture in its own right. This has led to the conclusion that there was actually considerable overlapping between the two, even while new elites were developing. The current argument most widely followed is that an elite culture developed under the Tudors, especially during the reign of Elizabeth, but that it retained contact with the more popular culture until the two began to pull apart during the reign of Charles I. This theme will be investigated further after a brief examination of 'popular' and 'elite' culture.

There were several types of culture which could be described as 'popular'. One was a form which affected the entire population. Examples included religious processions and ritual, or the celebration of festivals. Another was a culture which was seen as popular in a vulgar sense. This might arise from forms of punishment, such as the pillory and stocks, which provided a major form of entertainment. Or it might be castigated by the authorities – a case in point being witchcraft – on the grounds that it might upset the social balance or challenge religious orthodoxy. Indeed, the number of prosecutions for witchcraft increased considerably during the reign of Elizabeth and continued to rise steadily under the Stuarts.

'Elite' culture was, by definition, the preserve of the few rather than of the many. It comprised therefore those changes which were socially selective in their impact. One example was a more sophisticated form of architecture, as can be seen with Hampton Court, Nonsuch, Somerset House, Longleat, Hatfield and Audley End. Considerable investment was applied to terraced gardens, furnishings, paintings, tapestries, wall-hangings, busts, plate, books and ornaments. Above all, the Tudor period is associated with refinement and social graces adopted by the aristocracy. The greatest form of cultural expression was literary, with writers of unprecedented importance such as Elyot, More, Wyatt, Spenser, Marlowe, Sidney and Shakespeare. But there was also progress in navigation and exploration, described in Hakluyt's *Voyages and Discoveries*, and music, with the compositions of Byrd, Tallis, Weelkes and Gibbons. As yet, however, little advance was made in medicine or the sciences: their heyday was to be the seventeenth century.

What were the main influences on the emergence of an elite culture? One was Renaissance humanism, which brought a considerable increase in literacy among the upper classes. Developments in printing made reading more practical, and the houses of the well-to-do would have had a considerable number of books. Women, too, became more directly involved in the process. There was also an increase in the number of schools, and a humanist education came to be considered more important than the traditional training for warfare or the knight-hood, the earlier preserves of the aristocracy. Higher education was more widely favoured and opened up a vital route of mobility for the gentry. The same applied to the legal profession as many followed a few terms at Oxford or Cambridge with a course at the one of the Inns of Court in London. Another key influence was the Reformation. In its attack on Catholic ritual it carried a strong wave against superstition and was, in this respect, an influence for rationalism. It also assisted the switch in the cultural emphasis from the religious to the secular, while the dissolution of the monasteries played a major part in promoting the architecture and fine arts associated with domestic buildings.

To what extent were elite culture and popular culture in conflict with each other? On the one hand, there were areas of shared experience. These included the rituals of the church. Shaped and reshaped by government policy, whether during the reigns of Henry VIII, Edward VI, Mary or Elizabeth, they affected all levels of society. Astrology, too, continued to exercise an influence among all classes, as did the various feast days and fairs. Indeed, it has been argued that the culture of the elite was harmonised with the people during the reign of Elizabeth, but subsequently it polarised during the reign of Charles I. In some respects the Elizabethan period showed a great deal of common awareness among the population of a shared heritage. Some historians have pointed to the court as playing an important role here. According to Smith, 'the Elizabethan Court always remained a "popular" institution, in touch with the feelings and aspirations of the great majority of the Queen's subjects'. This was in contrast with the situation during the reign of Charles I, when the reverse happened. 'By the reign of Charles I the situation had changed beyond recognition. Charles, like Elizabeth, maintained a splendid and ceremonious Court, but increasingly, as the years passed, that Court was more and more out of touch with and unsympathetic to the cultural aspirations of the masses, unashamedly esoteric where the Elizabethan Court had been avowedly popular.'[19] Williams followed the same argument. He believed that 'the elite still participated in much of the culture of the literate populace, especially in the London theatre. Only in the course of the following century did the two worlds draw apart, so that the culture of the upper classes became largely isolated from the festivities of the common people.'[20]

The argument for cohesion and an Elizabethan harmony subsequently giving way to division is an attractive one. Perhaps it is partly true. But there is an alternative possibility. There already existed a popular culture. An elite culture also developed under the Tudors. For a while the two did harmonise during the reign of Elizabeth. This was partly because of the initiative from above, in the form of the court, and partly because of the social mobility of the groups below. Nevertheless, there were already strong indications of growing divergence, even polarisation, under the Tudors; these were not, therefore, entirely the responsibility of the Stuarts.

The Tudor elites had experienced a growth of education which made them much more receptive to literary culture and meant that they were less influenced than the lower levels of society by the more traditional forms of entertainment. It could also be argued that, as English became increasingly standardised as the language of the law and of culture, there was bound to be a divergence between a national version, used by the elites, and the more local vernacular forms, used by the lower orders.

There were also examples of the government and authorities regarding the expression of many traditional cultural forms and activities with more and more suspicion, reflecting the growing contempt held for these by the elite. Superstition of various kinds became a target, especially witchcraft, which was proscribed by statutes passed in 1542,

1563 and 1581. The peak period for prosecutions for witchcraft was 1580–1600. The victims were nearly always from the lower orders, and were often women or vagrants. There is a strong case for saying that the increase in anti-witchcraft legislation represents the polarisation of cultural as well as social attitudes. Whereas in the Middle Ages, superstition had permeated all levels of society, the sixteenth century saw superstition under attack from two areas – Protestant Reformation and Renaissance humanism. The former brought it under deep suspicion, the latter provided an alternative approach to the elite who were influenced by it. The lower orders fell into a rut of fear, which was exacerbated by the dislocation of society by the economic pressures such as population growth, inflation and agricultural change. Hence superstition turned inwards as a destabilising force which most affected those who were already socially destabilised. Those who benefited from the economic changes, or who were upwardly mobile, were largely unaffected by the panic created. Ironically, the same groups continued to be attracted by astrology. But this could be justified as more 'scientific', a cover for its real role of superstition for the elite.

There was also a more obvious divergence in the outward connection between culture and wealth. This showed itself especially in the form of domestic architecture and building. During the Tudor period the main investment in architecture moved away from churches and cathedrals into domestic houses. More emphasis was given to the display of status through architectural refinement. The number of stately homes increased considerably as a direct result of the dissolution of the monasteries. Above all, the splendour of the Elizabethan court provided the patronage for much of the literature of the period. As in the past, artists and writers had to settle for serving the elite in order to finance their interest. The Elizabethan period therefore saw a growing divergence between the social manners and graces of the different parts of the population. These were calculated to set the aristocracy apart from the rest and were therefore the most consciously elitist of all.

Questions

1. In what ways were 'popular' and 'elite' cultures distinct from each other?
2. In what ways did they overlap?

SOURCES: THE TREATMENT OF THE POOR

Source 1: From the Act for Punishment of Vagabonds and Relief of the Poor, 1572.

... All the parts of this realm of England and Wales be presently with rogues, vagabonds and sturdy beggars exceedingly pestered, by means whereof daily happen in the same realm horrible murders, theft and other great outrage, to the high displeasure of Almighty God, and the annoyance of the Common Weal....

... All and every person and persons whatsoever they be, being above the age of fourteen years, being hereafter set forth by this Act of Parliament to be rogues, vagabonds and sturdy beggars ... shall upon their apprehension be brought before one of the Justices of the Peace or Mayor or chief officer ... to be presently committed to the Common jail of the said county....

... If such person or persons be duly convicted of his or her roguish or vagabond trade of life ... then immediately he or she shall be adjudged to be grievously whipped, and burnt through the gristle of the right ear with a hot iron of the compass of an inch about....

And forasmuch as charity would that poor aged and impotent persons should as necessarily be provided for, as the said rogues, vagabonds and sturdy beggars repressed ... the Justices of the Peace, Sheriffs, Bailiffs and other officers ... shall ... make diligent search and enquiry of all aged, poor, impotent and decayed persons born within their said divisions and limits, or which were dwelling within three years next before this present parliament, which live or of necessity be compelled to live by alms of the charity of the people ... and shall upon that search made ... make a register book containing the names and surnames of all such aged, decayed and impotent poor people....

Source 2: From the Act for Punishment of Vagabonds, 1598.

... And be it enacted ... that every person which is by this present Act declared to be a rogue, vagabond or sturdy beggar, which shall be, at any time after the said feast of Easter next coming, taken begging, vagrant, wandering or misordering themselves in any part of this realm or the dominion of Wales, shall upon their apprehension ... be stripped naked from the middle upwards and shall be openly whipped until his or her body be bloody and shall be forthwith sent from parish to parish by the officers of every the same the next straight way to the parish where he was born, if the same may be known by the party's confession or otherwise; and if the same be not known, then to the parish where he or she last dwelt before the same punishment by the space of one year, there to put him or her self to labour as a true subject ought to do....

Source 3: From the 1598 Poor Law.

Be it enacted ... that the churchwardens of every parish, and four substantial householders. .. shall be called Overseers of the Poor of the same parish, and they or the greater part of them shall take order from time to time ... for setting to work of the children of all such whose parents shall not by the same persons be thought able to keep and maintain their children, and also all such persons married or unmarried as having no means to maintain them, use no ordinary and daily trade of life to get their living by: and also to raise weekly or otherwise (by taxation of every inhabitant and every occupier of lands in the same parish in such competent sum and sums of money as they shall think fit) a convenient stock of flax, hemp, wool, thread, iron and other necessary ware and stuff to set the poor on work, and also competent sums of money for and towards the necessary relief of the lame, impotent, old, blind and such other among them being poor and not able to work.... And ... it shall be lawful for the said churchwardens and overseers, or the greater part of them, by the assent of any two Justices of the Peace, to bind such children as aforesaid to be apprentices, where they shall see convenient, till such man child shall come to the age of four and twenty years, and such woman child to the age of one and twenty years. ...

Source 4: From D.M. Palliser, *The Age of Elizabeth*, published in 1983.

The Tudor policy of dealing with poverty and vagrancy was twofold: to punish and deter the vagrants and to relieve the 'deserving' poor. In both cases the older histories concentrate on statutory action, as though new measures were not tried until parliament had legislated, and were then immediately enforced throughout the country. Yet statutes, if a useful barometer of what governments and parliaments thought desirable, are a poor guide to what actually happened. Charitable individuals, justices and town councils did much in advance of national legislation, and indeed often provided the example and inspiration for that legislation: equally, unpopular laws were often not enforced or only reluctantly and partially enforced, despite all the threats and entreaties that the Privy Council could muster.

Questions

1. How do Sources 1, 2 and 3 distinguish between the different types of poor?
2. Compare the terms in Sources 1, 2 and 3 for the treatment of the poor.

3. 'Parliament determined the way in which the poor were treated in Elizabethan England.' Using Sources 1 to 4, and your own knowledge, comment on this viewpoint.

Worked answer: How do Sources 1, 2 and 3 distinguish between the different types of poor?

[Advice: This question requires concise but precise information from the three sources. Structure the argument as a direct response, using specific references, and avoid overlapping with Question 2.]

These sources make a basic distinction between two main types of poor: those who were worthy of help and those who were not. The latter are referred to in Sources 1.1 and 1.2 as 'rogues, vagabonds and sturdy beggars', or those who were unwilling to work, even though they were physically able to do so, and who roamed the countryside begging or committing criminal acts. Those who were genuinely unable to work were classed as the 'impotent' poor, described in Sources 1.1 and 1.3 as 'aged', 'decayed', 'lame', 'old', 'blind' or children without parental support; unlike the 'able' poor, they were entitled to support.

9

THE 'BRITISH' QUESTION

BACKGROUND

There had always been an interaction between the various components of the geographical area described as the 'British Isles', whether military, diplomatic, religious or cultural. During the high Middle Ages these had been part of a process of Anglo-Norman and Angevin expansion, although the most important direction was into the continent via France. For example, Henry II (1154–89) had governed England, Normandy, Anjou, Maine, Touraine, Poitou, Aquitaine, Gascony and Brittany. The Celtic fringe of Wales, Scotland and Ireland had formed only a loose bond to this empire, through the person of their ruler. At this stage, therefore, 'Britain' made little sense as a political term.

The first of the Celtic regions to develop a firmer attachment to England was Wales, reduced and brought fully under the English crown by Edward I (1272–1307). The union remained intact, although it was threatened by revolts during periods of instability in England under, for example, Richard II (1377–99) and Henry IV (1399–1413). The experience of Scotland was somewhat different. English rule, imposed by Edward I in 1304, was ended during the reign of Edward II at Bannockburn (1314). For nearly three centuries Scotland remained fully independent and, for much of this time, hostile to England. The situation in Ireland was the most complex. English monarchs such as Henry II and Edward I managed to establish some form of hegemony over the clans within the western area known as the Pale, only for this to be weakened under kings such as Edward III (1327–77), who had more important priorities elsewhere. Throughout the late Middle Ages Ireland remained 'subdued' in the way that Scotland was not – but not yet 'subject' in the manner of Wales.

During the fifteenth century a major change occurred in the nature of England's dominions. Edward III and Henry V (1413–22) conducted successful military campaigns which consolidated their hold over English possessions in France. But the long reign of Henry VI (1422–61) saw the loss of almost all of these: by 1453 only Calais remained of all the original possessions of Henry II. Deprived of its French possessions, England was forced to focus on relations with its own borderlands and more immediate Celtic neighbours. Tudor England, which emerged from the cauldron of civil war, was no longer the superpower that Angevin England had once been. Instead, it was to be fully stretched in competing with France and Spain, both recently united and in the ascendant. These took an increased interest in the internal state of the British Isles, and in the opportunities presented to destabilise England. Between 1485 and 1603 the Tudors therefore sought stability and, as far as possible, control over the outlying areas of Britain – the northern borderlands of England, the rival kingdom of Scotland, the divided tributaries of Ireland and a more or less pacified Wales.

They encountered mixed success. The closest relationship was with Wales, partly because of the direct connection with the dynasty established by Henry Tudor. This was confirmed by the Act of Union between England and Wales (1536) during the reign of Henry VIII. The administrative structures introduced by the Tudors were considered so successful at the time that there were those who advocated their use in Ireland as well. The latter had also been subject to clarifying legislation, including the 1494 Statute of Drogheda (better known as Poynings Law), which stated that the consent of the English monarch was required for the summoning of any Irish Parliament or the passing of any Irish law, and the Act of 1542 making Ireland a kingdom. Yet the situation in Ireland remained highly volatile and Elizabeth's government was faced with several major rebellions which had to be put down by military action; any peace achieved by 1603 was the result of conquest rather than mutual agreement. By contrast, Scotland proved to be more of a threat to the earlier Tudors than to Elizabeth, allying with France against Henry VIII and Edward VI and periodically threatening the border areas of England. During the second half of the sixteenth century, however, relations steadily improved – largely as a result of the spreading influence of Protestantism in Scotland. The succession crisis in England also ensured that the two thrones would be united under James VI of Scotland, who became James I of England in 1603.

The Celtic areas all played a significant role in what was once called the English Civil War, but which has been renamed by some historians 'the war of the three kingdoms' or the 'pan-British crisis'. The problems experienced by the Stuarts affected Scotland and Ireland as much as England and Wales, and a solution was sought in 1707 by the union of England (including Wales) and Scotland under the name of 'Great Britain'. This provided for a single Parliament to which Scotland would send sixteen peers and forty-five MPs, but the Scottish law and legal systems were unchanged. A similar process was attempted in 1800–01 by the Act of Union between Great Britain and Ireland, to establish the 'United Kingdom'. But whereas 'Britishness' was largely accepted as providing integration between England-Wales and Scotland, it was regarded by a substantial majority in Ireland as an alien influence, imposed by force. Most of the nineteenth century was therefore taken up with various forms of opposition to British 'rule' and with the search for solutions; the failure of these produced a more drastic outcome. In 1921 the provinces of Munster, Leinster and Connaught formed a new Irish Free State (later Eire). The province of Ulster was partitioned, three counties joining the Irish Free State and the other six retaining a constitutional link with Britain as part of the renamed 'United Kingdom of Great Britain and Northern Ireland'.

This chapter looks at only a small part of this extended outline. The Tudor period could, however, be seen as crucial to the origins of a new 'British' entity. Analysis 1 looks at the ways in which the Tudors, especially Elizabeth, confronted the problems of pacification and administration in Wales and Ireland, usually seen respectively as the most and least successful examples of integration into a 'British' system. Analysis 2 switches the focus to relations between England and an independent Scotland and the extent to which the reign of Elizabeth saw the emergence of an Anglo-Scottish state by 1603. Analysis 3 explores the more general issue of whether these developments could be seen as developing a potential 'Britishness' – and considers the various perspectives which historians have recently given this.

ANALYSIS 1: COMPARE TUDOR AND ELIZABETHAN RULE IN WALES AND IRELAND.

During the Middle Ages both Wales and Ireland had developed strong indigenous cultures while, at the same time, experiencing internal feuding and political fragmentation. Under the Tudors England had greater success in bringing Wales within its orbit than it did with Ireland.

P. Williams represented the usual view – that the political history of Wales between 1543 and the death of Elizabeth 'largely consisted of the implementation of the Henrician system'.[1] In Ireland, by contrast, earlier expedients attempted by Henry VII and Henry VIII collapsed under Elizabeth. Direct comparisons between Wales and Ireland need to be based on the implementation of English administrative and legal control, the threat of and response to disorder and rebellion, and religious and cultural connections. In each case it will be apparent that the integration of England and Wales was more successful than that of England and Ireland – but Williams's representation of the latter as 'almost uniformly disastrous'[2] also needs careful consideration.

The Tudor monarchy certainly had a stronger bond with Wales than with Ireland. A background of conquest under the Plantagenets, especially Edward I, and subsequent inheritance of land meant that the crown's actual ownership of land was much more substantial in Wales than in Ireland.[3] In Ireland Henry VIII tried to compensate for this by replacing feudal relationships, based on loyal chieftains, with direct rule under Lord Lieutenants selected from London; he also upgraded his own sovereignty from 'Lord' to 'King' of Ireland and attempted to redefine his relationship with the chieftains by surrender and regrant of land as fiefs to earls. From the outset there were more grounds for resistance from Ireland than from Wales.

The administrative and legal integration of Wales into England had occurred largely before the accession of Elizabeth. The principality itself and the marches with England had fragmented during the later Middle Ages to such an extent that they offered little resistance to the encroachment of English influence. This meant that it was relatively easy for Henry VIII, through the statutes of 1536 and 1543, to extend the English system of shires to Wales and, in the process, to remove the autonomy of the marches. He also introduced Welsh representation in the Westminster Parliament, established Justices of the Peace and enforced English law. This was all in part due to the willingness of competing units to accept the imposition of overall stability since these lacked the strength to resist England, having only the capacity to damage each other. Ireland had also been localised, but in larger units which were capable of dominating substantial areas and therefore resisting English attempts at imposing central control. Henry VIII recognised the difference between the relatively harmonious response from Wales and the outright defiance from Ireland. Hence Ireland was treated as a separate case: there was no act of union, as in Wales. Any reforms would have to be adapted to its own developments and traditions. This is why, instead of an act of union incorporating it into

England, Ireland was made into a kingdom by the Act for the Kingly Title of 1541. 'English' Ireland was confined to the Pale, under the Lord Lieutenant, the English legal system, and an Irish parliament and a new gentry which claimed to be English. Beyond the Pale the nobility were divided between those who were pro- and those who were anti-English.

While there was little left for her to do in Wales, Elizabeth inherited a substantial task of state-building in Ireland. Her reign therefore saw a contrast between consolidation in one area and the need to bring about change in response to the crises which developed in the other. In Ireland she tried two main policies. One was the use of plantations – not a method tried in Wales, where there was insufficient local hostility to warrant it. The Ulster plantation was largely unsuccessful. By the time of his death in 1576 its second organiser, Walter Devereux, Earl of Essex, had come to the conclusion that only fortified garrisons would control Ulster. Funds for this were not forthcoming and the scheme was abandoned. The Munster plantation survived a little longer, but was eventually destroyed in the uprisings in 1598. The second method adopted by Elizabeth was to try to bring Ireland into line with the sort of changes already made in Wales. Indeed, historians such as C. Brady have argued that there were attempts to apply a 'Welsh policy'[4] to Ireland, a more moderate alternative to colonisation and dispossession. There were two approaches to this. One, advocated by Sir William Gerrard in *Observations on the government of Ireland* (1578), was a reconstruction along Welsh lines, confined initially to the Pale and then gradually applied to the rest of Ireland. The alternative, advanced by Lord Deputy Sir Henry Sidney, was a new administrative and legal system throughout Ireland (which involved overhauling the central offices of law and establishing regular assize courts, and the presentation of reform programmes to the Irish parliament). There was, however, strong opposition throughout Ireland, including the Pale itself. The proposals failed, Sidney was recalled and rebellion broke out in Munster. Although she did eventually succeed in subduing Ireland by military force, in the process imposing more control than her predecessors, Elizabeth also left a legacy of division and hostility.

In all of this there were differences in the roles of the upper classes: the aristocracy in Wales assisted the spread of English government, whereas that in Ireland largely resisted it. Some of the leading families in Wales had actually helped the Tudors to acquire the throne and subsequently derived their strength from their connection with England rather than from opposition to it. Rebellion therefore became less and less of a problem, violence turning instead into more localised riots or feuds. The situation in Ireland was different: the English crown could not depend on the aristocracy to sustain its direct control. This was always potentially more dangerous since in Ireland the great families had sway over larger areas than in Wales, often acting as the core of a regional power and able to raise private armies. The incidence of rebellion therefore increased. The first, which broke out in Ulster under Shane O'Neill, had to be put down by Mountjoy. The Fitzmaurice rebellion was more widespread, starting in 1579 and spreading through the three provinces of Munster, Leinster and Ulster. Its savage suppression by Lord Grey brought destruction throughout Munster. Equally serious was the rebellion of the Earl of Tyrone (1595), which had the additional element of attempted Spanish assistance. When Tyrone defeated an English army in 1598, Elizabeth was forced to reconsider her normal constraints on expenditure and financed Essex's counter-campaign. But Essex merely made a truce and returned to England, which meant that the job had to be completed by Mountjoy. Although Elizabeth did succeed in crushing revolts in Ireland, pacification was never achieved on the basis of acceptance of English rule.

Underlying political and social developments were fundamental religious differences between Wales and Ireland. Although the two countries had a not dissimilar religious composition by the middle of the sixteenth century, they moved in opposite directions thereafter: from the beginning of Elizabeth's reign Catholicism retreated in Wales while it increased rapidly in Ireland, especially after 1580.

The Reformation was accepted with little conflict in Wales, whereas in Ireland it was contested from the outset. Although there was some evidence of early indigenous movements in Cardiff, Carmarthen and Haverfordwest, Protestantism spread in through an English Reformation rather than through a Welsh one; from 1560, for example, Welsh bishops followed instructions to use the new English Prayer Book in their dioceses. Catholicism was steadily eroded and the seminary priests had less of an impact on Wales than they did in southern England. In Ireland, by contrast, there was widespread refusal to use the Prayer Book imposed under Edward VI, while Mary's reign saw the weakening of Protestantism and the chance for Catholicism to rally. Elizabethan changes deepened the antagonism between Catholics and Protestants still further. The Irish parliament attempted to reimpose Protestantism through an Act of Uniformity in 1560. This was, however, difficult to enforce: even within the Pale there was strong resistance. There were also religious influences behind the rebellions against Elizabeth. For example, James Fitzmaurice Fitzgerald declared in 1579 that he was at war with a 'she-tyrant' who had no right 'to pronounce' on 'matters of faith' and had therefore 'deservedly forfeited her royal authority'.[5] Similarly, Hugh O'Neill in 1598 aimed to 'reform all things to the will of God'.[6] In direct contrast to Wales, there was a huge influx of Catholic priests from seminaries in Spain and the Spanish Netherlands, while sons of the Irish gentry were educated at schools founded specifically for the Irish; examples included Alcala (1590), Salamanca (1592), Lisbon (1593), Douai (1594) and Antwerp (1600).

The acceptance of the Reformation in Wales, and its rejection in much of Ireland, was in part a result of linguistic influences. But for these, the religious changes in Wales might have been seen as little more than a pragmatic political compromise. A key factor was the translation of many of the key religious texts into Welsh during the reign of Elizabeth. A Welsh version of the Bible was authorised by Parliament in 1563 and versions of the Prayer Book and New Testament in 1567; subsequent versions of the Prayer Book followed when required. The use of Welsh was therefore vital for the acceptance of the Church of England there. In Ireland, on the other hand, a Gaelic New Testament was not introduced until 1598 and a Book of Common Prayer not until 1608. The integration of Wales into England actually promoted a revival of the Welsh language, while attempts to control Ireland played no similar role for Gaelic.

Finally, there were differences in the economic conditions of the two areas. Not surprisingly, the frequency of war in Ireland caused devastation and famine, which were picked up in contemporary accounts (see Source 1.2 below). Wales experienced a respite, during which agriculture had a chance to recover and consolidate. More positively, the reign of Elizabeth started a trend in changing the direction of Ireland's trade. In the first half of the sixteenth century the main volume had been from ports in the south and west and with the continent, particularly with Spain. As a result of the growth of English influence, the bulk of trade switched to England and went through the east-coast ports of Dublin and Drogheda. This meant that, at the very time that Ireland was resisting English attempts to subdue it politically, economic links were growing in strength. Whether these links would eventually bring about a fuller integration on the Welsh model, or simply strengthen the pro-English minority within an otherwise hostile Ireland, was to become one of the key issue of the next four centuries.

Questions

1. Did Ireland 'progress' or 'regress' under Elizabeth?
2. Did the reign of Elizabeth make any fundamental difference to Wales?

ANALYSIS 2: WHY – AND TO WHAT EXTENT – DID ELIZABETH'S REIGN SEE A CLOSER RELATIONSHIP BETWEEN ENGLAND AND SCOTLAND?

There can be little doubt that important changes had taken place in the relationship between England and Scotland between 1558 and 1603. At the beginning of the reign Scotland was a largely hostile state, given to reviving from time to time the 'auld alliance' with France. Henry VIII had already tried to solve this problem, partly by military action (for example, at Flodden in 1513), and partly through his 'rough wooing' – an unsuccessful attempt to force upon the Scots a marriage between Prince Edward and Queen Mary Stewart. The reign of Edward VI had seen further conflict with both Scotland and France, and the Duke of Somerset tried to weaken Scotland through a policy of border garrisons. When Mary of Guise became regent in 1554 England faced a serious potential challenge: a claim to the English throne by her daughter, Mary Stewart, a Scottish Catholic indebted to France. In 1559 it must have seemed that England's basic security and newly established religious settlement was under threat – from the forces of the continental Counter Reformation about to enter through the open Scottish back door.

By 1603 the situation had apparently been transformed. The two countries had been at peace for nearly half a century. More than that, a new alliance between Scotland and England had replaced the 'auld alliance' between Scotland and France. Scotland had also become less of a threat to the English borders: as P. Williams argued, 'the Scottish frontier ceased to be the "postern gate" for England's enemies'.[7] The threat of the continental Counter Reformation had largely disappeared as both countries had a common bond in Protestantism, albeit under different administrative structures. Finally, the dynastic connection was no longer a threat; rather it was a form of security. James VI of Scotland was no Anglophobe and his accession to the throne as James I in 1603 was seen by many as the best solution to the absence of an English heir and the possibility of renewed Anglo-Scottish discord in the future. Throughout Elizabeth's reign a Scottish heir had never been more than a heartbeat way from the English throne. In 1558 it was the Catholic Mary Stewart; in 1603 it was the latter's Protestant son, James.

The reasons for these changes are varied and complex. The long-term dynastic connection provided by the marriage between Margaret Tudor, daughter of Henry VII, and James IV of Scotland; their son, James V, married Mary of Guise, whose daughter, Mary Queen of

Scots, was the mother of James VI. Elizabeth's refusal to marry ensured the lack of any direct heir and the transition of the Tudors to the Stuarts. With it came the connection between Scotland and England. But it took a unique series of events in Scotland to ensure that England accepted the connection as valid. The 1559 uprising of the Scottish Lords of the Congregation resulted in the overthrow and expulsion of Mary of Guise and the signing of the Treaty of Berwick with England; the new regime then proceeded to introduce a Protestant Reformation in Scotland, based on a Presbyterian structure. Mary of Guise's daughter, Mary Stewart, returned as Mary Queen of Scots in 1560 and, although a staunch Catholic, initially accepted the new Protestant order. But the scandals involving Mary and her various partners provoked her arrest in Scotland; she had married Bothwell, the murderer of her former husband, Darnley, who in turn had disposed of her lover, Riccio. Mary fled south to England, where she was eventually imprisoned and executed, while her son, James ascended the Scottish throne as a Protestant – an outcome much more acceptable to England. Even so, sensational though they were, these specific developments have to be set against a general background of improved relations between England and Scotland.

Probably the most important influence was the recently established religious connection between England and Scotland, where the former Catholic ascendancy had been replaced in the lowland areas by the Calvinist branch of the Protestant Reformation. Scotland was now seen as part of a common cause against the Catholic Counter Reformation embodied in the papacy, Spain and the Guise faction in France. In this sense the religious links between England and Scotland were strengthened by an apocalyptic vision of its enemies as well as by a common core of doctrine. An important consequence was the Anglo-Scottish treaties of Edinburgh (1559) and Berwick (1586). There were also strong cross-border links between various branches of Protestantism, often cutting across official differences. For example, English Presbyterians such as Cartwright and Travers had close relations with the Scottish Presbyterian kirk, while more moderate Puritans within the Church of England made common cause with Scottish episcopalians like Archbishop Adamson of St Andrews. Religious connections were, in turn, facilitated by the development of closer linguistic links between England and Scotland. The use of English, or lowland Scots, became increasingly widespread north of the border, while the Gaelic-speaking area shrank further into the west and central highlands. Formal English expanded the form of printed texts. Scotland used the Geneva Bible, which had been the work of English exiles in Switzerland during the reign of Mary Tudor, along with the *Book of Common Order*. Major works written by Scots, including Knox's *History of the Reformation*, were published not only in English, but also in England, thus strengthening the latter's cultural hold. English was increasingly favoured by Scottish writers, whether in prose or the poetry of William Drummond and William Alexander. Many Scots also went to school in England, or spent time at either Oxford or Cambridge.

To what extent were closer relations due to deliberate English policy? On two vital occasions England showed remarkably little direct involvement. It is true that in 1559 Elizabeth ordered an English fleet to the Firth of Forth and troops to Berwick – but her main concern was the landing of a French force; once this had withdrawn, English troops were pulled out rapidly. Similarly, between 1578 and 1585 she took no direct action to assist the Scottish Protestants faced with a direct threat from the supporters of Mary, even though help was much needed. In both cases, two arguments can be advanced. One is that the English reaction to events in Scotland was deliberately restrained and cautious; this view was put by J. Dawson, who argued that 'English policy had shown an unprecedented awareness of Scottish sensibilities in the negotiations and in the assistance which had been provided for the Scots'.[8] The reward for Elizabeth's departure from the rougher methods applied under Henry VIII and Edward VI was a more compliant neighbour prepared to allay some of its earlier suspicions about England's aggression. The alternative view is that Elizabeth instinctively disliked the prospect of intervention and probably did much to persuade Cecil to adopt a course of inaction. Throughout her reign she expressed herself in the strongest terms about the sanctity of the ruler against rebellion by subjects. Besides, there was always the danger that promoting rebellion elsewhere could backfire at home. She was also unsympathetic to the new Scottish regime and its main influence – John Knox. The latter had disgusted her with the views expressed about female rulers in *The First Blast of the Trumpet against the Monstrous Regiment of Women* (1558), even though Knox's main targets had been Mary Tudor and Mary of Guise. Hence Elizabeth did as little as possible, showing disdainful caution rather than calculated restraint. Scotland therefore controlled its own destiny between 1559 and 1567, irrespective of Elizabeth's policies.

There is a similar contrast in interpretations of Elizabeth's relations with James VI, from the time of his accession to the Scottish throne in 1567 until his eventual succession to the English throne in 1603. On the one hand, it has been argued that Elizabeth took the initiative in keeping the relationship alive and promoted formal and informal contacts between the two courts. She also did her best to pacify James after the execution of his mother, Mary Queen of Scots, in 1587 by completely disavowing any connection with the final decision. On the other hand, she has been seen as reluctant to provide any meaningful support to James. She never acknowledged that he had any claim to the English succession and frequently withheld part or all of the annual pension which had been guaranteed to him in the Treaty of Berwick. She even thought that James had no qualification for 'strong kingship'.[9] Perhaps this was as well: James's candidature had many supporters at the English court, who welcomed the prospect of a pliable monarch who would not try to impose Scottish ascendancy over England.

In fact, James had been far more enthusiastic about creating a genuine Anglo-Scottish state than Elizabeth had ever been, yet in this he was ultimately to be disappointed. For there were limits to the integration between the two countries achieved by 1603 – in both religious and secular terms. Although their religious ideas and beliefs had strong Calvinistic links, the ecclesiastical structures of the two countries remained essentially different. Elizabeth was strongly opposed to any changes within the Church of England, above all to the ideas of the radicals and Presbyterians, since this would destroy her own role and overturn the 1559 religious settlement. 'Let me warn you', she wrote to James VI in 1590, 'that there is risen, both in your realm and mine, a sect of perilous consequence, such as would have no kings but a presbytery.'[10] Nor was Elizabeth responsive to Scottish episcopalians, since she did not consider that Anglicanism could be exported northwards – any more than Presbyterianism should be important southwards. The Scottish kirk similarly stood on its own organisational base and traditions, even after the accession of James to the English throne in 1603. In 1604 the commissioners of the Scottish synods summed up the dilemma: 'how could the kirks be united, unless one gave place to the other?'[11] There was also a background of strong political suspicion, which was never fully allayed. The relationship between James and Elizabeth was always problematic. This was emphasised particularly by S. Doran. Even after the Treaty of Berwick, 'deep seams of mutual suspicion and acrimony lay just below the surface of the two monarchs' profession of loving friendship'.[12] The union of crowns actually occurred without the confirmation of any will or testament from Elizabeth. Nor did it bring political integration in the manner of Wales. The two countries already had their own traditions and institutions which, despite their cultural and religious affinity, were not fully compatible. Scotland therefore retained its own legal system and administration. There was even debate as to whether a Scot could be seen in England as an 'English citizen' in the 'eye of the law'. The overall nature of Anglo-Scottish integration was therefore somewhat elusive. It was obvious that something important had happened by 1603, but it was hard to place any structures on it.

Questions

1. How 'deliberate' was the growing friendship between England and Scotland during the reign of Elizabeth?
2. Which were more important in binding England to Scotland: religious or secular influences?

ANALYSIS 3: HOW FAR COULD IT BE SAID THAT A 'BRITISH' STATE HAD EMERGED BY 1603?

The very concept of 'Britain' and 'Britishness' involves the concentration of polity and nationality within the islands off the north-west coast of Europe rather than a straddling of territories in both the islands and the continental mainland.

A key factor in the evolution of 'Britain' was, therefore, the end of the Anglo-French empire of the Angevin kings. This changed the main pre-occupation from expansion in Europe to consolidation within the British Isles. Admittedly it took time for the lesson of defeat in the Hundred Years War to sink in. Henry VIII, for example, tried to compete on equal terms with Spain and France, the new superpowers of the continent, and to win back small areas of territory across the Channel. He temporarily succeeded with the acquisition of Tournai in 1514, although this was bought back by France four years later. The transition in policy really occurred during the reign of Edward VI (1547–53), when Lord Protector Somerset redefined the key objective. France was increasingly perceived as an *indirect* threat – through the support it gave to Scotland against England; hence he turned his main attention to Scotland. When Mary (1553–58) tried, but failed, to save Calais as England's last outpost in France, England had to give up all pretensions to a continental presence. From the time of her accession in 1558 Elizabeth accepted the retreat of England from Europe and made no attempt to revive sovereign claims there. Hence, even when France collapsed into internal turmoil with the religious wars (1562–98), Elizabeth made no attempt to regain territory. Instead, she focused on the growing threat from Spain – and the implications that this had for

English relations with Scotland and English rule in Ireland. Her perspective was, therefore, more distinctively 'British' than that of her predecessors.

The disrupted connection with Europe was not just dynastic; it also had strong diplomatic and religious influences. The 'turning' points here might be seen as the Treaty of Cateau Cambrésis (1559) and the mid-century interaction between the Protestant Reformation and the Catholic Counter Reformation. The former ended for a while the great dynastic rivalry between the Valois and Habsburg interests in Europe, while the latter partially reshaped the balance of power in Europe in terms of religious conflict. The Reformation, re-established in England, extended to Wales and springing up in Scotland, simultaneously brought a new perspective of an 'island Britain' struggling with hostile ideological influences from without and seeking to establish a common ideological base within.

The growth of 'Britain' therefore followed the disentanglement of England from France and Europe. But it also involved four further processes. One was control by 'lowland' England over the northern border areas. Another was the integration of Wales into England, establishing a direct constitutional link between 'principality and 'kingdom'. The third was the development of partnership between England and Scotland, initially as two separate 'kingdoms' which were eventually to be brought under one 'crown'. The fourth, and most difficult, was the pacification of Ireland and the spread of English political and cultural influence in selected regions.

Whether the Tudors in general, and Elizabeth in particular, gave 'Britain' and 'Britishness' a *positive* dimension depends very much on the vantage point from which their policy is viewed. Traditionally, historians have seen the evolution of Britain as the 'push' of England (especially 'lowland' England) to the border areas and the Celtic 'fringes': A.L. Rowse, for example, argued in 1955 that, in Elizabeth's reign, 'we can watch the momentum of the process out of which the United Kingdom was forged' (see Source 2.3 below).[13] More recently G.R. Elton[14] and A.G.R. Smith[15] maintained that much depended on Tudor administrative efficiency and consolidation, while P. Williams[16] contrasted the strong success in Wales with the continuing crisis in Ireland. In each case the earlier Tudors were accredited with starting the 'push' which Elizabeth intensified. A different perspective was put by S.G. Ellis, who emphasised that Tudor policies were 'pulled' into the border and Celtic areas rather than 'pushed' out from the English core. His re-evaluation was based on 'the thesis that the outlying territories were central, rather than peripheral, to the problems of Tudor government'.[17] Far from being a steady increase in momentum, Tudor policy was actually quite sporadic. Ellis identified an 'early Tudor phase' to 1534, which involved 'piecemeal and conservative tinkering with the inherited structures and problems'; this was followed by 'a much more radical, interventionist strategy' which meant 'great strains on relations between the crown and the political communities of the borderlands'.[18] These two possibilities – 'push' and 'pull' – are not necessarily exclusive of each other and will be taken in conjunction in what follows.

Logically, a key component in the development of 'Britain' was the completion of 'England'. The south and midlands ('lowland' England) had already been brought under central control, together with parts of the northern regions of Yorkshire and Lancashire. But the border counties of Cumberland, Westmoreland, Northumberland and Durham had traditionally been semi-autonomous, Durham, for example, as a county palatine. The integration of these areas into the rest of England had been attempted by Henry VIII and Edward VI. The former had reinforced the Council of the North in the 1530s in an attempt to undermine the powers of the great northern magnates: the Nevilles, Dacres and Percys had their wardenship of the marches removed. Their power was, however, restored by Mary, and Elizabeth, faced with renewed threats of rebellion, was obliged to continue where Henry VIII had left off. In 1563 she deprived the Dacres of the west march wardenship and, following Northumberland's rebellion in 1569, the heirs were confined to their possessions in the south and were deliberately cut off from their strongholds in the north. Instead, lesser northern or southern families were appointed to the wardenships. But this was very much a last resort. In a clear combination of 'push' and 'pull' influences, the crown was drawn – by an endemic threat from the periphery – into imposing a solution from the centre. In one respect this succeeded. There were no further uprisings in the area after 1569 and the security risk was further reduced by England's improved relations with Scotland. But a price was paid in terms of effective government within the region as opposed to central control over it. The southern appointments like Willoughby and Hunsdon were unable to control the rivalry between the remaining northern families. As a result, the area suffered from as much lawlessness and disorder as it had at the beginning of the reign.

The integration of Wales into England (Analysis 1) was greatly assisted by the Welsh connections of the Tudor dynasty whereas, of course, the north of England had had much closer contacts with Richard III, the dynastic rival to Henry Tudor. Administratively Wales was not dissimilar to the north of England in the sense that there were border areas and marcher lordships. But the Welsh equivalents offered less resistance and the Tudors had more immediate success in dealing with them. The key difference was that the border areas of the north were a potential danger because of the threat posed by Scotland, whereas the threat from Wales had already been largely subdued. Perhaps, therefore, Henry VIII's most successful 'push' was his transformation of the principality into shires in 1536 and 1543. The English Reformation was similarly imposed upon Wales by an Act of Uniformity enforcing the use of the Prayer Book. But Wales was far from being merely a victim in this relationship. Religious influences from England were converted into a more local change through extensive translations into the Welsh language. This meant that the 'push' was consolidated by the subsequent 'pull'. Indeed, P. Jenkins has gone so far as to say that the religious integration of England and Wales can 'be seen as a decisive victory in the process of national unification'.[19] Although there were remaining problems in both cases, the arrangement proved permanent. Hence 'England and Wales' was a very real starting point for 'Britain', preceding even the completion of 'England' itself.

The next component of 'Britain' was the development of a 'partnership' between 'England and Wales' and 'Scotland'. The latter had long been seen as a threat which had drawn England – often reluctantly – into a series of conflicts. Before Elizabeth it had in effect been a hostile foreign power. After 1558, however, it moved towards England because of a variety of changes in the gravitational pull – international relations and religion in particular (see Analysis 2). By 1603 there was the further influence of dynastic union with the accession of James VI as James I – the Stewarts becoming the Stuarts. Yet there was never an equivalent to the conciliar and shire reforms which were introduced in Wales and attempted in Ireland. Before the Commonwealth period there was no real temptation to impose an English administrative structure on to Scotland. Identities were still sometimes divergent, remaining so until 'Britain' was properly created by the Act of Union in 1707. The result was not the same as the integration achieved between England and Wales. Yet, paradoxically, Scotland and England were more closely related by a common language, which provided the basis for longer-term intellectual and economic cohesion in the form of the Enlightenment, the Industrial Revolution and the development of the British Empire in the nineteenth century.

The place of Ireland has always been more difficult to fit into any notion of 'Britain'. During the Middle Ages it had been more directly influenced by England than had Scotland, while the introduction of

Poynings Law clearly indicated the 'push' policy of the early Tudors in a way which did not affect Scotland. Yet there was a clear difference between Scotland and Ireland. If England was drawn into Scotland it was to settle its own border areas and to neutralise any direct Scottish threat. These objectives were sufficiently limited to prevent a more direct assertion of the English administrative structure on to Scotland. Ireland was a different matter. Internal instability was endemic, which meant that English influence was continuously drawn in. Various solutions were, of course, imposed, ranging from Henry VIII's attempts at administrative reform to Elizabeth's resort to the plantations or the 'Welsh' expedients suggested to her (see Analysis 1). The problem was that Ireland became increasingly difficult to dominate as a result of the Counter Reformation. Although the various rebellions were put down by military force, success was only temporary. There was no acceptable foundation for future 'Britishness'; instead 'British' became synonymous with 'greater English' – and both with 'imperialism' rather than 'integration'. The perception of the Irish 'problem' dated from the reign of Elizabeth. Future solutions diverged more than anywhere else in the United Kingdom.

By the time of Elizabeth's death (or rather, James I's accession) in 1603, a recognisable 'Britain' had emerged. As yet, however, it was both tentative and unstable. A great deal more ground had to be covered before it was distinctively recognised within the European state system. Under the Stuarts it was more volatile and was constantly threatened with extinction, although the influence of Scotland and Ireland has now been acknowledged in the conflicts of the 1640s, the 'English Civil War' now being seen more as the 'wars of the three kingdoms'. In the eighteenth and nineteenth centuries the internal bond tightened between England-Wales and Scotland as 'Britain' expanded outwards as an imperial power. At the same time, the very process of 'British' imperialism came to be perceived in Ireland as an intrusive and disuniting force. These trends were all incipient by 1603, but a further three centuries were needed for them to develop fully.

Questions

1. Were Tudor policies 'pushed' or 'pulled' into the areas beyond 'lowland England'?
2. Was 'Britain' under the Tudors any more than a 'greater England'?

SOURCES

1. THE TROUBLES IN ELIZABETHAN IRELAND

Source 1.1: From W. Durant, *The Story of Civilization, vol. VII: The Age of Reason Begins*, published in 1961.

[Elizabeth's] record in Ireland subtracted from her glory. She underestimated the difficulty of conquering, in an almost roadless country, a people whose love of their land and their faith was their only bond to life and decency. She scolded her deputies for failures that were due in part to her own parsimony; they were unable to pay their troops, who found it more profitable to rob the Irish than to fight them. She vacillated between truce and terror, and never followed one policy to a decision. She founded Trinity College and Dublin University (1591), but she left the people of Ireland as illiterate as before. After the expenditure of £10,000,000, the peace achieved was a desert of desolation over half the lovely isle, and, over all of it, a spirit of unspeakable hatred that only bided its time to kill and devastate again.

Source 1.2: Two extracts from Edmund Spenser, *A View of the State of Ireland*.

A. Sure it is ... a most beautiful and sweet country as any is under heaven: seamed throughout with many goodly rivers, replenished with all sorts of fish, most abundantly sprinkled with many sweet islands and goodly lakes, like little inland seas, that will carry even ships upon their waters, adorned with goodly woods fit for building of houses and ships ... also full of good ports and havens opening upon England and Scotland, as inviting us to come to them, to see what excellent commodities that country can afford, besides the soil itself is most fertile, fit to yield all kinds of fruit that shall be committed thereunto. And lastly, the heavens most mild and temperate, though somewhat more moist than the part towards the west.

B. For, notwithstanding that [Munster] was a most rich and plentiful country, full of corn and cattle, that you would have thought they should have been able to stand long, yet ere one year and a half they were brought to such wretchedness as that any stony heart would have rued the same. Out of every corner of the woods and glens they came creeping forth upon their hands, for their legs could not bear them; they looked like anatomies of death; they spake like ghosts crying out of their graves; they did eat the dead carrions, happy where they could find them; yea, and one another soon after, insomuch as the very carcasses they spared not to scrape out of their graves; and if they found a plot of watercresses or shamrocks, there they flocked as to a feast for the time, yet not able long to continue there withal; that in short space there were none almost left, and a most populous and plentiful country suddenly left void of man and beast; yet, sure, in all that war there perished not many by the sword, but all by the extremity of famine which they themselves had wrought.

Source 1.3: From Sir Robert Naunton, *Fragments Regalia*, published in 1641.

The Irish action we may call a malady, and a consumption of [Elizabeth's] times, for it accompanied her to her end, and it was of so profuse and vast an expense, that it drew near unto a distemperature of state, and of passion in herself, for, towards her last, she grew somewhat hard to please, her armies being accustomed to prosperity, and the Irish prosecution not answering her expectation, and her wonted success; for it was a good while an unthrifty and inauspicious war, which did much disturb and mislead her judgement; and the more, for that it was a precedent taken out of her own pattern.

For as the Queen, by way of division, had at her coming to the crown, supported the revolted states of Holland, so did the King of Spain turn the trick upon herself, towards her going out, by cherishing the Irish Rebellion.

Source 1.4: From M. Cronin, *A History of Ireland*, published in 2001.

The day of the Irish chieftain had finally passed. The old customs and laws of Ireland, which had ruled the different chieftains and kings, became obsolete and only English law ruled over the country. That law was underwritten by the royal administration in Dublin Castle. The destruction of the chieftains meant that many aspects of Irish life, which they had guaranteed and perpetuated, slipped into obscurity. . . . There were some continuities which survived the defeat of the Irish under O'Neill. The Irish language remained the most commonly used form of the vernacular, the Catholic religion remained as the most practised amongst the population and violent dissent against English rule, although muted, did not disappear. In one of those quirky coincidences which plague history, the submission of O'Neill to Mountjoy as the representative of Elizabeth took place on 30 March 1603, shortly after the Queen had died. The Elizabethan era had, almost in its last minutes, witnessed the submission of Tudor Ireland to the English throne.

Questions

1. Who were 'O'Neill' and 'Mountjoy' (Source 1.4)?
2. Compare the arguments of Sources 1.1 and 1.4.
3. Comment on the usefulness and reliability of Sources 1.2 and 1.3 to the historian studying sixteenth-century Ireland.

4. 'The key factor in the distress of Ireland was the policy of Elizabeth's government.' How far do Sources 1.1 to 1.4, and your own knowledge, support this view?

2. HISTORIANS ON ELIZABETHAN 'BRITAIN'

Source 2.1: From S.G. Ellis, 'Tudor State Formation and the Shaping of the British Isles', published in 1995.

The Tudors had inherited a balanced polity, in which the political influence of the lowlands was offset by the military and strategic value of semi-autonomous borderlands. The imposition of the highly centralized administrative structures of lowland England on the borderlands led to serious and continuing tensions between the court and local political communities and destroyed this balance. After their incorporation, Wales and the far north of England presented fewer problems, since they were smaller, and more easily dominated from London. . . . Then, however, Tudor politicians faced the problem of how to deal with two new borderlands – Scotland and Gaelic Ireland – which were even larger, more remote and 'uncivilized', a problem which previous experiences now left the English state singularly ill equipped to tackle. The military conquest of Ireland left a bitter legacy of racial and religious animosity. The Dublin administration was controlled by an unrepresentative clique of New English adventurers, with little indigenous support, and dependent on an army to maintain its authority. Moreover, the strategy of hiving Ireland off into a dependent kingdom, controlled from London but without a substantial input into the political process there, was an unfortunate precedent and a major and continuing source of political instability in the developing British state. Beguiled by this precedent, English politicians saw Ireland as a model for the integration of Scotland into the English state, even though the circumstances of the dynastic union precluded its application there – at least in the short term. Thus, it is hard not to see in this Tudor legacy of state formation the origins of the pan-British crisis of 1638–60 once described as the English Civil War.

Source 2.2: From N. Davies, *The Isles: A History*, published in 1999.

Such were the fruits of Burghley's 'British policy'. He lived long enough to see all parts of the Isles subordinated in one degree or another to the dominant English crown. England and Wales had been one kingdom since 1536. England and Ireland had lived in union under the Tudors since 1541. Cornwall's divergent tendencies had been silenced since 1549: those of the North since 1570. England and Scotland, since 1586, were converging towards a path of common destiny. Queen Elizabeth's death and the submission of the Earl of Tyrone occurred in March 1603 within a few days of each other. *De facto*, if not yet evenly *de jure*, all the Isles lay within the English obedience.

Source 2.3: From A.L. Rowse, *The Expansion of Elizabethan England*, published in 1955.

In spite of everything – climate, foreign intervention, the distraction and strain of war abroad, the constant threat of invasion, the changes of course in policy and person, the hesitations on the part of the government, the compromises of the Queen, the discouragements, the disgust of everybody sooner or later with Ireland … the expansion of English power went on. Only the power of an ordered state, whatever its temporary recessions and retreats, was irresistible. There was no possibility of an ordered state in Ireland – and little enough in Scotland – except the English state. In Elizabeth's reign we can watch the momentum of the process out of which the United Kingdom was forged, as at no other time – except for the brief interval of Cromwell's Commonwealth.

Questions

1. Compare the ways in which Sources 2.1 to 2.3 consider the impact of Elizabethan policies on England's future relationship with Scotland, Ireland and Wales.
2. 'By 1603 Elizabethan policies towards the English borderlands, Scotland, Ireland and Wales had been largely successful.' Using Sources 2.1 to 2.3, and your own knowledge of the historical and historiographical contexts, comment on this view.

NOTES

1. ELIZABETH AND HER GOVERNMENT

1 Quoted in J. Lotherington (ed.), *The Tudor Years* (London 1994), p. 214.

2 J.D. Alsop, 'Government, Finance and the Community of the Exchequer', in C. Haigh (ed.), *The Reign of Elizabeth I* (London 1984), p. 119.

3 Ibid., p. 123.

4 Quoted in K. Randell, *Elizabeth I and the Government of England* (London 1994), p. 55.

5 P. Williams, *The Later Tudors* (Oxford 1995), p. 313.

6 See John Lingard, *A History of England from the First Invasion by the Romans to the Accession of William and Mary in 1688*, vol. VIII (Boston and New York 1855).

7 J.A. Froude, *History of England from the Fall of Wolsey to the Defeat of the Spanish Armada* (London 1904).

8 See J.R. Green, *A Short History of the English People* (London 1874), ch. 7.

9 M. Creighton, *Queen Elizabeth* (London 1896), p. 304.

10 See A.F. Pollard, *History of England from the Accession of Edward VI to Elizabeth* (London 1910).

11 See J.E. Neale, *Queen Elizabeth* (London 1934).

12 S.T. Bindoff, *Tudor England* (Harmondsworth 1950), p. 309.

13 See A.L. Rowse, *The England of Elizabeth* (London 1950); and A.L. Rowse, *The Expansion of Elizabethan England* (London 1955).

14 Rowse, *The England of Elizabeth*, p. 266.
15 Quoted in C. Haigh (ed.), *The Reign of Elizabeth I* (London 1984), p. 14 n.
16 Haigh, *The Reign of Elizabeth I*.
17 A.G.R. Smith, *The Government of Elizabethan England* (London 1967).
18 G. Donaldson, *Scotland, James V–James VII* (Edinburgh 1965), pp. 236–37.
19 For an analysis of this view see S.J. Lee, *The Mid Tudors: Edward VI and Mary, 1547–1558* (London 2007), especially p. 124.
20 See G.R. Elton, *The Tudor Revolution in Government* (Cambridge 1953).
21 G.R. Elton, *England under the Tudors* (Cambridge 1955), p. 222.
22 Bindoff, *Tudor England*, p. 146.
23 W.R.D. Jones, *The Mid-Tudor Crisis* (London 1973), p. 1.
24 See D. Loades, *The Reign of Mary Tudor* (London 1979); D. Loades: *The Mid-Tudor Crisis, 1545–1565* (Basingstoke 1992).
25 See A.G.R. Smith, *The Emergence of a Nation State* (London 1984).
26 See P. Williams, *The Later Tudors: England, 1547–1603* (Oxford 1995).
27 Rowse, *The England of Elizabeth*, p. vii.
28 Donaldson, *Scotland*, p. 236–37.
29 C. Russell, 'England in 1637', in M. Todd (ed.), *Reformation to Revolution: Politics and Religion in Early Modern England* (London 1995), p. 138.
30 Haigh, *The Reign of Elizabeth*, p. 19.
31 J. Guy, *Tudor England* (Oxford 1988), p. 456.
Source 1.1: Quoted in A.G.R. Smith, *The Government of Elizabethan England* (London 1967), p. 1.
Source 1.2: Edward Rishton's continuation of Nicolas Sanders, *Rise and Growth of the Anglican Schism* (London 1877 edition), p. 325.
Source 1.3: Quoted in J.E. Neale, *Queen Elizabeth* (Jonathan Cape, London 1934), p. 295–96.
Source 1.4: Quoted in C.S. Marcus, J. Mueller, M.B. Rose, eds.: *Elizabeth I: Collected Works* (University of Chicago Press, Chicago, 2000), pp. 339–40.
Source 2.1: John Lingard, *A History of England from the First Invasion by the Romans to the Accession of William and Mary in 1688* (Boston and New York 1855), vol. VIII, pp. 424–29.

Source 2.2: J.A. Froude, *History of England from the Fall of Wolsey to the Defeat of the Spanish Armada* (Longmans Green, London n.d.), vol. XII, p. 511.

Source 2.3: J. Hurstfield, *The Elizabethan Nation* (New York and London 1964), p. 96.

Source 2.4: J.P. Kenyon, *The Stuarts* (Batsford, London 1958; Fontana edition. 1966), p. 11.

Source 2.5: C. Haigh (ed.), *The Reign of Elizabeth I* (Macmillan, London 1984), pp. 18–19.

2. ELIZABETH AND PARLIAMENT

1 See John Lingard, *A History of England from the First Invasion by the Romans to the Accession of William and Mary in 1688* (Boston and New York 1855), vol. VIII.

2 See A.F. Pollard, *The Evolution of Parliament* (London 1920)

3 See J.E. Neale, *Elizabeth I and her Parliaments*, 2 vols. (London 1953, 1957); and J.E. Neale, *The Elizabethan House of Commons* (London 1949).

4 See G.R. Elton, 'Parliament in the Sixteenth Century: Functions and Fortunes', *Historical Journal*, 22 (1979); and G.R. Elton, 'Parliament in the Reign of Elizabeth', in M. Todd (ed.), *Reformation to Revolution: Politics and Religion in Early Modern England* (London 1995).

5 See M.A.R. Graves, 'The Management of the Elizabethan House of Commons: The Council's "Men-of-Business" ', *Parliamentary History*, 2 (1983); and M.A.R. Graves, *Elizabethan Parliaments, 1559–1601* (Harlow 1987).

6 Graves, *Elizabethan Parliaments*, p. 76.

7 G.W.O. Woodward, *Reformation and Resurgence* (London 1963), pp. 47–48.

8 G.R. Elton, 'Parliament', in C. Haigh, (ed.), *The Reign of Elizabeth I* (Basingstoke 1984), p. 100.

9 G.R. Elton, *The Parliament of England, 1559–1581* (Cambridge 1986).

10 Quoted in Sir Thomas Smith, *De Republica Anglorum* (1565), ed. L. Alston, (Cambridge 1906), p. 48.

11 Graves, 'Management of the Elizabethan House of Commons', p. 20.

12 J.E. Neale, 'The Commons' Journals of the Tudor Period', *Transactions of the Royal Historical Society*, 4th ser., 3 (1920).

13 Graves, *Elizabethan Parliaments*, p. 57.

14 Neale, *Elizabeth I and her Parliaments*, vol. I, pp. 319–20.

15 Sir Simonds D'Ewes, *Journals*, 1682, p. 16; quoted in D. Cook, *Documents and Debates: Sixteenth Century England, 1450–1600* (Basingstoke 1980), p. 96.

16 Quoted in Cook, *Documents and Debates*, p. 92.

17 Quoted in ibid., p. 97.

18 Graves, *Elizabethan Parliaments*.

19 Elton, 'Parliament', in Haigh, *The Reign of Elizabeth*, p. 100.

Source 1.1: Sir Thomas Smith, *De Republica Anglorum* (1565), ed. L. Alston (Cambridge University Press, Cambridge 1906).

Source 1.2: *The Journal of the House of Commons*, vol. I, p. 104.

Source 1.3: G.W. Prothero, *Statutes and Constitutional Documents, 1558–1625* (Oxford University Press, Oxford 1913), p. 124.

Source 2.1: John Lingard, *A History of England from the First Invasion by the Romans to the Accession of William and Mary in 1688* (Boston and New York 1855), vol. VIII.

Source 2.2: J.E. Neale, *Elizabeth I and her Parliaments, vol. II: 1584–1601* (Jonathan Cape, London 1957), p. 434.

Source 2.3: G.R. Elton, 'Parliament in the Reign of Elizabeth I', in M. Todd (ed.), *Reformation to Revolution: Politics and Religion in Early Modern England* (Routledge, London 1995), pp. 98–99, 113–14.

Source 2.4: M.A.R. Graves, *Elizabethan Parliaments, 1559–1601* (Longman, Harlow 1987), pp. 78–79.

3. THE 1559 RELIGIOUS SETTLEMENT

1 See A.F. Pollard, *History of England from the Accession of Edward VI to Elizabeth* (London 1910).

2 J.R. Green, *A Short History of the English People* (London 1874; Macmillan edition 1911), p. 376.

3 See J.E. Neale, *Elizabeth I and her Parliaments, vol. I* (London 1953), and J.E. Neale, *The Elizabethan House of Commons* (London 1949).

4 P. McGrath, *Papists and Puritans under Elizabeth I* (London 1967), p. 13.

5 See W.P. Haugaard, *Elizabeth I and the English Reformation: The Struggle for a Stable Settlement of Religion* (Cambridge 1958), pp. 98–99.

6 W.J. Sheils, *The English Reformation, 1530–1570* (London 1989), p. 153.

7 D. MacCulloch, *The Later Reformation in England, 1547–1603* (Basingstoke 1990), p. 29.

8 Ibid.

9 Ibid., p. 27.

10 N.L. Jones, 'Elizabeth's First Year: The Conception and Birth of the Elizabethan Political World', in C. Haigh (ed.), *The Reign of Elizabeth I* (Basingstoke 1984), p. 52.

11 Sheils, *The English Reformation*, Document 15c.

12 W.R.D. Jones, *The Mid-Tudor Crisis, 1539–1563* (London 1973), p. 109.

13 P. Williams, *The Later Tudors* (Oxford 1995), p. 458.

14 Quoted in Haugaard, *Elizabeth and the English Reformation*, p. 200.

15 J. Warren, *Elizabeth I: Religion and Foreign Affairs* (London 1993), p. 35.

16 Quoted in P. Collinson, *Archbishop Grindal, 1519–1583: The Struggle for a Reformed Church* (London 1979), p. 101.

17 Williams, *The Later Tudors*, p. 457.

18 Quoted in R. O'Day, *The English Clergy: The Emergence and Consolidation of a Profession, 1558–1642* (Leicester 1979), p. 130.

Source 1.1: *Statutes of the Realm* (London, Record Commission 1810–28), vol. IV, part I, p. 352.

Source 1.2: *Statutes of the Realm* (London, Record Commission 1810–28), vol. IV, part I, pp. 356–57.

Source 1.3: William Camden, *History of the Most Renowned and victorious Princesse Elizabeth, Late Queen of England* (3rd edition, London 1635), p. 2.

Source 1.4: W. Allen, *A True, Sincere, and Modest Defence of English Catholiques* (1584), pp. 7–11.

Source 2.1: J.R. Green, *A Short History of the English People* (Macmillan edition, London 1911), pp. 376–77.

Source 2.2: S. Doran, *Elizabeth I and Religion* (Routledge, London 1994), pp. 6–7.

Source 2.3: D. Loades, *Revolution in Religion: The English Reformation, 1530–1570* (University of Wales Press, Cardiff 1992), p. 30.

Source 2.4: P. Williams, *The Later Tudors* (Oxford University Press, Oxford 1995), p. 236.

4. CATHOLICISM AND THE CATHOLIC 'THREAT'

1 Quoted in P. Johnson, *Elizabeth: A Study in Power and Intellect* (London 1974), p. 349.
2 Quoted in ibid., p. 347.
3 Quoted in ibid., p. 348.
4 A.L. Rowse, *The England of Elizabeth* (London 1959; 1964 edition), p. 443.
5 Johnson, *Elizabeth*, p. 342.
6 J.R. Green, *A Short History of the English People* (London 1874; Macmillan edition 1911), p. 310.
7 G.R. Elton, *England under the Tudors* (London 1955), p. 309.
8 A.G. Dickens, *The English Reformation* (London 1964; Fontana edition 1977), pp. 423–24.
9 P. McGrath, *Papists and Puritans under Elizabeth I* (London 1967), p. 17.
10 Ibid.
11 See J. Bossy, *The English Catholic Community, 1570–1850* (London 1975).
12 Elton, *England under the Tudors*, p. 306.
13 J. Guy, *Tudor England* (Oxford 1988; 1990 edition), p. 300.
14 C. Haigh, 'The Church of England, the Catholics and the People', in C. Haigh (ed.), *The Reign of Elizabeth I* (London 1984), p. 201.
15 Ibid., p. 202.
16 Guy, *Tudor England*, p. 301.
Source 1.1: J.B. Black, *The Reign of Elizabeth, 1558–1603* (Clarendon Press, Oxford 1936), p. 148.
Source 1.2: *Statutes of the Realm* (London, Record Commission 1810–28), vol. IV, part I, pp. 350–55.
Source 1.3: *Dodd's Church History of England*, ed. M. A. Tierney (1839–43), vol. III, App., pp. ii–iii.
Source 1.4: Ibid., pp. iv–xvi.
Source 2.1: A.G. Dickens, *The English Reformation* (London 1964; Fontana edition 1977), pp. 423–24.
Source 2.2: J. Guy, *Tudor England* (Oxford University Press, Oxford 1988; 1990 edition), p. 300.
Source 2.3: S. Doran, *Elizabeth I and Religion* (Routledge, London 1994), p. 63.
Source 2.4: P. Johnson, *Elizabeth: A Study in Power and Intellect* (Weidenfeld and Nicolson, London 1974), pp. 342–43.

5. PURITANISM AND THE PURITAN 'THREAT'

1 P. Williams, *The Later Tudors* (Oxford 1995), p. 487.
2 See R.H. Tawney, *Religion and the Rise of Capitalism* (London 1926).
3 See E. Troeltsch, *The Social Teaching of the Christian Churches* (trans. New York 1931).
4 P. Collinson, *English Puritanism* (Historical Association 1983), p. 7.
5 See P. Collinson, *The Religion of the Protestants* (Oxford 1983).
6 S. Doran, *Elizabeth I and Religion* (London 1994), p. 30.
7 H.J. Hillerbrand (ed.), *The Protestant Reformation*: extract from Calvin's reply to Sadoleto.
8 J. Warren, *Elizabeth I: Religion and Foreign Affairs* (London 1993), p. 43.
9 Quoted in ibid., p. 47.
10 Quoted in M.M. Knappen, *Tudor Puritanism* (Chicago 1939), p. 235.
11 G.R. Elton (ed.), *The Tudor Constitution: Documents and Commentary* (Cambridge 1962), pp. 435–36.
12 Quoted in J.E. Neale, *Elizabeth I and her Parliaments*, vol. II (London 1957), p. 273.
13 Quoted in C. Read, *Lord Burghley and Queen Elizabeth* (London 1960), p. 294.
14 J.R. Green, *A Short History of the English People* (London 1911 edition), p. 468.
15 P. Johnson, *Elizabeth: A Study in Power and Intellect* (London 1974), p. 356.
16 Elton (ed.), *The Tudor Constitution*, pp. 435–36.
17 J. Guy, *Tudor England* (Oxford 1988; 1990 edition), pp. 304–05.
18 P. Lake, 'Calvinism and the English Church, 1570–1635', in M. Todd (ed.), *Reformation to Revolution: Politics and Religion in Early Modern England* (London 1995), p. 188.
19 A.L. Rowse, *The England of Elizabeth* (London 1959; 1964 edition), p. 466.
20 Ibid., p. 488.
21 Quoted in C. Haigh (ed.), *The Reign of Elizabeth I* (Basingstoke 1984), p. 14.
22 J. Hurstfield, *Elizabeth I and the Unity of England* (London 1960), pp. 94–95.
23 J.R.H. Moorman, *A History of the Church in England* (London 1953), p. 221.
24 Hurstfield, *Elizabeth I*, p. 93.

25 G.R. Elton, *England under the Tudors* (Cambridge 1955), p. 460.
26 See C. Hill, *Society and Puritanism in Pre-Revolutionary England* (London 1964).
27 See C. Russell, *The Causes of the English Civil War* (Oxford 1990).
28 See K. Sharpe, *The Personal Rule of Charles I* (New Haven 1993).
29 See N. Tyacke, 'Puritanism, Arminianism and Counter-Revolution', in M. Todd (ed.), *Reformation to Revolution: Politics and Religion in Early Modern England* (London 1995).
Source 1.1: J. Strype, *The Life and Acts of Edmund Grindal* (Oxford 1821), pp. 566–69.
Source 1.2: E. Cardwell, *Documentary Annals of the Reformed Church of England, 1546–1716* (Oxford 1839), vol. I, p. 373.
Source 1.3: J. Strype, *The Life and Acts of John Whitgift* (Oxford 1822), vol. I, pp. 229–30.
Source 2.1: S.T. Bindoff, *Tudor England* (Penguin, Harmondsworth 1950), pp. 242–43.
Source 2.2: J. Guy, *Tudor England* (Oxford University Press, Oxford 1988; 1990 edition), pp. 304–05.
Source 2.3: J. Hurstfield, *Elizabeth I and the Unity of England* (Edinburgh University Press, London 1960), pp. 94–95.
Source 2.4: A.L. Rowse, *The England of Elizabeth* (London 1959; 1964 edition), p. 488.

6. FOREIGN POLICY

1 J.B. Black, *The Reign of Elizabeth, 1558–1603* (Oxford 1936), pp. 285–86.
2 D.J.B. Trim, 'Seeking a Protestant Alliance and Liberty of Conscience on the Continent', in S. Doran and G. Richardson (eds.), *Tudor England and its Neighbours* (London 2005), p. 141.
3 Ibid., p. 142.
4 D. Loades, *Elizabeth I* (London 2003), p. 151.
5 G.D. Ramsay, 'The Foreign Policy of Elizabeth I', in C. Haigh (ed.), *The Reign of Elizabeth I* (London 1984), p. 145.
6 P. Williams, *The Later Tudors* (Oxford 1995), pp. 306–07.
7 J. Hurstfield, *Elizabeth I and the Unity of England* (London 1960), p. 87.
8 Trim, 'Seeking a Protestant Alliance', p. 41.
9 Ramsay, 'Foreign Policy', p. 159.

10 R. Pollitt, 'John Hawkins' Troublesome Voyages: Merchants, Bureaucrats and the Origins of the Slave Trade', *Journal of British Studies*, May (1973).

11 R.B. Wernham, *Before the Armada: The Growth of English Foreign Policy, 1485–1588* (London 1966), p. 320.

12 C. Wilson, *Queen Elizabeth and the Revolt of the Netherlands* (London 1970), p. 16.

13 S. Doran, *England and Europe, 1485–1603* (Harlow 1986), pp. 76–77.

14 Doran, *England and Europe*, Document 19.

15 R. Harding, *The Evolution of the Sailing Navy, 1509–1815* (London 1995), p. 23.

Source 1: J.B. Black, *The Reign of Elizabeth 1558–1603* (Oxford 1936), pp. 285–86.

Source 2: A.L. Rowse, *The Expansion of Elizabethan England* (Macmillan, London 1955), p. 346.

Source 3: D.J.B. Trim, 'Seeking a Protestant Alliance and Liberty of Conscience on the Continent', in S. Doran and G. Richardson (eds.), *Tudor England and its Neighbours* (Macmillan, London 2005), pp. 169–70.

Source 4: D. Loades, *Elizabeth I* (Hambledon and London, London 2003), p. 151.

7. THE DEVELOPMENT OF THE ECONOMY

1 D.M. Palliser, *The Age of Elizabeth: England under the Later Tudors, 1547–1603* (London 1983), p. 60.

2 E. Lamond (ed.), *A Discourse of the Common Weal of the Realm of England* (London 1893), p. 186.

3 Quoted in M. Saxon, 'The Economy and Society in Tudor England', in J. Lotherington (ed.), *The Tudor Years* (London 1994), p. 443.

4 Lamond, *A Discourse*, p. 188.

5 See D.C. Coleman, *The Economy of England, 1450–1750* (Oxford 1978).

6 See R.B. Outhwaite, *Inflation in Tudor and Early Stuart England* (London 1969).

7 Ibid., p. 60.

8 Coleman, *Economy of England*, p. 25.

9 Ibid, pp. 25–26.

10 See E. Kerridge, *The Agricultural Revolution* (London 1967).

11 Ibid., p. 15.

12 See G.E. Mingay, *The Agricultural Revolution: Changes in Agriculture, 1650–1880* (London 1977).

13 See A.G.R. Smith, *The Emergence of a Nation State* (Harlow 1984).

14 See J. Thirsk (ed.), *The Agrarian History of England and Wales, vol. IV: 1500–1600* (Cambridge 1967) and J. Thirsk, *England's Agricultural Regions and Agrarian History, 1500–1750* (London 1987).

15 Mingay, *Agricultural Revolution*, 'Introduction'.

16 Thirsk, *England's Agricultural Regions*, pp. 57–58.

17 Smith, *Emergence of a Nation State*, p. 171.

18 See J.U. Nef, *The Rise of the British Coal Industry*, vol. I (London 1932).

Source 1.1: Figures from a larger table in D.M. Palliser, *The Age of Elizabeth: England under the Later Tudors, 1547–1603* (Longman, London 1983), p. 40.

Source 1.2: From E.A. Wrigley and R.S. Schofield, *The Population of England and Wales, 1541–1871* (Arnold, London 1981), p. 528.

Source 1.3: Figures from text of F.C. Spooner, 'The Economy of Europe, 1559–1609', in R.B. Wernham (ed.), *The Counter-Reformation and the Price Revolution, 1559–1610*, vol. III of *The New Cambridge Modern History* (Cambridge University Press, Cambridge 1968), pp. 32–33.

Source 1.4: Figures for Europe from Spooner, 'Economy of Europe', pp. 33–34. Figures for Scotland, Wales and Ireland from text of J.A. Sharpe, 'Economy and Society', in P. Collinson (ed.), *The Sixteenth Century, 1485–1603* (a volume in The Short Oxford History of the British Isles Series) (Oxford University Press, Oxford 2002), p. 33.

Source 2.1: Quoted in M. Saxon, 'The Economy and Society in Tudor England', in J. Lotherington (ed.) *The Tudor Years* (Hodder and Stoughton, London 1994), pp. 443–44.

Source 2.2: Figures from a larger table in D.M. Palliser, *The Age of Elizabeth: England under the Later Tudors, 1547–1603* (Longman, London 1983), p. 164.

Source 2.3: Ibid., p. 164.

Source 2.4: From a table in ibid., p. 158.

8. SOCIETY AND CULTURE

1 Quoted in A.G.R. Smith, *The Emergence of a Nation State: The Commonwealth of England, 1529–1660* (London 1984), p. 181.
2 Ibid.
3 Ibid., p. 184.
4 See L. Stone, *The Crisis of the Aristocracy, 1558–1641* (Oxford 1965).
5 See D.M. Palliser, *The Age of Elizabeth: England under the Later Tudors* (London 1983).
6 See A.L. Beier, *The Problem of the Poor in Tudor and Early Stuart England* (London 1983), p. 5.
7 See P. Slack, *Poverty and Policy in Tudor and Stuart England* (Harlow 1988), ch. 2.
8 Quoted in ibid., p. 20.
9 J. Pound, *Poverty and Vagrancy in Tudor England* (Harlow 1978), p. 85.
10 Slack, *Poverty and Policy*, p. 182.
11 Quoted in S.J. Lee, *Crime, Punishment and Protest, 1450 to the Present Day* (Harlow 1994), p. 7.
12 P. Williams, *The Later Tudors* (Oxford 1995), p. 212.
13 Ibid., p. 213.
14 See J.S. Cockburn (ed.), *Crime in England, 1500–1800* (London 1977).
15 Williams, *The Later Tudors*, p. 215.
16 F.G. Emmison, *Elizabethan Life: Disorder* (ChelmsFord 1970).
17 Smith, *Emergence of a Nation State*, p. 189.
18 Williams, *The Later Tudors*, p. 232.
19 Smith, *Emergence of a Nation State*, p. 211.
20 Williams, *The Later Tudors*, p. 453.
Source 1: *Statutes of the Realm* (London, Record Commission 1810–28), vol. IV, part I, pp. 590–93.
Source 2: *Statutes of the Realm* (London, Record Commission 1810–28), vol. IV, part II, p. 899.
Source 3: *Statutes of the Realm* (London, Record Commission 1810–28), vol. IV, part II, pp. 896–97.
Source 4: D.M. Palliser, *The Age of Elizabeth: England under the Later Tudors, 1547–1603* (Longman, London 1983), p. 145.

9. THE 'BRITISH' QUESTION

1 P. Williams, *The Later Tudors* (Oxford 1995), p. 521.
2 Ibid.
3 C. Brady, 'Comparable Histories? Tudor Reform in Wales and Ireland', in S.G. Ellis and S. Barber (eds.), *Conquest and Union: Fashioning a British State, 1485–1725* (Harlow 1995), p. 68.
4 See ibid., pp. 77–86.
5 Quoted in M. Mac Craith, 'The Gaelic Reaction to the Reformation', in Ellis and Barber, *Conquest and Union*, pp. 144–45.
6 Quoted in ibid., p. 146.
7 Williams, *The Later Tudors*, p. 525.
8 J. Dawson, 'Anglo-Scottish Protestant Culture and Integration in Sixteenth-Century Britain', in Ellis and Barber, *Conquest and Union*, p. 91.
9 S. Doran, 'Loving and Affectionate Cousins? The Relationship between Elizabeth I and James VI of Scotland, 1586–1603', in S. Doran and G. Richardson (eds.), *Tudor England and its Neighbours* (London 2005), p. 210.
10 G. Donaldson, 'Foundations of Anglo-Scottish Union', in S.T. Bindoff, J. Hurstfield and C.H. Williams (eds.), *Elizabethan Government and Society: Essays Presented to Sir John Neale* (London 1961), p. 305.
11 Quoted in C. Russell, *The Causes of the English Civil War* (Oxford 1990), p. 38 (spelling has been updated).
12 Doran, 'Loving and Affectionate Cousins', p. 205.
13 A.L. Rowse, *The Expansion of Elizabethan England* (London 1955; 1962 edition), p. 116.
14 See G.R. Elton, *Reform and Reformation: England, 1509–58* (London 1977).
15 See A.G.R. Smith, *The Emergence of a Nation State: The Commonwealth of England, 1529–1660* (London 1984).
16 P. Williams, *The Later Tudors* (Oxford 1995), p. 525.
17 S.G. Ellis, 'Tudor State Formation and the Shaping of the British Isles', in Ellis and Barber, *Conquest and Union*, p. 62.
18 Ibid., p. 41.
19 P. Jenkins, 'The Anglican Church and the Unity of Britain: The Welsh Experience, 1560–1714', in Ellis and Barber, *Conquest and Union*, p. 117.
Source 1.1: W. Durant, *The Story of Civilization, vol. VII: The Age of Reason Begins* (Edito-Service S.A., Geneva 1961), p. 30.

Source 1.2: Quoted in H. Morley (ed.), *Ireland under Elizabeth and James the First* (Routledge, London 1890), pp. 143–4.

Source 1.3: Quoted in R. Salter (ed.), *Elizabeth I and her Reign: Documents and Debates* (Macmillan, Basngstone 1988), p. 103.

Source 1.4: M. Cronin, *A History of Ireland* (Palgrave, Basingstoke 2001), pp. 62–63.

Source 2.1: S.G. Ellis, 'Tudor State Formation and the Shaping of the British Isles', in S.G. Ellis and S. Barber (eds.), *Conquest and Union: Fashioning a British State, 1485–1725* (Longman, Harlow 1995), pp. 61–63.

Source 2.2: N. Davies, *The Isles: A History* (Macmillan, London 1999), pp. 411–12.

Source 2.3: A.L. Rowse, *The Expansion of Elizabethan England* (Macmillan, London 1955; 1962 edition), pp. 115–16.

SELECT BIBLIOGRAPHY

The following have been especially helpful in the preparation of this book.

PRIMARY SOURCES

Of particular importance are the *Statutes of the Realm* (London, Record Commission 1810–28), vol. IV, William Camden, *History of the Most Renowned and victorious Princesse Elizabeth, Late Queen of England* (3rd edition, London 1635), W. Allen, *A True, Sincere, and Modest Defence of English Catholiques* (1584) and E. Cardwell, *Documentary Annals of the Reformed Church of England, 1546–1716* (Oxford 1839). More general and accessible are D. Cook (ed.), *Documents and Debates: Sixteenth Century England, 1450–1600* (Basingstoke 1980), R. Salter (ed.), *Documents and Debates: Elizabeth I and her Reign* (Basingstoke 1988), and G.R. Elton (ed.), *The Tudor Constitution: Documents and Commentary* (Cambridge 1962).

GENERAL HISTORIES

Most general histories of the Tudors include detailed sections on the reign of Elizabeth. Old staples are J. Lingard, *A History of England from the First Invasion by the Romans to the Accession of William and Mary in 1688* (Boston and New York 1855), vol. VIII, J.A. Froude,

History of England from the Fall of Wolsey to the Defeat of the Spanish Armada (London 1904), J.R. Green, *A Short History of the English People* (London 1911 edition) and A.F. Pollard, *A History of England from the Accession of Edward VI to the Death of Elizabeth* (London 1910). These are good examples of the earlier views of the Tudor regime which prevailed for much of the first half of the twentieth century. Very influential in the 1950s and early 1960s were S.T. Bindoff, *Tudor England* (London 1950) and G.R. Elton, *England under the Tudors* (Cambridge 1955). An entertaining – but traditional – account of the period is provided in W. Durant, *The Story of Civilization, vol. VII: The Age of Reason Begins* (New York 1957). More recent general histories, which reflect extensive changes in interpretation on Elizabeth, are A.G.R. Smith, *The Emergence of a Nation State* (London 1984), J. Guy, *Tudor England* (Oxford 1988) and P. Williams, *The Later Tudors: England, 1547–1603* (Oxford 1995). Standard textbooks include R. Lockyer, *Tudor and Stuart Britain, 1471–1714* (Harlow 1985 edition), G.W.O. Woodward, *Reformation and Resurgence* (London 1963) and J. Lotherington (ed.), *The Tudor Years* (London 1994).

BIOGRAPHIES AND DETAILED COVERAGE OF THE REIGN

Two major works of the 1930s were J.E. Neale, *Queen Elizabeth* (London 1934) and J.B. Black, *The Reign of Elizabeth, 1558–1603* (Oxford 1936). Other well-known works are A.L. Rowse, *The England of Elizabeth* (London 1959), A.L. Rowse, *The Expansion of Elizabethan England* (London 1955), J. Hurstfield, *Elizabeth I and the Unity of England* (London 1960), P. Johnson, *Elizabeth: A Study in Power and Intellect* (London 1974), E. Jenkins, *Elizabeth the Great* (London 1958), L.B. Smith, *The Elizabethan Epic* (London 1966) and D. Loades, *Elizabeth I* (London 2003).

INTERPRETATIVE COMPILATIONS

The following contain a variety of views on a range of issues: R.L. Greaves, *Elizabeth I, Queen of England* (Lexington, Mass. 1974), C. Haigh (ed.), *The Reign of Elizabeth I* (London 1984), M. Todd (ed.), *Reformation to Revolution: Politics and Religion in Early Modern England* (London 1995), S. Doran and G. Richardson (eds.), *Tudor England and its Neighbours* (London 2005) and S.G. Ellis and

S. Barber (eds.), *Conquest and Union: Fashioning a British State, 1485–1725* (Harlow 1995).

GOVERNMENT AND PARLIAMENT

Readable introductions are T.A. Morris, *Tudor Government* (London 1999) and K. Randell, *Elizabeth I and the Government of England* (London 1994). Three major works, now controversial, are J.E. Neale, *Elizabeth I and her Parliaments, 1559–1581* (London 1953), J.E. Neale, *Elizabeth I and her Parliaments, 1584–1601* (London 1957) and J.E. Neale, *The Elizabethan House of Commons* (London 1949). These are discussed in G.R. Elton, 'Parliament in the Reign of Elizabeth I', in M. Todd (ed.), *Reformation to Revolution: Politics and Religion in Early Modern England* (London 1995), and M.A.R. Graves, *Elizabethan Parliaments, 1559–1601* (London 1987). Other reference works are C. Read, *Lord Burghley and Queen Elizabeth* (London 1960), N.L. Jones, 'Elizabeth's First Year: The Conception and Birth of the Elizabethan Political World', in C. Haigh (ed.), *The Reign of Elizabeth I* (Basingstoke 1984) and L. Strachey, *Elizabeth and Essex* (London 1928).

FOREIGN POLICY

J. Warren, *Elizabeth I: Religion and Foreign Affairs* (London 1993) provides an accessible introduction. Other works include R. B. Wernham, *Before the Armada: The Growth of English Foreign Policy, 1485–1588* (New York 1966), S. Doran, *England and Europe, 1485–1603* (Harlow 1986), S. Doran and G. Richardson (eds.), *Tudor England and its Neighbours* (Basingstoke 2005), C. Wilson, *Queen Elizabeth and the Revolt of the Netherlands* (London 1970), G.D. Ramsay, 'The Foreign Policy of Elizabeth I', in C. Haigh (ed.), *The Reign of Elizabeth I* (London 1984) and D.J.B. Trim, 'Seeking a Protestant Alliance and Liberty of Conscience on the Continent', in S. Doran and G. Richardson (eds.), *Tudor England and its Neighbours* (London 2005).

RELIGIOUS ISSUES

A lucid – and traditional – introduction to religious changes is J.R.H. Moorman, *A History of the Church in England* (London 1953). A

Catholic perspective is put by P. Hughes, *The Reformation in England*, vol. II (London 1954) and J. Bossy, *The English Catholic Community, 1570–1850* (London 1975). Highly influential in its assertion that the Protestant Reformation spread 'from below' is A.G. Dickens, *The English Reformation* (London 1964). The most important of the recent works are J.J. Scarisbrick, *The Reformation and the English People* (London 1984), F. Heal and R. O'Day (eds.), *Church and Society in England, Henry VIII to James I* (London 1977), D. MacCulloch, *The Later Reformation in England, 1547–1603* (Basingstoke 1990), C. Haigh (ed.), *The English Reformation Revised* (Cambridge 1987), W.J. Sheils, *The English Reformation, 1530–1570* (Harlow 1989), D. Loades, *Revolution in Religion: The English Reformation, 1530–1570* (Cardiff 1992), P. Collinson, *The Religion of Protestants* (Oxford 1982), S. Doran, *Elizabeth I and Religion* (London, 1994) and R.J. Acheson, *Radical Puritans in England, 1550–1660* (London 1990). Other works used in compiling this book are J. Strype, *The Life and Acts of Edmund Grindal* (Oxford 1821), J. Strype, *The Life and Acts of John Whitgift* (Oxford 1822), W.P. Haugaard, *Elizabeth I and the English Reformation: The Struggle for a Stable Settlement of Religion* (Cambridge 1958), M.M. Knappen, *Tudor Puritanism* (Chicago 1939), W. Haller, *The Rise of Puritanism* (New York 1938), P. McGrath, *Papists and Puritans under Elizabeth I* (London 1967), P. Collinson, *Archbishop Grindal, 1519–1583: The Struggle for a Reformed Church* (London 1979) and R. O'Day, *The English Clergy: The Emergence and Consolidation of a Profession, 1558–1642* (Leicester 1979). There is also an important chapter in C. Haigh (ed.), *The Reign of Elizabeth I* (London 1984); this is C. Haigh, 'The Church of England, the Catholics and the People'. There are also contributions to M. Todd (ed.), *Reformation to Revolution: Politics and Religion in Early Modern England* (London 1995): P. Lake, 'Calvinism and the English Church, 1570–1635', P. Collinson, 'Protestant Culture and the Cultural Revolution', and N. Tyacke, 'Puritanism, Arminianism and Counter-Revolution'.

ECONOMIC AND SOCIAL

Excellent coverage of the main issues is provided in D.M. Palliser, *The Age of Elizabeth: England under the Later Tudors 1547–1603* (London 1983) and D.C. Coleman, *The Economy of England, 1450–1750* (Oxford 1978). More specific topics are dealt with in R.B. Outhwaite, *Inflation in Tudor and Early Stuart England* (London 1969), E.A.

Wrigley and R.S. Schofield, *The Population of England and Wales, 1541–1871* (London 1981), E. Kerridge, *The Agricultural Revolution* (London 1967), G.E. Mingay, *The Agricultural Revolution. Changes in Agriculture 1650–1880* (London 1977), J. Thirsk (ed.), *The Agrarian History of England and Wales, vol. IV: 1500–1600* (Cambridge 1967) and J. Thirsk, *England's Agricultural Regions and Agrarian History, 1500–1750* (London 1987). Various aspects of society are covered in L. Stone, *The Crisis of the Aristocracy, 1558–1641* (Oxford 1965), A.L. Beier, *The Problem of the Poor in Tudor and Early Stuart England* (London 1983), P. Slack, *Poverty and Policy in Tudor and Stuart England* (Harlow 1988), J. Pound, *Poverty and Vagrancy in Tudor England* (Harlow 1978) and J.S. Cockburn (ed.), *Crime in England, 1500–1800* (London 1977).

THE BRITISH QUESTION

Particularly useful is a series of chapters in S.G. Ellis and S. Barber (eds.), *Conquest and Union: Fashioning a British State, 1485–1725* (Harlow 1995). These include S.G. Ellis, 'Tudor State Formation and the Shaping of the British Isles', C. Brady, 'Comparable Histories? Tudor Reform in Wales and Ireland', P. Jenkins, 'The Anglican Church and the Unity of Britain: The Welsh Experience, 1560–1714', M. Mac Craith, 'The Gaelic Reaction to the Reformation' and J. Dawson, 'Anglo-Scottish Protestant Culture and Integration in Sixteenth-Century Britain'. Some of the ideas in the last of these seem to have been inspired by essays: G. Donaldson, 'Foundations of Anglo-Scottish Union' and R.D. Edwards, 'Ireland, Elizabeth I and the Counter-Reformation', both in S.T. Bindoff, J. Hurstfield and C.H. Williams (eds.), *Elizabethan Government and Society: Essays Presented to Sir John Neale* (London 1961). Other important material is in S. Doran, 'Loving and Affectionate Cousins? The Relationship between Elizabeth I and James VI of Scotland, 1586–1603', in S. Doran and G. Richardson (eds.), *Tudor England and its Neighbours* (London 2005), P. Collinson (ed.), *The Sixteenth Century, 1485–1603* (a volume in The Short Oxford History of the British Isles series) (Oxford 2002), H. Morley (ed.), *Ireland under Elizabeth and James the First* (London 1890), J.C. Beckett, *A Short History of Ireland* (London 1952; 1966 edition), M. Cronin, *A History of Ireland* (Basingstoke, 2001) and K. Kenny, *Ireland and the British Empire* (Oxford 2004).

INDEX